Blake's late prophecies, *The Four Zoas*, *Milton*, and *Jerusalem*, feature a conflict between the poet–prophet Los and a Spectre embodying all he most opposes: intellectual skepticism, religious despair, and a systematic philosophical logic of contraries which is for Blake an abstraction from, and a negation of, his ideal of "life." Lorraine Clark traces the analogy between Blake's Spectre and Søren Kierkegaard's concept of "dread," whose spirit of negation and irony he seeks to conquer, in both its philosophical and aesthetic manifestations. Using Kierkegaard's philosophy to illuminate Blake's prophecies, Lorraine Clark shows these concepts to offer the basis for a profound critique both of romanticism, as it has come to be identified with the spirit of dialectic, and of the postmodern irony which it has spawned. The attempt shared by both writers to rescue an ideal of life from its abstraction within idealist dialectics is itself deeply romantic, and offers a dramatization of tensions – between skepticism and affirmation, religion and nihilism, philosophy and poetry – central to our understanding of romanticism.

BLAKE, KIERKEGAARD, AND THE
SPECTRE OF DIALECTIC

BLAKE, KIERKEGAARD, AND THE SPECTRE OF DIALECTIC

LORRAINE CLARK

Trent University, Peterborough, Ontario

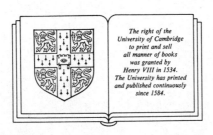

The right of the
University of Cambridge
to print and sell
all manner of books
was granted by
Henry VIII in 1534.
The University has printed
and published continuously
since 1584.

CAMBRIDGE UNIVERSITY PRESS

Cambridge
New York   Port Chester
Melbourne   Sydney

Published by the Press Syndicate of the University of Cambridge
The Pitt Building, Trumpington Street, Cambridge CB2 1RP
40 West 20th Street, New York, NY 10011–4211, USA
10 Stamford Road, Oakleigh, Melbourne 3166, Australia

First published 1991

Printed in Great Britain at the University Press, Cambridge

British Library cataloguing in publication data
Clark, Lorraine
Blake, Kierkegaard, and the Spectre of dialectic.
. 1. Dialectics. Philosophical perspectives.
1. Title 100

Library of Congress cataloguing in publication data
Clark, Lorraine.
Blake, Kierkegaard, and the Spectre of dialectic / Lorraine Clark.
p.   cm.
Includes bibliographical references.
ISBN 0 521 39509 7
1. Blake, William, 1757–1827 – Philosophy. 2. Kierkegaard, Søren, 1813–1855 – Aesthetics.
3. Polarity (Philosophy) in literature. 4. Romanticism.
5. Dialectic. 6. Blake, William, 1757–1827.
7. Kierkegaard, Søren, 1813–1855. I TITLE.
PR4148.P5C43   1991
821'.7–dc20   90-24297 CIP

ISBN 0 521 395097 hardback

CE

For my parents,
John Hosie Clark and Rosamond Bailey Clark
and for Donald Kjelmyr

This mode of thought, from which a definite type of man is bred, starts from an absurd presupposition: it takes good and evil for realities that contradict one another (not as complementary value concepts, which would be the truth), it advises taking the side of the good, it desires that the good should renounce and oppose the evil down to its ultimate roots – it therewith actually denies life, which has in all its instincts both Yes and No ... And even here, life is still in the right – life, which does not know how to separate Yes from No –:

Nietzsche, The Will to Power

For a Line or Lineament is not formed by Chance a Line is a Line in its Minutest Subdivisions Strait or Crooked It is Itself & Not Intermeasurable with or by any Thing Else Such is Job but since the French Revolution Englishmen are all Intermeasurable One by Another Certainly a happy state of Agreement to which I for One do not Agree. God keep me from the Divinity of Yes & No too the Yea Nay Creeping Jesus from supposing Up & Down to be the same Thing as all Experimentalists must suppose

Blake, Letter to Cumberland, April 12, 1827

An observation for theologians: King Lear, Act IV, Scene 6: "Aye and no too was no good divinity."

Kierkegaard, Journal

Contents

Acknowledgements

I wish to thank all who have contributed both directly and indirectly to my work on this book: Lee Patterson and Lorraine Miller Richey, profoundly formative intellectual influences long before the book was begun; Leo Damrosch, for his encouragement at a critical early juncture when I was losing faith in the project; Paul Cantor, who first suggested I explore the role of the Spectre in Blake's poetry, and who has provided invaluable criticism, advice, and support ever since the project's inception. My greatest intellectual debt is to Don Hirsch, whose lucidity of perception and generosity of spirit are very rare indeed.

I am grateful to the Canada Council for funding several years of graduate work on this project; to Kevin Taylor of Cambridge University Press; and to my first and final anonymous readers, whose exceptionally lucid, rigorous, yet generous reports made this a much better book, for all its faults, than it would otherwise have been.

Finally, I am deeply grateful to my parents, John and Rosamond Clark; to my friends and colleagues Andy Silber and Eugene Hill for their staunch personal and intellectual support; and to Adele Davidson for her wit and quiet wisdom over the course of our long friendship. My greatest immediate debt is to my husband, Donald Kjelmyr, who has patiently read and discussed every stage of this book with me, and who shares with Blake and Kierkegaard a stubbornly polemical temperament and an enduring passion for ideas. Like them, he often speaks in paradoxes but can always explain them when he pleases.

A note on texts and abbreviations

All Blake quotations are from David Erdman's *The Poetry and Prose of William Blake*, with commentary by Harold Bloom (Garden City, NY: Doubleday & Co., 1982). For convenience I have included Erdman's page numbers after Blake's plate and line numbers. Blake's most frequently cited works are abbreviated as follows:

BA	The Book of Ahania
BU	The Book of Urizen
FZ	The Four Zoas
GA	The Ghost of Abel
J	Jerusalem
M	Milton
MHH	The Marriage of Heaven and Hell
VLJ	A Vision of the Last Judgment

Kierkegaard's most frequently cited works are also abbreviated, as follows, from the following translations and editions:

CD   *The Concept of Dread*, transl. Walter Lowrie (Princeton: Princeton University Press, 1944).

CI   *The Concept of Irony*, transl. Lee M. Capel (Bloomington and London: Indiana University Press, 1965).

CUP   *Concluding Unscientific Postscript*, transl. David F. Swenson and Walter Lowrie (Princeton: Princeton University Press, 1941).

E/O   *Either/Or*, vol.I, transl. David F. Swenson and Lillian Swenson (Princeton: Princeton University Press, 1944).
Either/Or, vol.II transl. Walter Lowrie (Princeton: Princeton University Press, 1944).

FT   *Fear and Trembling*, transl. Walter Lowrie (Princeton: Princeton University Press, 1941).

PV   *The Point of View for my Work as an Author*, transl. Walter Lowrie (New York: Harper & Row, Publishers, Inc., 1962).

R   *Repetition*, transl. Walter Lowrie (Princeton: Princeton University Press, 1941).

SUD *The Sickness Unto Death*, transl. Walter Lowrie (Princeton: Princeton University Press, 1941).

Introduction

No, everything has its dialectic, not indeed such a dialectic as
makes it sophistically relative (this is mediation), but a dialectic
by which the absolute becomes manifest as the absolute by
virtue of the dialectical.

Johannes Climacus, *Concluding Unscientific Postscript*

I will compel thee to rebuild by these my furious waves
Death choose or life thou strugglest in my waters, now choose
life.

Blake, *The Four Zoas*

Blake scholarship has been persistently rife with analogues, and the
appearance of yet another is likely to meet with skepticism if not
outright dismay.[1] But the idea of an analogue in Kierkegaard is a
compelling one: despite Blake's Nietzschean moments, Kierkegaard's radically individual Protestantism or "Christianity" – the
tension between religion and nihilism in his work – has always
suggested a better analogue for Blake, whose figure of Christ in his
last poem *Jerusalem* invokes at least a theological remnant of sorts.
Deconstructive and poststructuralist criticism have brought this
latent analogue into sharper prominence, for it has been increasingly observed of both authors that they are curiously at once
"proto-deconstructive," one might say (although I must apologize
for this extraordinarily ugly adjective), and anti-deconstructive.[2]
Indeed, Kierkegaard has been thoroughly deconstructed to the
point that he has himself become a master deconstructionist who
brings his corrosive skepticism to bear on the question of religion or
any metaphysics of presence.[3] Blake thus far has proved more
resistant to such dissolution, and it is interesting to speculate why
this should be so. "Blake has not – apparently – been very interesting to poststructuralism and vice versa," W.J.T. Mitchell has
recently remarked; yet the late Paul de Man suggested to Mitchell,

as he recounts it, that this is because Blake is himself such a deconstructionist that "there are no secrets or repressions" to be exposed by deconstructive analysis.[4] Mitchell further and more interestingly suggests that in fact Blake may be "the secret agenda of poststructuralist romantic criticism, the marginal figure who infiltrates the center" (91). More than this, he may be "the repressed Other who haunts and indirectly *dominates* the [poststructuralist] discourse from which he is excluded" (my emphasis); and it is this provocative insight – the insight in turn linking Blake most compellingly with Kierkegaard – that my study explores.

The observation that Blake and Kierkegaard are at once deconstructive and anti-deconstructive duplicates the observation in earlier scholarship that they are at once Hegelian and anti-Hegelian.[5] This duplication is no accident, for both observations rest on the profound insight that their notion of "dialectic" *mirrors* – that is to say, both repeats and inverts – the logic of dialectic informing Hegelianism, romantic irony, and (I shall argue) deconstruction. What Blake and Kierkegaard fundamentally share is an eccentric idea of dialectic: Kierkegaard's famous "either/or," which stands in fierce opposition to the "both-and" logic not only of Hegelian mediation, but of Schlegelian romantic irony and in turn of deconstruction. (Deconstruction's affinities with romantic irony are hotly disputed, but this dispute remains an open one, and I shall engage it in chapter v).[6] Kierkegaard characterizes Hegelian dialectic and Schlegelian romantic irony as equally "spectral," an abstract parody of the true dialectic of contraries constituting his ideal of "life." And it is in a very similar spectre of "Negation" – a spectre which "mediates" and hence negates life's contraries – that Blake–Los comes to define his greatest opponent.

Briefly, my argument is that in his new focus on the struggle of Los and the Spectre in *The Four Zoas*, *Milton*, and *Jerusalem*, Blake turns from a Hegelian "both-and" dialectic of Orc and Urizen in his early works to something very like a Kierkegaardian "either/or." This new dialectic of Los and the Spectre, truth and error, life and death, is in fact a complex inversion of the Orc–Urizen dialectic – an inversion which mirrors and yet radically transvalues that earlier dialectic. This transvaluation is rather in the nature of a conversion experience, embodying the same paradox of violent repudiation yet equally violent embrace. The act of repudiation in "either/or" is at the same time an act of embrace, a kind of "both-and" – and it is this

difficult paradox which constitutes the heart of our difficulties with
Blake and Kierkegaard. Kierkegaard's entire body of work is a
sustained struggle against, yet embrace of, both Schlegel's romantic
irony (which he calls "the aesthetic") and the Hegelian system ("the
ethical"), a struggle with system to deliver individuals from that
system. And it is a very similar struggle not merely between opposing principles or "contraries" but between two entire dialectics – a
systematic dialectic of negation and an unsystematic dialectic which
at once incorporates and rejects the both-and logic of idealist negation – that Blake dramatizes in the struggle between Los and the
Spectre of Urthona. Their shifting mirror relationship, their
shadowy resemblance, masks a profound opposition: the opposition
of life and death, the "either/or" with which Blake and Kierkegaard
finally confront us.

The dialectic of Los and the Spectre of Urthona which Blake
worked out during his three years at Felpham and made into the
central dynamic of *Milton* and *Jerusalem* was an extraordinary
breakthrough for him, a solution (as he saw it) to the problem of
"the contraries" which had dogged him throughout his career. For
although he never wavered from characterizing life as a dynamic
interaction of contraries, he struggled throughout his career with
different ways of representing that interaction. His continual rewor-
king of the *Songs of Innocence and Experience* was part of this struggle, as
was his sustained engagement with the battle between Orc and
Urizen which Frye has so thoroughly explicated.[7] Blake's increasing
dissatisfaction with this static Orc cycle, as Frye has called it, and
final abandonment of that battle with the appearance of the Spectre
of Urthona is the crisis or turning point around which this study
revolves.

This turn is also familiar to readers as the turn from Blake's "Two
Classes of Men" (*The Marriage*) to the "Three Classes of Men"
(*Milton* and *Jerusalem*), and from "the Two Contraries" to "the Two
Contraries and the Reasoning Negative." He further confusingly
titles these two contraries "the Reprobate" and "the Redeemed,"
and calls the third class of men "the Elect." The dialectic is further
complicated by the fact that the two contraries are within Los, while
the "reasoning negative" is the Spectre.

Unravelling the dynamics of this dialectic will be the task of this
study. For the moment, the point is that the new and crucial
feature in this later dialectic is the addition of a third element: the

Reasoning Negative or Negation (the Third Class of Men or the Elect):

> There is a Negation, & there is a Contrary
> The Negation must be destroyd to redeem the Contraries
> The Negation is the Spectre; the Reasoning Power in Man
> This is a false Body: an Incrustation over my Immortal
> Spirit; a Selfhood, which must be put off & annihilated alway
> To cleanse the Face of my Spirit by Self-examination.
> (M, ii, 40:32–37; 142)

This negation or Spectre threatens to reconcile or mediate the contraries of life within Los, reducing them from absolutes to mere relativities within a system. But Blake despises such mutual accommodation as a blurring of distinctions which reduces the passion or energy of life, and relegates this kind of "marriage" to the secondary realm of Beulah – "To where the Contraries of Beulah War beneath Negations Banner" (M, ii, 34:23; 134).

Because Los must cast off this negation, Blake's dialectic of Los and the Spectre is one of exclusion not inclusion, emphatically not a happy marriage of contraries. And it is this new, central emphasis on casting off, on decisively differentiating between men and their spectres, between "sheep" and "goats," and between truth and error, which makes Blake's dialectic so resistant to the all-inclusive, both-and logic not only of Hegelian dialectic but of idealist dialectics in general. His dialectic of life is the activity of clarifying muddled perception into clear-cut differentiation or what he calls "minute discrimination" (VLJ; 560). As Blake cogently summarizes his dialectic,

All Life consists of these Two Throwing off Error & Knaves from our company continually & recieving Truth or Wise Men into our Company Continually.... to be an Error & to be Cast out is a part of Gods Design No Man can Embrace True Art till he has Explord & Cast out False Art ... whenever any Individual Rejects Error & Embraces Truth a Last Judgment passes upon that Individual. (VLJ; 562)

Hegelian readings of Blake's dialectic result largely from taking as the law of Blake's dialectic his famous aphorism from *The Marriage* that "Without contraries is no progression" (MHH 3; 34). But this is the very doctrine that Blake later repudiates – at least in its original sense, and as it is commonly understood – in *Milton* and *Jerusalem*. As Leo Damrosch has observed, Blake's final dialectic of contraries does not keep them "forever opposed in [the] mutual immanence" of the Hegelian system,[8] but decisively casts one off:

It is tempting to understand Blake's aphorism ["Without Contraries ... " etc.] as pointing to a Hegelian *Aufhebung,*the dialectic that simultaneously annuls each stage and raises it to a higher one. But the developed Blakean myth has no place for the upward spiral that absorbs each preceding stage, emphasizing instead that the Spectral or Satanic must be expelled utterly. ... Blake's movement away from the optimistic "progression" of *The Marriage of Heaven and Hell* and toward the drastic exclusion of "negation" represents a recognition that much in our experience is radically unassimilable.[9]

If, for Blake, "All Life consists of these two throwing off Error & Knaves from our Company continually & recieving Truth or Wise Men into our Company Continually," life is not a gradual progression towards some increasingly visible goal or truth, but the repeated activity of casting off error and embracing truth. And in each act of embracing truth, that truth is whole and complete, not partial or a mere approximation of some final truth. As Damrosch points out, "Blake maintains ... , as Hegel would not, that the whole is fully present in each particular member, and is unwilling to hold as Hegel does that the particulars are necessarily finite and transitory" (151). In other words, Blake's contraries (synonymous with "particulars") are not merely parts adding up to some larger all-inclusive whole, but are wholes in themselves. Further, as Damrosch remarks, whatever Blake may mean by "progression" must be something very different from the usual Hegelian understanding of it as a gradual, incremental movement towards an absolute goal: "Blake's system is often called dialectical, but it is so only in a special sense, envisioning truth as the simultaneous union of all particulars rather than as the sequential development that we ordinarily expect in dialectic" (27–28). More recently, Steven Shaviro has perhaps best described Blake's real sense of progression as "the continuation of a lived tension of opposites:"

Dialectical progression always implies the "Abstract objecting power" (J 10:14, E151) of negation and comprehension, whereas Blake insists upon the positivity of both contraries, their active and continuing opposition. "Progression" thus has a very special meaning for Blake, implying the continuation of a lived tension of opposites, rather than any sublation or furthering resolution.[10]

Martin Nurmi similarly observed years ago that Blake's dialectic was anti-Hegelian – a dialectic of "being" not "becoming" – and in this remark we find I think the crux of Blake's (and not incidentally, of Kierkegaard's) opposition to the idealist dialectics of both-and logic or becoming:

Blake is not a Hegelian. Though he uses the word "progression" in *The Marriage*, his contrary forces do not, like Hegel's "thesis" and "antithesis," constitute a world process of "becoming." Indeed, Blake's Human world, in which the contraries freely interact, is not one of becoming at all, for it is perfect; the only "progression" there is in it is that of continued creativeness. And, of course, Blake would have nothing to do with anything as abstractly systematic as Hegel's dialectic.[11]

Nurmi's observation isolates a number of central anti-Hegelian features: Blake's objection to the idea of infinitely progressing towards, but never reaching, a final goal or absolute; his emphasis instead on the repeated embrace of that absolute (what Nurmi calls "continued creativeness") in the visionary experience; and his rejection of an abstract, systematic notion of contraries. Furthermore, Nurmi points out, Blake would abhor the Hegelian synthesis of contraries: "Nowhere in Blake's use of contraries does he provide for such a synthesis, except possibly in the very general one of the unity of Human life. And that is not really a Boehmian (or Hegelian) synthesis, because the contraries remain unchanged" (33). Here again Nurmi provides us with a critical phrase – "the very general ... unity of Human life" – and with a critical distinction: that between "synthesis" and "unity." For Blake's idea of unity is that of "life" – and most of the problems with his dialectic of human life stem from the problematic nature of that almost by definition indefinable ideal. Life for Blake is a unity but not a synthesis; it has a shape (Los) but not a fixed shape (Urizen or the Spectre); and it is a dynamic struggle but not therefore mere indeterminate flux, the endless striving of infinite becoming.

In all of these ways, then, Blake seems fundamentally anti-Hegelian. Yet in fact he is both Hegelian and anti-Hegelian; and further, he is so both at the beginning and at the end of his myth. It is true that in his change from a Hegelian dialectic of contraries to an anti-Hegelian dialectic of contraries and negations he might seem to have been "converted" from a systematic dialectic of becoming to an anti-systematic dialectic of being. But his turn from one to the other, as I hope to show, merely makes explicit an anti-Hegelianism – a rejection of "negation" – that was present all along; and in his rejection of Hegelianism he does not so much reject it as re-evaluate and "master" it. This is why Hegelian readings of Blake are not strictly wrong and why we continue to have the sense, rightly, that Blake is in some way Hegelian.

This Hegelian anti-Hegelianism is the very structure of Kierkegaard's "either/or," which, like Blake's dialectic of Los and the Spectre, incorporates yet radically transvalues the Hegelian logic of negation. It is a structure which may take us some considerable way towards explicating many of the apparent contradictions within Blake's thought. For, like the relationship of Los to the Spectre, the structure of either/or is such that it rejects yet contains both-and logic. Like Blake, Kierkegaard rejects the both-and logic of "Becoming" for a dialectic of "Being" in which the final vision of life is (to quote Shaviro once more) as an "active and continuing opposition" of contraries, "a lived tension of opposites, rather than any sublation or furthering resolution." For Kierkegaard, the Hegelian *Aufhebung* of contraries was a bloodless abstraction, the final evaporation of the romantic ideal of life through the agency not just of Hegel but of all the post-Kantian idealist systems. "The calamity of romanticism," he pronounced, "is that what it grasps is not actuality" (*CI*, 319). Just as Blake came to see in the course of his career that his originally systematic dialectic of contraries (Orc and Urizen) abstracted from and hence destroyed his ideal of life, so Kierkegaard came to see in the course of the romantic age that all the systematic idealist dialectics abstracted from and thereby destroyed life. Their easy mediation of contraries within what Kierkegaard called the "higher unity" of the Hegelian *Aufhebung* and the "higher madness" of Schlegel's romantic irony (*E/O*, II, 174) was a mediation which could occur only in the abstract realm of thought, not in the concrete realm of life. For Kierkegaard, "both-and" logic is life-denying because it blurs the absolute distinctions or minute discriminations in which life consists; it does not encourage choosing among alternatives, but rather suggests that all alternatives are equal. Life for Kierkegaard as for Blake is the activity of sharpening distinctions or "contraries" to the point at which they become absolute and one embraces truth in a moment of unmediated fusion with it.

Kierkegaard's dialectic, like Blake's, emphasizes subjectivity over objectivity, the individual over the system, exclusion over inclusion, passion over reason, truth and error over good and evil. It proceeds not through a series of gradual, mediated steps towards some absolute goal, but through a series of unmediated leaps, each of which is absolute in itself, a crisis of vision or "choice" which is also a "Last Judgment" differentiating truth from error, life from death. Its focus is what Kierkegaard calls "the instant," the moment of break-through when truth or the eternal enters time, the moment Blake refers to as the "Moment in each Day that Satan cannot find / Nor can his Watch Fiends find it" (M, II, 35:42–43; 136).

In apparently rejecting the mediations of both-and for the unme-diated leaps or decisive "crises" of either/or, however, Blake and Kierkegaard nonetheless retain both-and logic as essential to their vision of life, and it is this which makes them so difficult to explicate. The Spectre of both-and logic is the spirit of indeterminacy, per-spectivism, Becoming, and "error" who dissolves or relativizes life's contraries into undecidable oppositions; "either/or" attempts to reintroduce "decidability" into this prior dissolution. Blake and Kierkegaard thus try to "master" or "dominate" (Mitchell) the logic of indeterminacy or error as Blake–Los tries to master the Spectre. Yet it is critical to see that this spectre is also essential to their ideal of life, which is why, again, one can call them both Hegelian and anti-Hegelian, deconstructionist and anti-deconstruc-tionist. Both see this spectre of indeterminacy as central to their vision of life as flux; but because they do not want life to be *only* flux (the flux of pure Becoming that is Hegelian, Schlegelian, and deconstructive), they try to master this indeterminacy in the service of their truth of life. They attempt to reconstitute an idea of Being out of its prior dissolution within the Becoming of idealist dialectics (or less anachronistically in Blake's case, out of its dissolution in his Orc cycle of pure Becoming); and in this sense they might be said to respond to what Tilottama Rajan terms a "proto-deconstructive crisis" in nineteenth-century thought.[12]

The difficult logic informing their attempted reconstitution of "Being," the conversion of a spectral "both-and" into a living "either/or," is what this study attempts to explicate. This logic is a peculiarly negative one, which is why Blake and Kierkegaard are so notoriously difficult. The starting point of their dialectic, for example, is not a state of alienation requiring a mediation of contra-ries, but a state of mediation or dissolution requiring their differenti-ation. Their dialectic does not attempt to grasp "inclusively" the whole of life (as does the both-and system), but to consolidate "exclusively" the state of "error," in a "Last Judgment" or act of choice that sharply differentiates "error" from a truth of life that ideally (but not inevitably, and this is its precariousness) stands revealed in stark opposition by this consolidation. The Spectre "who will not defend Truth" must "be compelled to / Defend a Lie," as Blake puts it, "that he may be snared and caught and snared and taken / That Enthusiasm and Life may not cease" (J, 1, 9:29–31; 152).

This battle with the spectre of negation or error has an extraordinary vitality that I would like this study to convey. But to do so requires walking a fine line between two orthodoxies that are equally determined to collapse Blake (perhaps) and Kierkegaard (certainly) into either orthodox evangelical Christian theologians or into master deconstructionists. Deconstructionist readings of Kierkegaard dismiss resistance to their orthodoxy as a reactionary retreat into the staid Kierkegaard of early Kierkegaard scholarship, the Kierkegaard of evangelical Christianity. Conversely, Christian readings of Kierkegaard, while generally acknowledging the radicalism of that Christianity, nonetheless fail to grant the extraordinary precariousness of Kierkegaard's reconstituted Being – a precariousness that cannot, I would insist, *after* Kierkegaard be sustained. But I want to argue that it is sustained in Kierkegaard himself, as it is in Blake – and that this extraordinary tension between religion and nihilism is Blake's "wiry bounding line of life" attenuated to its very breaking point. Through their negative dialectic Blake and Kierkegaard do I think reconstitute a precarious Being out of its dissolution within Becoming, and my study traces this vigorous attempt. But because they reconstitute Being *for the sake of* Becoming or life, that Being is reduced to a mere limit, "the bound or outward circumference of energy." In this radically attenuated form it becomes dispensable to those who follow Kierkegaard; yet in his own thought it is critical to distinguish between a precarious Being and no Being at all, and thus to insist on a critical, however tenuous, distinction from a Nietzschean/deconstructive Becoming. Blake and Kierkegaard retain a certain *moderation* that critically distinguishes them from Nietzsche – the moderation behind their struggles with dialectic, as I shall argue. To collapse them at the very outset into either orthodoxy of religion or of deconstruction destroys not only this moderation but the vitality at the heart of their romantic ideal of life, the vitality at the heart of romanticism itself. I shall argue indeed that their ideal *is* finally "life" and not a Platonic truth or orthodox God; and those who would too easily dismiss this reading as theological are well advised to keep this in mind. Blake and Kierkegaard want to rescue "actuality" or "life" (what Kierkegaard also calls "existence") from its formalistic abstraction within idealist dialectics, and it is the extraordinary vitality of the attempt itself that may best testify to its success.

In some ways this alliance of Blake and Kierkegaard may seem an unlikely one, not only because of the historical gap between them, but because of political and perhaps temperamental differences. Blake's England was, from the 1770s through the early 1800s, in the throes of division over first of all the American revolution and later England's response to the French revolution and involvement in the Napoleonic wars. And Blake responded as a political liberal to these events, always championing the cause of liberty against tyranny in all its guises. Kierkegaard, writing in Denmark in the 1840s, was by contrast a political conservative who championed the monarchy and deplored the increasing democratization of Denmark, a movement which he saw as consolidating the slide into mediocrity brought upon "Christendom" by the Hegelian systematic philosophy. The only revolution he witnessed was the bloodless revolution of 1848 – and his sympathies were decidedly not with the revolutionists.[13]

Yet Blake and Kierkegaard seem to have had uneasy and controversial relations with the realm of politics, and may well themselves transcend or expose the conservative–liberal opposition as an illusory one, in the pattern we will come to see as characteristic of their thought. It is generally accepted that although Blake did not become a political conservative he significantly moderated his early revolutionary ideas.[14] And while Kierkegaard is called a conservative, he spent most of his life attacking the political and social *status quo* in Denmark, the complacently institutionalized bourgeois society of Hegelian Christendom. More significantly, both at times seem to repudiate politics in the name of a radical individualism. Kierkegaard remarks that it is an "illusion" "to believe that corruption comes from a king, an emperor, a Pope, a tyrant, or a national leader; if only he can be toppled, the earth will be saved. ... Any reformation which is not aware that fundamentally every single individual needs to be reformed is *eo ipso* an illusion."[15] This finds an almost uncanny echo in Blake's rather bitter remark

I am really sorry to see my Countrymen trouble themselves about Politics. If Men were wise, the Most arbitrary Princes could not hurt them If they are not Wise the Freest Government is compell'd to be a Tyranny[.] Princes appear to me to be Fools Houses of Commons & Houses of Lords appear to me to be fools; they seem to me to be something Else besides Human Life. (Public Address; 580)

As the appropriation of such philosophers as Nietzsche and Heidegger to serve both right- and left-wing political agendas surely attests, attempts to claim relationships of entailment between philosophy and politics are in any case precarious ones at best.[16] Independently of their political differences, Blake and Kierkegaard attack all rationalistic abstractions from life, particularly those which seem to them to be turning the individual into an atomistic, isolated ego, "selfhood," or "spectre." Both also clearly belong within the long Inner Light Protestant tradition dating from Luther, a tradition persistently dualistic in the qualitative disjunction – the "either/or" – it perceives between the inner and the outer, the spiritual and the natural man (again, the battle of Los with the Spectre). They share as well the logic of idealist dialectics, a logic of contraries rooted in the theology of Jacob Boehme, generally acknowledged as the father of German idealism. And this logic of contraries is a very limited one; it does not allow for an infinite or even a very wide range of permutations. The narrowness of this rigidly systematic logic may well have been what roused their energies in stubborn opposition – and what arguably forced them into similar strategies of circumvention.[17]

A more telling objection to their alliance may well be the more subjective matter of personal temperament. I shall be arguing that "either/or," grounded as it is in the inner life of the individual, is a profoundly "temperamental" dialectic, the expression above all of a deeply polemical temperament which Blake and Kierkegaard should accordingly share. Yet Blake was a visionary and Kierkegaard a skeptic – or so at least they might appear at first glance. Blake seems by most accounts to have been subject to extremes of emotion, from debilitating melancholy to ecstatic visionary trances. But he seems to have consistently abhorred furtiveness and secrecy; his fundamental impulse is towards honesty, openness, or what Kierkegaard might call "revelation" as opposed to hiddenness. And it is clear that although he often felt blocked and thwarted, he also experienced moments of great fulfillment and serenity. Kierkegaard, by contrast, was apparently a much more secretive and even furtive individual, whose life may have been (as skeptical readings would have it) an extended exercise in deception.[18] If Blake was, as Samuel Palmer called him, "a man without a mask,"[19] Kierkegaard may have been, next to Nietzsche, the man of masks *par excellence*. Deconstructionist readings deny that a single author, "Kierkegaard," ever emerges or reveals himself from behind his various pseudonyms;[20] and one might speculate equally about whether Kierkegaard ever felt he had experienced the kind of personal revelation that Blake claimed to have experienced in the person of Christ.

Blake hated all calculation, what he would call the "cool villainy" of intellect so different from the (for him) forgivable sins of excessive emotion. He wanted his art to be rooted in life not intellect – and as more than one critic has proposed, it is rooted in *his* life, a life of ideas governed not by reasoned logical relationships but by painful emotional crises. This is precisely Kierkegaard's claim for his dialectic of "either/or" – that unlike Hegel's rational, systematic dialectic abstracted from the turbulent crises of existence, his dialectic is rooted not only in the life of the individual situated in existence, but in the biographical crises of *his* life as an individual equally firmly situated in existence. Yet skeptics insist that there is something very calculated about Kierkegaard's entire authorship, a persistent self-consciousness and manipulation of supposedly real events that dissolves its claims for a grounding in the "authenticity" of emotional crisis or life.

This difference between the secretive, skeptical Kierkegaard and the visionary Blake may to some extent simply mark the difference between the philosopher and the poet; and one can point out that, in the end, both writers are philosopher–poets in the embrace of philosophy and poetry so characteristic of the romantic age. More to the point, however, is the widespread recognition of Blake's skeptical (again, "deconstructive") tendencies – a hiddenness to his writing that is something more than unintentional obscurity and that is in tension with his vatic and visionary moments. Like Kierkegaard, Blake experienced intensely the two-edged sword of reason or intellect: the extent to which it could be fruitfully employed on the one hand in corrosively exposing the illusion or "error" around him, but the extent to which on the other hand it could escape his control and turn on him, radically undermining his faith in life. This again is what Los's battle with the Spectre dramatizes: a deeply-felt polarization in Blake's psyche between affirmation and negation, revelation and concealment, faith and skepticism, certainty and uncertainty. This polarization persistently confronts his interpreters with a "contradiction between the two most commonly received images of the poet: that of Blake as systematizer, as sage and teacher, as essentially doctrinal poet, and that of Blake as dramatic poet and master of irony who rarely or never speaks *in propria persona.*"[21] This description applies equally well to Kierkegaard, whose authoritative stance on the one hand yet refusal to speak *in propria persona* once again suggests almost uncanny alliance with Blake.

If Blake is a highly rational philosopher–poet, Kierkegaard is equally a poet–philosopher. His poetic tendencies almost need no remark, for he articulates on explicit theoretical grounds why a preoccupation with fictional technique is essential to his authorship. Poetry – that is, "the aesthetic," the playful oscillations and radical perspectivism of Schlegelian romantic irony – is essential to his vision of life, and thus permeates his entire authorship to the point that it threatens to dissolve his authority altogether (again, as the deconstructionist reading argues). The indeterminacies of aestheticism might seem therefore to dissolve Kierkegaard entirely into an "irrational" poet; yet curiously, these indeterminacies are also what make him a philosopher. For his point is that the Schlegelian aestheticism that dissolves the decidability of contraries is essentially no different from the Hegelian rationalism that similarly relativizes or dissolves the contraries of life. The rational and the aesthetic are two forms of a single "irony" united in the person of the philosopher–poet.

These ironic or skeptical dissolutions of reason and poetry must again, however, be "mastered" in the service of his truth of life; they must be forced into determinate shape or consolidated as "error." Here again the aptness of Blake's Spectre should be apparent; for Los's labor to make the Spectre work for him at his forge is none other than his attempt to "master" an all-dissolving skepticism and aestheticism in the service of his similar truth of life. For Blake, as for Kierkegaard, although the irony of reason and aesthetics is essential to life, life remains something always "beyond" it, and it is in this sense that life for them "masters" skeptical irony as Los masters the Spectre.

Since life is beyond both philosophy and poetry (beyond both reason and aesthetics), this means of course that in a certain sense

Blake and Kierkegaard are not only philosopher-poets but also resolutely anti-philosophical and anti-poetic, in the name of their higher truth of life. Orthodox Christian readings call this truth God; yet as deconstructionists correctly point out, in his attack on orthodox religion Kierkegaard is also anti-theological. But the deconstructionist orthodoxy claims that Kierkegaard's higher truth is poetry or aesthetics – that like the romantic ironist Kierkegaard aesthetically "creates" life in an endless flux of creation and destruction. This aesthetic reading is what I shall dispute, not however in the name of an orthodox theological Being, but in the name of his higher truth of life. Deconstructionists identify life with a condition of idealist/ Nietzschean Becoming; but it is precisely this identification that Kierkegaard tries to resist. He is certainly anti-philosophical and anti-theological in the name of life; he is also, however, as deconstructionists will not acknowledge, anti-poetic in the name of life. Kierkegaard insists on critically distinguishing between "choosing" one's life versus either "knowing" it (through a philosophical "reason") or "creating" it (through a romantic–ironic aestheticism or "will"). Skeptical readings collapse Kierkegaard's "choosing" into "creating," which is how Kierkegaard becomes a deconstructionist and a poet;[22] and I would agree that, after Kierkegaard, this collapse is inevitable. But again, Kierkegaard's vitality lies in his struggle *not* to collapse "choosing" into "creating" – not to collapse life into the formalist abstractions of philosophy, theology, or aesthetics, all forms of irony that for him dissolve life into a shadow-boxing of fictions. Kierkegaard is not Nietzsche; and for very similar reasons, neither is Blake. They are not only Hegelian and anti-Hegelian, deconstructive and anti-deconstructive; they are philosophical and anti-philosophical, aesthetic and anti-aesthetic, theological and anti-theological, in the extraordinary balancing-act that makes them so notoriously difficult, with the "difficulty" Kierkegaard claims is life itself.

The point of this analogy, then, is two-fold: to explicate the dynamics of Blake's curiously eccentric or negative dialectic in *The Four Zoas*, *Milton*, and *Jerusalem* – his turn from Orc and Urizen to Los and the Spectre – and to illuminate in turn thereby the tension between nihilism and religion that is the informing energy of romanticism. I am arguing that Blake–Los's central task in the last prophecies is to confront his readers with a moment of Kierkegaardian *choice*, a moment precariously suspended between and beyond philosophical "knowing" and aesthetic "creating" – "beyond" them not in some theological realm but in the realm of life or actuality. Blake exhorts his readers not to "know" themselves or to "create" themselves, but to *choose* themselves. Others have noted the centrality of this Blakean moment of choice, but in ways that have tended to aestheticize it as a matter of mere stylistic choice or as a moment of deconstructive *aporia*.[23] But through "choice" or "decisiveness" Blake attempts to master or dominate this aesthetic *aporia* by forcing it out of its undecidability or indeterminacy; for him, as for Kierkegaard, "decisiveness is precisely the eternal protest against all fictions" or rationalistic abstractions from life (*CUP*, 203). This moment of choice appears with remarkable frequency throughout Blake's poetry: in the consolidation of the Spectre as "error," in the paradox of the Blakean incarnation-as-crucifixion and Last Judgment (as David Wagenknecht has recently so astutely noted),[24] in the apparently undecidable verbal oppositions in such poems as "The Clod and the Pebble" (as Jerome McGann was one of the first to note),[25] in the radical perspectivism that so pervades every facet – verbal, visual, and philosophical – of Blake's myth. This perspectivism was first noted by Frye, whose observation that the worlds of Eden, Beulah, Generation and Ulro are simply the different perspectives adding up to "Four-fold Vision" has been radicalized in the new attention to Blake's perspectivism as sheer indeterminacy without any truth, ground, or "Being" to which this perspectivism finally points.[26] Frye was also the first to remark the perspectivism of the dialectic of Los and the Spectre – that their conflict is itself one of opposed perspectives on life; and the rhetoric of *Fearful Symmetry* is pervaded with the "either/or" of this perspectival opposition.[27] Again, the thrust of this study is to demonstrate how Blake and Kierkegaard attempt to use this perspectivism against itself, to prevent it from dissolving into a dialectic of pure Becoming, to master it as Los masters the Spectre.

The extraordinary tension implicit in the Blakean and Kierkegaardian idea of choice is also the tension or paradox at the heart of romanticism: its tension between transcendence and immanence, religion and humanism, or more radically, between religion and nihilism. Gerald Graff reminds us that in the debate over whether the romantics were humanists or nihilists, "both sides are right": critics such as Abrams and Wellek base their "optimistic" interpretation of romanticism on "what the romantics themselves

consciously intended," while critics such as J.Hillis Miller and
Harold Bloom base their "nihilistic" interpretation "on the logical
consequences of romantic ideas, independent of intentions."[28]
Again, this is another precarious (and much-disputed) distinction
whose dissolution I would like to resist. The logical consequences of
Blake's and Kierkegaard's ideal of life are, I would agree, inevitably
nihilistic; but it is in their intentions that their extraordinary vitality
resides. In their struggle with the Spectre of idealist dialectics, the
romantic ideal of life as paradox burns with the fierce intensity and
clarity of its moment of extinction.

This study is written not for Kierkegaardians but for Blake schol-
ars and romanticists. Kierkegaardians will find not a new Kierkegaard but one of the Kierkegaards they already know, the Kierkegaard who sustains a precarious difference from Nietzsche. Again,
this difference has been under such attack by deconstructionist
readings that its dissolution is regarded as a foregone conclusion; but
the debate should I think remain an open one. By privileging the
aesthetic Kierkegaard, deconstructionist readings have perhaps usefully corrected traditional Anglo-American theological readings
which may have underestimated the central role of "the poetic" in
Kierkegaard's thought. But these readings have become a new
orthodoxy which may be just as one-sided as the old theological one.
Kierkegaard himself exposes religious and deconstructive (aesthetic)
readings as two sides of the same coin; his ideal of "mastered irony"
is neither theological nor deconstructive but attempts to go beyond
both. The concept of mastered irony is in fact my central disagreement with deconstructionist readings, for they mistakenly call
"irony" that which "resists" "the System" (meaning the Hegelian
system or dialectic), and "mastered irony" that which is "sublated,"
"dialectized," or "reduced to a moment" within the System.[29] On
the contrary, I shall argue, for Kierkegaard irony *is* the System,
which negates, ironizes, and dissolves all real differences within
itself; only by *escaping* irony – by resisting or standing outside of the
ironizing, negating System with a firm foothold in *life* – does one
"master" irony in what is finally (at least ideally) an unironic
stance.

Aesthetic readings of Kierkegaard privilege the aesthetic by privileging *The Concept of Irony* as representative of the Kierkegaardian
irony elaborated in the later pseudonymous works.[30] My argument
is that *The Concept of Irony* is not representative of the pseudonymous

works but instead describes the "unmastered" philosophical (Hegelian) and aesthetic (Schlegelian) irony Kierkegaard so forcefully repudiates in the later works. *The Concept of Irony* ends with the tantalizing ideal of mastered irony which Kierkegaard then propounds with extraordinary consistency throughout the pseudonymous works: not the unmastered irony which dissolves and negates life, but the mastered irony which "now limits, renders finite, defines, and thereby yields truth, actuality, and content" (*CI*, 338–339). My claim, therefore, is that *Either/Or* more accurately represents the pseudonymous works as a whole and Kierkegaard's ideal of mastered irony properly understood. *Either/Or* initiates the sustained rhetoric of "decidability" which the pseudonymous works oppose to all idealist hermeneutics of undecidability or unmastered irony.

This Kierkegaard, however familiar, needs at this point I think to be rescued from his dissolution (or hardening) into either theological or aesthetic extreme. His familiarity also receives a new vitality from seeing it within the context of contemporary debates about the hermeneutics of undecidability, for Kierkegaard's complaint that such hermeneutics negate action and life – that they are simply untrue to our situatedness in life, to how we do and must live and act in the world – is finding increasing articulation within these debates.[31] Such debates have now gone beyond arguments about whether decidability (or determinacy) is possible (that possibility and indeed necessity being acknowledged even by deconstructionists),[32] and it is not my purpose to reiterate those arguments here. Rather, insofar as the study indirectly addresses those debates it is concerned with the implications of adopting a hermeneutics of undecidability as Kierkegaard – and less explicitly, Blake – unfold them. Blake's and Kierkegaard's terms as I deal with them here are largely ethical and religious (in a qualified sense) rather than political, and as such they may be of little interest to those primarily concerned with the politics of undecidability. But they are simply the terms of life as Blake and Kierkegaard conceive of it.

Despite his familiarity, this Kierkegaard of mastered irony thus serves I hope as more than merely innocuous and static background for explicating Blake. Not only can the analogy also yield implications for current theoretical debate, it may yield (perhaps even for Kierkegaardians) some new insight into Kierkegaard: first of all, in my argument for the essential moderation of his dialectic, and secondly, in my concluding argument that Kierkegaard may be not the first existentialist so much as the last romantic. While his polemic against romantic irony is a familiar topic in Kierkegaard scholarship, the argument for his own profound romanticism – made largely through this analogy with Blake – is not.

Because in opposition to the spectral abstractions of idealist logic "either/or" purports to be a dialectic of crisis or life, Chapter 1 opens with the biographical crises that marked Blake's and Kierkegaard's decisive turn from "both-and" to "either/or": Blake's crisis with William Hayley at Felpham, and Kierkegaard's crisis – his broken engagement – with Regina Olsen. (Again, skeptics insist that Regina became a poetic fiction and that this crisis was entirely manufactured; but in the interests of preserving Kierkegaard's vitality I must insist that this question remain open to debate.)[33] Both crises, I argue, involve rejecting the "marriage" or mediation of contraries for a reconstituted hierarchy of contraries symbolically expressed as the relation of father to son. Blake's rejection of Hayley as "error" and embrace or reconstitution of John Milton as "truth" marks his turn from a dialectic of contraries to one of contraries and negations; from the indeterminate Orc cycle of pure Becoming or Error to a reconstituted Being or Reason in the person of Milton himself.

Chapter 2 explores Blake's and Kierkegaard's identification of all life-denying formalist abstractions not with a Urizenic reason (as in Blake's early myth), but with the spectre of abstract *perspective*, a spectre of inaction, "jealousy," and "dread." Through explications of the Los–Spectre confrontations in *The Four Zoas*, *Milton*, and *Jerusalem*, it charts Blake's discovery of this idea and the way in which it inverts the old Orc–Urizen cycle, thus allowing Blake to "redeem the contraries," in a dialectic not of *inclusive contraries* (both-and) but of *exclusive perspectives* (either/or).

Chapter 3 turns to Kierkegaard's argument in the pseudonymous works that the root cause of the nineteenth century's abstraction from life in both its Hegelian and Schlegelian forms is its abolition of the principle of contradiction in the idealist dialectics of pure Becoming, which he dismisses as dialectics of Negation and Error. It explores the dynamics of the idea of "choice" whereby he hopes to reintroduce true contradiction or "difference" into life – the Being that has been dissolved within the dialectics of Becoming. This makes explicit the central parallel with Blake, thereby situating him relative to the romantic discourses of Hegelian and Schlegelian dialectic with which Kierkegaard is concerned. The dynamics of Kierkegaard's idea of choice are rather subtle, for this choice converts the idealist romantic logic of inclusive contraries into a logic of exclusive perspectives, precisely Blake's dialectic of Los vs. the Spectre, truth vs. error, life vs. death.

Chapter 4 concerns issues of sex and murder: how one re-establishes the grounds of human community "negated" by idealist ironies. Blake and Kierkegaard try to reconstitute or revitalize the sexual and ethical grounds or "contraries" of human community dissolved into pure *eros* on the one hand or stultified into bourgeois stolidity on the other. Their attempts to revitalize the sexual contraries and the ethical contraries of good and evil (the latter explored in readings of two acts of murder: Abraham's "sacrifice" of Isaac in *Fear and Trembling* and Cain's murder of Abel in Blake's poetic drama "The Ghost of Abel") provide the key to their attempt to refound an ideal community or "brotherhood" of life on mastered irony.

Chapter 5 explores the problems of irony and authority in language: how Blake and Kierkegaard try to reconstitute a notion of interpretive decidability out of its dissolution within the proto-deconstructive undecidabilities of romantic irony. I argue that their final appeal is neither to a "providential ethics of interpretation" nor to a Nietzschean or deconstructive "aesthetics of interpretation," but to the activity or life of interpretation itself.

The conclusion examines the figures of Christ and Socrates as the culminating symbols of the true contraries of Will and Intellect in Blake's and Kierkegaard's dialectic of life, and assesses the potent paradox of the incarnation as the central symbol for their truth of life as the paradox of choice or mastered irony: Los's mastery over the Spectre.

Every analogy must break down at some point; and that point in this study may be the idea of history. In keeping with his refusal to speculate on the shape of history or even on whether it has a shape, Kierkegaard professes only indignation that Hegel reduces the individual to "a scum upon the immanent development of infinity"(*CUP*, 485), and insists that no matter how many "mediations" a man may make of his life in retrospect, in his inner history, which "neither history nor world-history can take ... from him, ...

there rules ... an absolute either/or. An either/or still separates
enduringly that which was separated when he chose" (Judge
William, *E/O*, II, 179). Blake's vision of history as "the Seven Eyes of
God," seven attempts to awaken the sleeping Albion,[34] finds no
parallel in Kierkegaard, and to try to force one would be unwise and
probably futile. This breakdown is significant, for it suggests that
whatever absolute or truth stands revealed for Blake in sharp opposition to error is not so radically Other as Kierkegaard's version of
that truth. Blake can still envisage history or God as having a human
form – precisely the sort of mythologizing of the other that Kierkegaard refuses to do. The most that Kierkegaard will concede is that
"reality" may be "a system – for God" (as it cannot be for the
existing individual); but to speculate further on the shape of this
whole would contradict his entire philosophy, the point of which is
to relinquish the illusion that one can "see" the whole of life or
history (again, the illusory Hegelian standpoint abstracted from
life). Only by intensifying one's partial vision, one's finite perspective as an existing individual, can one perhaps indirectly grasp this
whole of life, a whole that nonetheless for Kierkegaard resists not
only rational comprehension but also poetic mythologizing of the
sort in which Blake engages. This difference further suggests why it
has been harder to make a radical ironist of Blake than of Kierkegaard; for Blake's mythologizing of history in contrast to its apparent blankness for Kierkegaard is clearly one of the kinds of details
that point to a persistently visionary and religious dimension in
Blake. But despite the issue of history, the ground of the analogy I
think holds firm: the basic idea that for both Blake and Kierkegaard,
the absolute or truth of life becomes manifest not through "mediation" but through "differentiation," a consolidation of error
against which that truth emerges in sharp opposition in the moment
of "Last Judgment" or choice. Both see this dialectic of negative
differentiation as their only hope for preserving the qualitative
otherness of transcendence from the dissolutions of irony; and that
Kierkegaard refuses to conceptualize or mythologize this otherness
may simply mark a greater philosophical consistency than we see in
Blake. For not only does Blake still continue to mythologize this
other, he refers to such mysteriously vague traces of transcendence as
"the Eternals" and "the Divine Assembly." It is however the greatly
attenuated quality of this theological remnant or "ground" – its
emptiness yet its presence as a necessary "limit" – that I am

suggesting Blake fundamentally shares with Kierkegaard. The question of history I leave to others more interested and more qualified to pursue.

My purpose is simply to explore the complex dynamic of Blake's turn to Los and the Spectre in the last prophecies as the true dialectic of life, a dynamic made more visible perhaps by a possible philosophical analogue in Kierkegaard. This focus on the Spectre is admittedly a narrow one; but despite nearly universal acknowledgement of his central role in the late prophecies no such extended study exists.[35] And to understand the Spectre is to understand more clearly the nature of the radical perspectivism and "error" so central to Blake's myth – its affinities with yet precarious differences from an all-dissolving Nietzschean perspectivism. "Perspectivism," "unmastered irony," and "error" are indeed the critical terms in this study, for my claim is that in Blake and Kierkegaard we see most clearly the origins of the perspectivism, irony, and error central not only to romanticism but to postmodern thought. Blake and Kierkegaard together are among the earliest and most rigorous advocates of the ironic or perspectival view of life, which sees life as radically contingent perspectives or "points of view." Like the Nietzschean and postmodern ironist, they employ perspectivism and error to dissolve the dogmatic "foundational" authorities of theological and philosophical Being or Truth. At the same time, however, unlike the postmodern ironist they see the problems with this dissolution: that perspectivism or unmastered irony can impose a new kind of tyranny, skeptically dissolving into spectral abstractions the very action and life it hoped to capture. This awareness – that one cannot live and act according to the skeptical negations of radical perspectivism – is what leads Blake and Kierkegaard to try to reconstitute foundational ideas of reason, being, truth, and individual selfhood or agency out of their dissolution; it leads them to try to reconstitute philosophy, one might say, out of poetry.[36] They attempt this not, however, on orthodox foundational grounds but on the grounds of perspectivism itself: they attempt to reconstitute Being for the sake of Becoming, reason for the sake of passion or will, philosophy for the sake of poetry or life. This heroic attempt accounts both for their success and (perhaps) for their ultimate failure. It also accounts for their profound affinities with, yet curiously intractable resistance to, the discourses of Hegelian mediation, Schlegelian romantic irony, and poststructuralist poetics within which critics have attempted to locate them. This same stubborn resistance, I shall argue, is what makes them finally most profoundly "romantic," decisively differentiating them from their postmodern successors.

Through the analogy with Kierkegaard, then, I hope to suggest directions for situating Blake relative to the critical discourses he has thus far so successfully resisted. Such an attempt is not designed to tame or extinguish the Blakean tyger that has resisted easy assimilation within these discourses, the tyger I shall argue is at the heart of romanticism. Nor is it an attempt to equate this tyger with the "rough beast" that Mary Lynn Johnson suggests is slouching towards Blake studies to be born[37] – although that may well be the outcome of my study. On the contrary, it is designed to keep Blake's tyger burning bright – like life, "beyond" these discourses and their gods.

CHAPTER I

The Spectre and the logic of error

Thou art in Error Albion, the land of Ulro
One error not remov'd, will destroy a Human Soul
Repose in Beulah's night till the Error is remov'd
Reason not on both sides.
                                    Blake, *Jerusalem*

We read in fairy tales about human beings whom mermaids
and mermen enticed into their power by means of demoniac
music. In order to break the enchantment it was necessary for
the person who was under the spell to play the same piece of
music backwards without making a single mistake. This is very
profound, but very difficult to perform, and yet so it is: the
errors one has taken into oneself one must eradicate in this way,
and every time one makes a mistake one must begin all over.
                                    Judge William, *Either/Or*

Crises in their personal lives contributed in large measure to the
erratic evolutions of Blake and Kierkegaard as poet–philosophers.
True to their own dialectic of crisis, of the individual, and of "life,"
they perceived certain events in their lives as decisive turning points
for their thought and literary production. "At the first glance I saw
that he was a poet," says Kierkegaard's Constantine Constantius,
" – for this reason, if for no other, that an occurrence which, if it had
happened to a commonplace man would quietly have come to
nothing, assumed in his case the proportions of a cosmic event" (*R*,
137). By Kierkegaard's account, such a momentous event marked
the beginning of his career, and one equally momentous certainly
marked the nadir of Blake's – a three-year period of intense despair,
out of which he recovered to write his last prophecies.

Both of these "cosmic" events were confrontations with the
spectre of mediation or compromise, confrontations from which
both men emerged triumphantly – or perhaps not so triumphantly –

"unmediated." For Kierkegaard, the central event in his life, or so he claimed, the occasion behind virtually all his pseudonymous works, was his aborted engagement to Regina Olsen in 1841.[1] With what he would have us believe to be characteristic absolutism, he apparently felt upon meeting her that either he would marry this woman or he would never marry. He did not marry her, and he never married. He was not, however, as one might expect, the rejected party; on the contrary, he himself called off the wedding and extricated himself with considerable anguish from the situation. He then seems to have spent the rest of his life wondering if he had done the right thing. The puzzle is why he did it at all; but on this point he remains (understandably) enigmatic.[2] The story appears in various places throughout his pseudonymous works, retold in a number of parables. The most suggestive of these is the Abraham–Isaac story which Johannes de Silentio analyzes in great detail in *Fear and Trembling*. Kierkegaard himself said that "*Fear and Trembling* reproduced my own life,"[3] and "If you can explain Abraham's collision [of the ethical with the religious sphere of life] you have explained my whole life."[4] Silentio's preoccupation is with Abraham's sacrifice of Isaac, where Abraham unexpectedly receives Isaac back again, "by virtue of the absurd." Abraham breaks the laws of conventional morality (which would call him a murderer) to serve the command of God; he renounces the finite (Isaac) at the bidding of the infinite, only to receive the finite back again, transformed into a great and unexpected gift (as was Isaac's birth to begin with). There is some speculation that Kierkegaard's "sacrifice" of Regina was meant to be a sacrifice of the same sort – that he hoped, having renounced her for religious reasons, to receive her back again.[5] Perhaps it was even his test to see whether God existed or not, for to receive her back, unexpectedly and impossibly, after having renounced her totally, would surely constitute a "proof." But he did not receive her back; in fact, she married another man, within a disconcertingly short interval after the rupture with Kierkegaard. Not only did God not demonstrate his existence; this "cosmic event" threatened to be merely mundane after all. Clearly Regina's perception of the situation was considerably less cosmic than Kierkegaard's; evidently she did not feel that either she would marry Kierkegaard or she would never marry.

Kierkegaard's response to this renunciation of marriage was to rush off to solitude in Berlin and write; in the two years following the event he wrote and published, in rapid succession, *Either/Or* (February 1843), *Two Edifying Discourses* (May 1843), and in October 1843, *Fear and Trembling, Repetition,* and *Three Edifying Discourses.* He sent *Either/Or, Fear and Trembling,* and *Repetition* to Regina, who read them aloud to her husband.[6] Formerly somewhat of an aesthete and a dilettante (spending ten years writing his graduate thesis, *The Concept of Irony,* for instance), Kierkegaard continued this astonishing pace and prolific output for the rest of his life, a fact which in itself might seem to argue for the authenticity of the crisis.[7]

He had renounced marriage, and his entire "literary" output – i.e., the pseudonymous works – re-enacts this struggle and this apparently momentous decision. It is also his attempt to justify that decision to himself; for unless his renunciation had some higher religious justification it was a meaningless gesture. His real task then was to justify God's ways to men, a task made the more difficult by the fact that God had not responded to Kierkegaard's sacrifice as he was supposed to have done. The onus was on Kierkegaard to keep the entire incident from collapsing into meaninglessness, an experiment which had backfired, an absurd tragedy of unfulfillment. It is no wonder he felt impelled to produce so prolifically; for if the event could be thus productive, that productivity alone would be some justification for it. "So costly this girl had to become to me, or so costly I had to make her for religious reasons," he says in his *Journal.*[8]

The pseudonymous works re-enact not only Kierkegaard's struggle and decision to renounce marriage, but also his struggle to reject the Hegelian system, for these were in fact the same struggle. Hegel was the great philosopher of marriage, whose own happily married bourgeois life broke with an entire tradition of philosophic isolation:

Particularly among philosophers, there were until the nineteenth century very few exceptions to the rule that men of learning, if not necessarily celibate, should at any rate be undisturbed by the domestic turmoil of marriage. In the Middle Ages, of course, most philosophers were clerics. But even after Luther set the example of a married clergy, and did it with such zest after all those years in the monastery, it continued to be taken for granted that a scholar, and particularly a philosopher, could not combine the high seriousness of his calling with marital frivolities and vexations. Then, too, philosophers doubtless were daunted by the example of the terrible-tempered Xantippe.

In Germany, it was the idealistic successors of Immanuel Kant who

decisively broke the pattern ... When the so-called German idealists ...
transferred the scene of philosophical thinking from the monkish cell to the
bourgeois household, the transfer manifested a new philosophical humanism. This was true in the life and work of Hegel above all. The culminator
of German idealism, Hegel could also be called, invoking his own view of
the philosophical task and a little poetic license, the first thoroughly
domesticated philosopher. For the first time philosophy found itself com-
fortably at home with the common life, in Marie Hegel's parlor.[9]

To Kierkegaard, the Hegelian system was as ponderously slow-
moving – as static, finally – as the institution of marriage itself. Like
marriage, it collapsed the cosmic into the mundane, the incommensurable into the commensurable; it collapsed the spirited, unmediated, passionate relations of love into the spiritless, systematic
relations of duty, social convention, and family love.[10]

This "error" which the entire nineteenth century around him
seemed to have "taken into itself," the error he had successfully
expelled from his own life as an individual, Kierkegaard methodi-
cally set out to eradicate. Step by step he carefully played backwards
the music of the Hegelian system, and it is a discordant, difficult,
jarring piece of music which results. Not objectivity but subjectivity,
not reason but passion, not collectivism ("the state") but individualism, not continuity but discontinuity, not "history" but "the
moment" – all these reversals mark his tortuous, negative way, his
systematic anti-systematic undoing of the Hegelianism he had taken
into himself.

The "cosmic event" marking a crisis in Blake's turbulent evolu-
tion as a poet was the famous episode in his garden at Felpham,
when John Milton descended from above and entered into Blake's
left foot – which "alters Blake's [poetic] *stance*," as Harold Bloom so
imperturbably informs us.[11] Objectively speaking this event might
seem of a somewhat different order than Kierkegaard's (considerably more cosmic indeed); but subjectively speaking as we are here,
this too was the culmination of Blake's decisive confrontation with,
and breaking away from, "commensurability."

His three-year sojourn at Felpham was a period of intense despair,
when he feared he was losing not only his productivity, but also his
poetic vision altogether. What appeared initially to be an ideal situation for poetic inspiration – a cottage in the country, solitude, plenty
of bread-and-butter commissions procured for him by his patron
William Hayley – became a nightmare of paralysis and self-doubt.

The story has been told many times – of Blake's clashes with Hayley, his obscure marital troubles, his bizarre trial for sedition, a trial which could only confirm that his general feelings of paranoia were no mere products of imagination.[12] Fundamentally, it is the story of Blake's confrontation with the spectre of compromise, a spectre which had haunted him throughout his career but which materialized with sudden, unexpected definition in the figure of Hayley. For Blake saw in his apparent benefactor the embodiment of all that blocked true poetic vision: a temptation to dependence on his beneficent fatherly patronage which would destroy Blake's fierce independence of imagination. Hayley's commissions demanded that Blake abandon visions for portraits, inspiration for convention, imagination for common sense, the exalted for the mundane. And these demands were made on entirely reasonable grounds – the grounds of simple survival, the basic financial neces-sity Blake had to acknowledge and could best meet by hiring himself out for this kind of work. "Reasonable" and "necessary" to be sure; but an unacceptable compromise to Blake's uncompromising tem-perament. Either one produced true art, inspired subjectively from within by visionary truths, or one produced false art, dictated by the muses of external, objective necessity and of public opinion and convention. One could not do both; at least, not if one was Blake. Being true to vision might – and should – produce material rewards as a consequence; but material necessity could not for Blake usurp the place of visionary truth as the primary motivation for his art. When it did, when the spectrous tyrant of objective necessity and obligation filled Blake's vision, he was paralyzed.

More accurately, he was probably paralyzed by ambivalence, by the very real temptation to take the easy, mediated route rather than the difficult, unmediated route to recognition. He had by this time spent years in isolation and neglect; here was a patron at last, who promised to mediate between Blake and his uncomprehending public. And perhaps it would not be such a compromise after all; perhaps his "visionary forms dramatic" were, as Hayley apparently told him, merely the phantasms of a madman, phantasms which needed these curbs of necessity and convention to make them comprehensible. Perhaps this discipline imposed from without was the true discipline, the true "bounding line" Blake's art needed: the discipline of objective reality or existence. Blake did after all want his art to be true to human experience or life – and were these not the demands of life which Hayley urged upon his art? This spectre bore an uncannily close resemblance to some truths Blake could not but acknowledge.

Blake's escape from this paralyzing ambivalence required an enormous effort of will, an act of decision by which he sharply differentiated himself from Hayley, rejecting all of Hayley's temptations to compromise. And this decision was indeed a "leap of faith," for by it he cast off the "corporeal friendship" of William Hayley to embrace instead the "spiritual friendship" of John Milton. This crisis of decision at Felpham, the subject matter of *Milton*, marks Blake's leap from paralysis into production, his rejection of the false art for the true. And this crisis marks also the sudden kaleidoscopic shift in Blake's myth from Orc and Urizen to Los and the Spectre, a new configuration which retains and yet transforms the earlier components of the myth to become the configuration decisive for Blake's last prophecies, particularly *Jerusalem*, where it consolidates with intense and final clarity.

This shift to the Los–Spectre dialectic in a sense "reverses" Blake's early Orc–Urizen dialectic, a pattern of logic which he now comes to see as "error." His new dialectic is the same yet not the same as his early one; it is an exact inversion of that earlier dialectic of contraries which merely makes explicit the error hidden within it and then casts (or attempts to cast) it off. This is the error which Blake now calls "negation" or "the Spectre." And where formerly he would not cast off Urizen as the solution to the Orc–Urizen conflict, he now casts off the Spectre in a Kierkegaardian either/or (although the nature of this casting-off is paradoxically, again as in Kierkegaard, in the nature of an embrace as well). Blake's move from an objective "Hegelian" dialectic to a subjective "Kierkegaardian" one would seem consistent with the generally accepted theory about the progressively inward-turning direction of his myth. His abandonment of belief in an actual historical revolution (Orc) and relocation of this revolution within the perception of the individual (Los) is essentially Kierkegaard's attempted internalization of Hegelian dialectic.

A more detailed account of this sudden turn to the Spectre must begin however with an account of the poetic event which was the catalyst. For something happened at Felpham which made the Spectre leap into sudden prominence. *Milton* not only records in a single "moment" this decisive event in Blake's life as a man and a poet, it also gives us in little the history of the entire progression of Blake's myth. For its history is that of his struggles to correct not only his own errors, but also the errors (as he saw them) of Milton's *Paradise Lost*. Blake's entire career is in a way a backwards retracing of Milton's steps, an attempt to undo Milton's errors, in which Blake finds himself merely repeating those errors and having to begin all over again.[13] The dialectic of his career is one of a progressive sharpening not only of Los (as truth) but also of the Spectre (as error). They emerge with equal and opposite intensities, the one an equally potent yet paradoxically shadowy analogy of the other.

The structure of *Milton* illustrates Blake's reversal of Hegelian dialectic with remarkable clarity. The poem as a whole moves not from "division" to "reconciliation" but the reverse: from a dissolution of contraries to their sharp differentiation. It moves from an initial state of "mediation" or unity to an exposure of this state as false or illusory, then to a decisive differentiation or casting-off of this state, and finally to a state of true unity and poetic vision. It begins, in the "Bard's Song," with the "corporeal friendship" of Blake–Palamabron and Hayley–Satan, a false friendship and a false poetic vision. The crisis of the Song is the exposing and casting-off of this false friendship, an expulsion of Satan or "error" which thus allows Blake to unite in true "spiritual friendship" with Milton. In the Bard's Song, Blake is cleansed of his error; in the rest of the poem's two books, Milton is cleansed of error in a step-by-step narrative retracing and correction of his steps in *Paradise Lost*, a progression which culminates in a decisive confrontation with his spectre. These two "negative" movements of Blake and Milton take place simultaneously with their positive embrace of each other and of Ololon, the emanation of true poetic vision and unity. For the poem's narrative events all occur in the "moment" – the "Moment in each Day that Satan cannot find" – the moment of decision and of incarnation when Blake brings Milton out of eternity and into time to be his ally against Hayley.

The poem even gives us a visual emblem of Blake's dialectic in the opening plate of the second book, a plate containing both forward and backward writing. The forward writing says merely "Milton Book the Second;" Blake makes us read laboriously backwards or else hold the plate up to a mirror to read (arching across the top of the plate): "How wide the Gulf Unpassable between Simplicity &

Insipidity," and below this, "Contraries are Positives A Negation is not a Contrary." Already Blake is concerned with drawing absolute distinctions: the "gulf unpassable" is presumably the qualitative difference between Milton's grand simplicity and Hayley's petty insipidity; and as we shall see, Blake and Milton are the "contraries" of which Hayley is the mere "negation."

Blake is "erroneously" allied with Hayley because Hayley–Satan has usurped Blake–Palamabron's poetic task and instruments – his "Harrow of the Almighty" – and tried to perform Blake's task himself. The patron has tried to be the poet: "he hath assum'd my place / For one whole day, under pretence of pity and love to me" (M, 1, 7:25–26; 101). But "my horses he hath maddened! and my fellow servants injur'd: / How should he know the duties of another?" (M, 1, 7:27–28; 101). And Blake's fear is that no one will recognize Satan's destructiveness, because it is so successfully concealed in "soft dissimulation of friendship" (M, 1, 8:35; 102) and "incomparable mildness" (M, 1, 7:4; 100): "Palamabron fear'd to be angry lest Satan should accuse him of / Ingratitude, & Los believe the accusation thro Satans extreme / Mildness" (M, 1, 7:11–13; 100). Worst of all, Satan himself is not really a hypocrite, but genuinely unable to see his own destructiveness: "Mean while wept Satan before Los, accusing Palamabron; / Himself exculpating with mildest speech. for himself believ'd / That he had not oppress'd nor injur'd the refractory servants" (M, 1, 8:1–3; 101). But "seeming a brother, being a tyrant," Satan must be exposed as such, and to this end "Palamabron called down a Great Solemn Assembly / That he who will not defend Truth, may be compelled to / Defend a Lie that he may be snared & caught & taken" (M, 1, 8:46–48; 102). Blake–Palamabron's strategy for exposing Satan is to make him reveal himself, which he does by making Satan angry; for "Satan flaming with Rintrahs fury hidden beneath his own mildness / Accus'd Palamabron before the Assembly of ingratitude! of malice:" (M, 1, 9:19–20; 103). Once he is angry, Satan loses control, raging amidst the Assembly and saying "I am God alone / There is no other! Let all obey my principles of moral individuality" (M, 1, 9:25–26; 103). His true enmity to poetic vision is revealed; the Assembly stands appalled; and he sinks down "a dreadful Death" (M, 1, 9:48; 103).

Anger, Rintrah's prophetic wrath, is the agent of redemption for Blake–Palamabron because it is a divisive rather than a mediating emotion, an emotion of sharp, antagonistic combat which Blake opposes to "pity," the soft, mediating emotion which caused all the trouble in the first place. Hayley–Satan is destroyed by his own anger not only because it reveals his true enmity, but because, unused to such a decisive, differentiating emotion, he cannot control it: "And Satan not having the Science of Wrath, but only of Pity: / Rent them asunder and wrath was left to wrath, & pity to pity. / He sunk down a dreadful Death" (M, 1, 9:46–48; 103). Hayley–Satan is unable to make qualitative distinctions, and this, finally, is his sin: he cannot see the difference between himself and Blake–Palamabron, the difference between his idea of art and Blake's, the difference which makes his attempted usurpation of Blake's role such a destructive parody of it.

Blake learned from this incident the saving value of anger: "If you account it Wisdom when you are angry to be silent, and / Not to shew it: I do not account that Wisdom but Folly" (M, 1, 4:6–7; 98). He learned from it in other words the destructive quality of "mediation" and the saving quality of "division," the very concept he had spent his life up to this point fighting against. And he had fought against it most vehemently in the person of John Milton, whose *Paradise Lost* for Blake embodied the tyranny of division in its most spectrous form.

Issues of "division," the qualitative distinction between man and God, are at the heart of all of Milton's central justifications of the ways of God to man in *Paradise Lost*. Even though Raphael assures Adam and Eve that they are different from God in degree but not in kind, there remains the inescapable, absolute difference in kind which the tree of knowledge seems to set up. That prohibition is none other than God's firm command to Adam and Eve to observe the qualitative disjunction between themselves and him, not to seek to know too much, not to seek equality with God. And for Blake (as for many others) this prohibition seemed directly responsible for the fall, for had it not been established, had this unattainable otherness not been set up to tempt Adam and Eve, they would not have fallen.

The second division in *Paradise Lost* which seems equally to make God responsible for the fall is the division of the sexes. For it is Eve's "separateness" from Adam which seems to make her particularly susceptible to the serpent; had she not insisted on wandering off on her own, he would not have found her alone and unprotected. Eve seems to be created inherently flawed by the very fact of her

physical and sexual separation from Adam, a separation typologi-
cally repeated in all her actions throughout the epic.

The third (and most famous) separation Blake objected to in
Milton's epic was the casting out of Satan, God's ultimate act of
division. For Satan cannot be redeemed; this tyrant will not forgive
him his sin – again, the sin of wanting to equal God. And Blake sees
no difference between the expulsion of Satan from heaven and all
the separations or acts of individuation in *Paradise Lost*, which is why
for him the very act of creation is Satanic.

Milton's justification of the ways of God lies in the concept of
freedom. God's greatest gift, apart from life, is freedom – that man
should be free to choose whether or not to worship God. Compelled
obedience is meaningless, for as God says,

> Not free, what proof could they have giv'n sincere
> Of true allegiance, constant faith or love,
> Where what they needs must do appeared,
> Not what they would? What praise could they receive,
> What pleasure I, from such obedience paid,
> When Will and Reason (Reason also is Choice)
> Useless and vain, of freedom both despoiled,
> Made passive both, had served Necessity,
> Not me?
>
> > *Paradise Lost* III:103–111

The only way Adam and Eve can be free to choose whether or not to
worship God is if they are offered some real, *qualitatively* real,
alternatives. It is this qualitative choice which the prohibition
symbolically represents. Only the prohibition gives Adam and Eve
the freedom to choose between obedience and disobedience; before
the prohibition, the choice and the freedom did not exist. Limitless
freedom is not freedom but necessity. And only Eve's separation
from Adam – just like Adam's separation from God – allows her to
choose between idolatry (worship of Adam) and true worship of
God. (Her apparent narcissism at the pool when she is first created is
yet another symbol or type of her freedom of choice, for her choice
here is between her own reflected image and Adam.)

The prohibition is Milton's "wirey bounding line," what shapes
the key ideas of *Paradise Lost*. It is a line of decisive differentiation, of
qualitative distinction, a line which seemingly fixes an "unpassable
gulf" between God and man, man and woman, and heaven and
hell. Yet this gulf for Milton does not mean that man is inherently

fallen: the sin is not division *per se*, but "idolatry," substitution of the wrong alternative for the right. Sin is the perversion or negation of value distinctions, for to worship someone or something other than God is to hold it up as equal or superior in value to God. It is to upset the proper *hierarchy* of values.

For Blake throughout most of his career, not idolatry but hierarchy (what Blake calls "jealousy") is the sin – that is, division *per se*, God's selfishly possessive withholding, via his prohibition, of his own knowledge and superiority. And it is the division between the sexes which keeps them in perpetual "torments of love and jealousy," fruitlessly trying either in torments of desire to cross the unpassable gulf, or in acts of selfish possessiveness and "chastity" to fix it more firmly between them. Each attempt at true freedom, each Orc who appears to liberate men from this tyranny, is bound down eventually and irrevocably by this "Chain of Jealousy."

Milton's wiry bounding line in other words looked very much to Blake like the line made by Urizenic dividers, a line which bound man a prisoner of a Urizenic spectre of abstraction, an "abstract non-entity." For it divided God off from man in splendid isolation, as someone outside of man remaining untouched by and oblivious to his torments. Blake's struggle throughout his career, then, is to expel this tyrannous spectre of division and abstraction by creating a "seamless" myth. This would mean that the division of man from God would be a division within God himself; not man but God falls, or man is fallen God. It should also mean that there would be no Satan who is irrevocably cast out as an irredeemable sinner; all parts of the fallen self should be taken up again into the whole. And it should finally mean that no acts of repentance, forgiveness, redemption, or grace are involved in the reintegration of the fallen self, for such acts by definition ratify the God–man distinction Blake wants to abolish.

Blake's problem, however, is that while he wants to get rid of Milton's dualism, he wants to maintain qualitative distinctions. He wants to get rid of *hierarchy* – a transcendent God who is superior to man, or in psychological terms, a reason which rules over passion. Yet at the same time, he wants to maintain the qualitative distinctions between transcendence and immanence, or between reason and passion. His ideal of life is always as the dynamic interaction of qualitatively distinct contraries – yet the unavoidable impasse he confronts is that contraries cannot be qualitatively distinct without hierarchy – that is, without elevating one contrary over the other. Qualitative distinctions are by definition hierarchical, yet it is just this which Blake refuses to accept.

This is why Blake struggles so long with different sets of contraries – innocence and experience, Orc and Urizen, Zoas and emanations, Rintrah and Palamabron (or wrath and pity), Los and the Spectre, truth and error. With each successive pair he tries to reformulate his ideal. But he has only two alternatives. Either his contraries will be qualitatively distinct, in which case they must by definition be hierarchical, with one contrary necessarily elevated above the other; or the contraries will be equal and opposite, non-hierarchical – in which case they will not be qualitatively distinct, not real contraries.

Blake wants neither of these alternatives, because either alternative seems to destroy his ideal of life. His polemical temperament and deeply religious absolutism make him want to choose one contrary rather than the other, in a kind of "either/or" moment of choice – a moment of unqualified, fervent embrace. But this seems too dogmatic and one-sided to be true to his ideal of life as something always changing. Such hierarchy seems clearly tyrannical, for one contrary dominates over the other by casting it off or else by subsuming it within itself. On the other hand, equallizing the contraries in an eternal "both-and" dialectic seems equally destructive of life, for they can only oscillate in perennial vacillation, with no end to dialectic. Blake wants life to be dynamic yet definite in shape; he wants neither the rigidity that dualism seems to impose on it nor the formless dissolution into flux which the equallizing of the contraries seems to produce. Striving is not all, for Blake; life must take definite form.

Blake's contraries of innocence and experience provide one example of this struggle between systematic "both-and" contraries and unsystematic "either/or" contraries. The relation between the states of innocence and experience was once vigorously contested in Blake studies, in a debate about precisely this issue: were the contraries "intellectual counters within a dialectic," equally necessary to life and hence "married" in a systematic unity? Or did Blake continually change his mind about them, repudiating innocence for experience and vice-versa? Despite W.J.T. Mitchell's rather waspish protest that this question of the systematic versus unsystematic nature of Blake's myth is a "dead isssue" which should be laid to rest, I resurrect it here because I am proposing that in Los and the

Spectre Blake found a way of dramatizing that very conflict and perhaps its solution.[14]

E.D. Hirsch argued in an early study, for example, that only the "unsystematic" view could account for the contraries' curious resistance to being systematized even by Blake's systematic title, *The Songs of Innocence and Experience, Shewing the Two Contrary States of the Human Soul*:

> the ... title has precisely the same problematical character that numerous readers have observed in the similarly systematic title of *The Marriage of Heaven and Hell*. The new title to the *Songs* pays lip service to a dialectical unity in which Innocence is just as important as Experience, but it fails to describe the fact that Innocence is in general satirized and experience celebrated. Blake *says* in *The Marriage* that the Devourer is necessary to the Prolific, but the work is primarily a celebration of the Prolific. In the systematic unity which the new title imposed on the *Songs*, he *implies* that Innocence is as permanent and as necessary to human existence as experience, but the addition of the countervolume is more a repudiation than a marriage.[15]

Despite his attempt to systematize the *Songs* in a dialectical unity, then, Hirsch argued that Blake still leaned towards a "repudiation" of one of the contraries rather than a "marriage." And he argued further that in the end Blake abandoned all attempts at a dialectical system, in a return to an even more transcendental or visionary state of innocence than that which he celebrated in his youth.

Hirsch's thesis has never been widely accepted, at least as it applies to the *Songs*; but whether it is right or wrong is not what is at issue here. For my immediate purposes, his thesis raises in a useful way some of the issues at stake in the debate over Blake's Hegelianism or anti-Hegelianism. First of all, it argued that Blake realized a dialectic of crisis or conversion is truer to experience or life than is the dialectic of both-and logic, in which contraries are merely "intellectual counters" rather than the polarities of lived experience. Hirsch's argument was largely an empirical one based on textual evidence, yet we also feel it to be intuitively true, I think, given Blake's emotional intensity, that he would be pulled towards one contrary, as Hirsch suggested, and that he would be given to radical reversals or re-evaluations of his own positions based not simply on reasoning but on lived experience. (This view of Blake's temperament is also borne out by G. E. Bentley's accounts of Blake's troubled friendships – his pattern of first idealizing and then rejecting various mentor figures.)[16] And despite the general lack of agreement with Hirsch's argument as it applies to the *Songs*, his more general thesis about the "unsystematic" or self-revisionary nature of Blake's myth is now not only widely accepted but often taken for granted.

This raises a second issue in the Hegelian anti-Hegelian debate, one that is a kind of corollary to the first. Part of Hirsch's argument that Blake's dialectic is rooted in life not logic depended upon his claim that Blake's myth is self-referential – i.e., that the changes in the myth are essentially self-corrections, repudiations of ideas that Blake later comes to see as "erroneous." This means that Blake conceived of his contraries as *sequential*, not *simultaneous*, and as thus fundamentally incompatible. This suggests that if Blake did experience or "live" these contraries as irreconcilable or mutually exclusive, he will try to dramatize or accurately mirror not the marriage of those contraries but the very irreconcilability or conflict which constituted that lived experience. The problem with this, however, as both Hirsch and more recently Steven Shaviro have pointed out, is that the very act of representing or conceptualizing the contraries presupposes an objective, atemporal, and hence abstract position outside those contraries as lived experience, a position which then effectively reconciles or "negates" them.[17] It is in part then a problem inherent in the nature of representation which may make Blake look systematic and abstracted from life despite all his struggles against such abstraction. How can he possibly escape this dilemma?

It arises again in his treatment of a second pair of contraries, Orc and Urizen. This is in a way the same pair of contraries, since to a certain extent they also represent the conflict between innocence and experience. But since Blake worked through their conflict separately from that of the *Songs* it deserves separate consideration; and because Orc and Urizen also represent passion and reason, they are more immediately useful for comparing Blake with Milton.

Orc and Urizen first appear as "the Prolific" and "the Devouring" in *The Marriage of Heaven and Hell*, and here Blake explicitly states that the two contraries of life must remain absolute, qualitatively distinct:

> Thus one portion of being, is the Prolific the other, the Devouring: to the Devourer it seems as if the producer was in his chains, but it is not so, he only takes portions of existence and fancies that the whole....

These two classes of men are always upon the earth, & they should be enemies; whoever tries to reconcile them seeks to destroy existence.

Religion is an endeavour to reconcile the two.

Note: Jesus Christ did not wish to unite but to separate them, as in the Parable of sheep and goats! & he says I came not to send Peace but a Sword. (MHH, 16; 40)

As numerous commentators have noted, even at this early stage in Blake's myth we see a marked anti-Hegelianism in his refusal to mediate or reconcile the two classes of men or the contraries.[18] Yet the "third thing" which threatens to mediate them, what Blake will later call "negation," does not explicitly appear, except perhaps in the term "religion." Nonetheless, the concept of negation is *implicitly* present, and is rejected as vehemently as it is in the later myth. But Blake had a long struggle to undergo before he realized with greater explicitness that the problem dogging his representation of the contraries was "negation," and that this struggle *with negation* rather than that *between the contraries* should be his real focus. The negation, in other words, took a long time to declare itself in its true shape, the shape of the Spectre of Urthona.

The Spectre of Negation consolidated himself as "error" only after Blake struggled with the contraries Orc and Urizen and came to realize that something was wrong with the logic of their relationship. He always wanted Orc and Urizen, the Prolific and the Devouring, to remain in productive strife, yet Orc continually threatened to annihilate Urizen (and vice-versa). Urizen is clearly a "villain" throughout Blake's early works (*America, The Book of Urizen, The Song of Los, The Book of Ahania,* and *The Book of Los*), while Orc is clearly the "hero" (in *The Book of Ahania* the Orc figure is called Fuzon). Yet Blake realizes he does not really want Orc to cast off Urizen but to unite fruitfully with him. Urizen has divided himself off from Orc as Milton's God cast off Satan; and to have Orc in turn cast off Urizen would make Orc repeat the mistakes of Milton's God and himself become a new Urizen. It would ratify the very God-man distinction in *Paradise Lost* which Blake is trying to overcome. There is only one alternative, however – to have Orc "swallow" Urizen instead of casting him off. But this would reduce Urizen's potency as an antagonist, render Orc's victory a feeble one, and again, make Orc a Urizenic tyrant. This is in fact what does happen to Orc: Blake discovers that he has allowed Orc to tyrannize one-sidedly over his myth to the exclusion of Urizen, just as Urizen previously tyrannized to the effective exclusion of Orc. Blake's dialectic of life has ended – there *is* no dialectic.

Blake in other words sees life, which should be a fruitful inter-action of reason and passion, as tyrannized over by reason. He therefore sets passion against this reason, only to find that passion without the bounds of reason is as tyrannical as reason without passion. Orc has triumphed, but to the destruction of the very life he was supposed to embody: "Once Man was occupied in intellectual pleasures & energies / But now my soul is harrowed with grief & fear & love & desire / And now I hate & now I love & Intellect is no more," Blake–Los laments in *Jerusalem* (III, 68: 65–67; 222). The excess of either principle leads to an excess of the other: an excess of reason leads to uncontrolled passion, and an excess of passion leads to a tyranny of reason. This means that Orc and Urizen are mutually implicated in the fall of man – that both are in some sense "equal." This is why in *The Four Zoas* Blake makes Luvah (Orc) and Urizen equally responsible for the fall of man into disunity, instead of blaming the fall on Urizen alone as in the early myth. Luvah has usurped Urizen's "Horses of Light" – but Urizen has voluntarily handed them over.

Blake discovers in other words that since they are mutually implicated in the fall, Orc and Urizen are not real contraries but different aspects of the same thing. Frye has carefully charted his increasing discovery of this "Orc cycle," his realization that Orc is not tyrannized over by a Urizen who is *different* from him, but that Orc *himself* declines inevitably into Urizen.[19] Innocence, revolution-ary energy, and desire inevitably decline into experience, stasis, and repressive reason. This is the cycle of life – but it is in fact a cycle of death.

Blake's struggle with these two sets of contraries thus demon-strates the two poles between which he was continually pulled throughout his career. The outcome of his struggle in the *Songs*, as Hirsch argued, may be an "either/or" celebration of one contrary – innocence – to the exclusion of experience. By contrast, his Orc–Urizen struggle, as Frye documented it, ends in the stalemate of a "both-and" dialectic which neutralizes both contraries in a static cycle. (Again, whether either or both of these arguments are "right" is for the moment less important than their highlighting of the nature of Blake's struggles with the contraries.) Blake ultimately rejects the both-and dialectic and, as Hirsch in a qualified sense rightly says, opts for something closer to "either/or." Yet really he wants neither of these alternatives, as I have said, and therefore opts for a very special kind of either/or which is neither both-and nor either/or as that is simply understood.

Blake's disillusionment with the static both-and Orc cycle is usually described as a disillusionment with the idea of political revolution. And his turn to Los as the new agent of redemption is described as a turn to the imagination or the visionary faculty as the new redeemer. In this sense, Los is seen as Blake's "solution" to his problem with the Orc cycle. But Los too proves inadequate on his own. Blake has rejected the Orc cycle as static, yet by introducing Los as the visionary or imaginative faculty which will put Orc and Urizen together in a dynamic unity he still does not solve his problem. He has overcome the problem of either Orc or Urizen taking over in a dogmatic tyranny which one-sidedly ends dialectic or the flux of life's contraries. Yet he has not escaped the trap of the Orc cycle itself, the systematic logic of contraries which he has just discovered to be static. Los is a "third thing" who therefore seems to transcend the Orc–Urizen trap – yet how does the introduction of Los solve the problem of how to put Orc and Urizen together in such a way that they form a dynamic unity of life rather than a static cycle of death? How is Los to unify Orc and Urizen without becoming, like "Religion," "an endeavour to reconcile the two" which "seeks to destroy existence"? In fact, as Blake has just discovered, the whole problem is that Orc and Urizen have *already* been "reconciled" within some higher invisible unity, which is why they are not real contraries, and why their conflict is static.

Blake must prevent Los from becoming simply a name for or an embodiment of this invisible higher unity which has mysteriously negated Orc and Urizen within itself. He must keep Los from being hierarchically superior to Orc and Urizen or else Los will be an abstract unity, an empty "container," and Orc and Urizen will be reduced to feeble "things contained," their energy negated in mutual accommodation.

Blake's multiplication of the contraries into the four Zoas seemed initially to be a successful strategy for doing this. It decentralized Orc and Urizen by making them merely two parts of a four-part schema; and theoretically at least it kept all four Zoas in dynamic equilibrium. No one Zoa was higher than any other; no Zoa would be cast out or excluded as the "original sinner" – all would be taken up again into the final whole. The entire structure of the poem was a more moderated or mediated one, not only because Orc and Urizen became just part of the Zoa scheme instead of the whole, but because the idea of repentance or acknowledgment of error became a new and prominent feature.[20]

But Blake still finds that he cannot avoid elevating Los qualitatively above the rest, as the agent of redemption. Los therefore runs the risk of seeming to be a kind of *deus ex machina* who reaches down from above and redeems the other Zoas up into himself. Such a unity would make Los into an abstract Urizenic God much like Milton's God, when Blake wants to insist above all that *man* must effect his own redemption.

Blake therefore introduces at this point the Spectre of Urthona as the final solution to his problems with the contraries. The Spectre is fundamentally the abstract form of Los, all of the qualities of abstraction which Blake wants to dispel from Los. He is the abstract transcendent unity which reconciles and hence "negates" the contraries, a parody of the concrete human unity which Blake wants Los to represent. The Spectre is the shadow or trace of Los's unfallen form – the qualitative transcendence from which Los has fallen, the "memory" of the unity-that-was. This is why the Spectre is truly in a sense Los's "real self," the eternal self from which Los has fallen, and why it is said of him that he "kept the Divine Vision in time of trouble" (J, II, 44:15; 193 and IV, 95:20; 255). In this sense he is a positive figure, absolutely necessary for reintegration to be possible. Yet he is also a negative figure who threatens to usurp Los's role in reintegrating the fallen parts, the abstract God of orthodoxy who tempts man to passively await his redemption instead of actively effecting it himself. His temptation is what causes Los to rage so furiously at the other Zoas in *Jerusalem*, crying "Why stand we here trembling around / Calling upon God for help; and not ourselves in whom God dwells" (J, II, 38:12–13; 184).

The Spectre represents, in other words, the abstract unity of death that stands opposed to the concrete unity of life which Blake wants Los to embody. He must be united with Los in the "Divine Human" – but this unity must for Blake be in a way more human than divine, a unity instigated by Los. What is most divine *is* what is most human, for Blake. The Spectre threatens to usurp Los by uniting with Enitharmon to create the true unity, the true poetic vision of life, and this is why the struggle of Los and the Spectre over Enitharmon is central to the confrontations in *The Four Zoas* and *Jerusalem*. But the marriage of the Spectre separate from Los to Enitharmon would produce an abstract unity, a parody of the true poetic vision. The Spectre's form of mediation would in fact ratify division, for although it would reintegrate the fallen Zoas, and reintegrate Los, Enitharmon, and himself, it would reintegrate them into an abstract unity removed from life.

With the appearance of the Spectre, then, Blake has simply given a form or shape to a principle of reconciliation or negation implicit even as early as *The Marriage*. He has made the implicit explicit; but in doing so he transvalues the early Orc–Urizen conflict from the dialectic of life to the static cycle of death, as we shall see. He will make the real dialectic of life the struggle between Los and the Spectre of Urthona; and this new dialectic will retain and yet transvalue the old Orc cycle. In the conflict of Los and the Spectre Blake changes the focus of his myth and in a very real sense repudiates his early formulation of this conflict. But his new dialectic is "the same yet not the same" as his early one; it is merely a new way of working out the same early ideal of life as the strife of contraries. It is this tenacious pursuit of the *same* ideal of life which is most responsible for our sense of Blake's great consistency despite the confusions of his myth – the consistency that leads some to call him dogmatic and systematic. The new dialectic makes what was *potential* – an ideal of contraries which excluded the error of reconciliation or negation – *actual*; and it is in this sense that the new dialectic constitutes a "leap" making it at once radically different from and radically identical with the early one.

This leap from potential to actual and from death to life is the essence of the radical change represented by Kierkegaard's "either/or." Blake's turn from contraries to contraries and negations thus itself enacts the very dynamic it proposes as the dynamic of life. We shall be investigating here the way in which this dynamic informs not only the structure of Blake's myth, but the vision of life that myth conveys. For the moment, however, we should return to Blake's spiritual crisis at Felpham to see why it should have been the catalyst for this leap.

What Blake discovered in the course of his struggles with the contraries was that he had to battle not one but two spectres – and that these spectres were paradoxically again one and the same. He realized increasingly that Los's "mediation," his attempted solution to Milton's error of Urizenic "division," was itself another form of abstraction, a repetition of the same error. Milton's qualitative divisions between God and man, reason and passion, might lead to the tyranny of abstraction – God and reason – over life. Yet the mediation of these divisions could only be effected within some higher unity which negated the energy of the contraries in an equally tyrannical abstraction from life. Further, mediation was an even greater danger to life than was division. For this spectre of false unity looked too much like the Los of true unity, and this hypocritical parody was far more dangerous than open opposition. Blake does want Los to unify life's contraries – but in a dynamic, *unsystematic* way. The Spectre is therefore doubly dangerous, because he does unify life's contraries; and most people will not see that he does so in a way which kills life. Milton's God of division is less dangerous because he at least openly declares that his activity is divisive: his prohibition is absolute and clearly stated. The Spectre by contrast pretends to mediate while thereby dividing men even more radically from life.

It was this revelation about the nature of "mediation" which was brought home to Blake with unexpected force by his encounter with Hayley at Felpham. For if Hayley's lack of discrimination, his blurring of the "unpassable gulf" between true and false, "simplicity" and "insipidity," Blake and himself, was what mediation led to, then mediation was even more dangerous to poetic vision than the original enemy of division. The tyranny of Milton, the tyranny of the "divisive" perspective which saw life's contraries as absolute, was not so tyrannical as that of Hayley, the tyranny of the "mediating" perspective which reduced life's contraries to equality and indeterminacy. The tyranny of the absolute was not so tyrannical as that of the relative holding itself up as the absolute. "Division" at least declared itself for what it was; "mediation" pretended to be what it was not.

This revelation allied Blake with Milton because he saw with sudden clarity Milton's justifications for the prohibition, the "unpassable gulf" of division in *Paradise Lost*. Blake's new focus in *The Four Zoas*, *Milton*, and *Jerusalem* therefore is on the crime of usurpation – Luvah's attempted usurpation of Urizen's horses of light, Hayley's attempted usurpation of Blake's poetic vocation, and the Spectre's attempted usurpation of Los. Usurpation is almost synonymous with Milton's concept of idolatry as the original sin: usurpation, like idolatry, depends on the notion of *hierarchy* – the idea that a qualitative distinction, the superiority of one contrary over another, is being violated by a claim of equality. Adam and Eve declare themselves God's equals; this is their sin. The Spectre declares himself Los's equal, and this is his sin. He also declares that life's contraries are equal – an equallizing that brings death into Blake's world as surely as Adam and Eve brought it into theirs.

Blake's embrace of Milton here then is a return to and embrace of qualitative distinctions or hierarchy. But this formulation is not exact enough for Blake's ideal. The Spectre after all represents *both* Hayley's and Milton's forms of abstraction, both mediation and division. Blake wants *neither* Milton's tyranny of the absolute nor Hayley's tyranny of the relative, but something in between – again, an ideal of life less rigidly defined and divided than Milton's God renders it, yet more distinct and formed than Hayley's blurring of distinctions does to it. Most correctly, he wants something in between yet closer to Milton than to Hayley, for he has just seen how dangerous Hayley's annihilation of distinctions can be and how essential an antidote Milton's qualitative distinctions provide.

This is why Milton and Hayley become for Blake two kinds of negative, a "contrary" and a "negation" respectively. Milton is a negative in the sense that he is an opponent. But he is a more "positive" negative ("Contraries are Positives," declares Blake, "a Negation is not a Contrary"), because battle with him generates life. Battle with Hayley destroys life; it negates it.

The negation must therefore be cast off; the contrary however can be embraced. But the contrary must be "redeemed" or "reconstituted" first; Milton must moderate his divisions before Blake can embrace him. He must cast off his personal spectre – the spectre of Urizenic division – and this is what he decides to do when he chooses to descend from eternity. He must fight simultaneously with his spectre Satan – the clearest instance of absolute division in *Paradise Lost* – and with Urizen, his abstract God, for this is in a way the same battle. If he can cast off this Satanic spectre of division and abstraction he will be able then to "humanize" Urizen. He comes, he says, "To bathe in the Waters of Life; to wash off the Not Human" (M, II, 41:1; 142). As he battles with the spectre he simultaneously meets Urizen "on the shores of Arnon" and makes his God over, this time in the image of man:

Silent they met, and silent strove among the streams of Arnon, . . .
But Milton took the red clay of Succoth, moulding it with care
Between his palms: and filling up the furrows of many years
Beginning at the feet of Urizen, and on the bones
Creating new flesh on the Demon cold, and building him
As with new clay a Human form in the Valley of Beth Peor.
(M, I, 19:6–14; 112)

He casts off in the figure of the spectre all his rationalistic qualities
which dehumanize his God and which prevent his alliance with Blake.

By casting off spectrous abstraction, Milton corrects all his
"errors" in *Paradise Lost*: his Satan, his Urizenic God, and finally his
"sinful" female, Eve. He is now able to embrace Ololon, his emanation, in a state of redemption and final unity denied to the sexes in
Milton's epic. He is not now in an illusory or false eternity as he was
at the beginning of the poem, but has by leaving that eternity
entered into the true eternity, the true unity of poetic vision, the
human unity, of his "reincarnation" within William Blake.

What Milton and Blake most fundamentally share through their
embrace is Blake's ideal of true reason or "intellect," the reason
which is not the oppressor but the bound or outward circumference
of energy. In his embrace of hierarchy Blake has moved closer to
embracing Milton's insistence that true *liberty* – Blake's "Jerusalem"
or ideal state of imaginative freedom – requires restraint, for Milton
the restraint of the prohibition or reason. And as Blake's return here
to values formerly rejected as repressive, authoritarian, and pater-
nalistic suggests, he embraces in Milton not only a brother and a
friend, but also a spiritual father. It is in this sense that Blake is
philosophically conservative or reactionary here: although he still
repudiates a tyrannical version of reason, he also repudiates his early
ideal of unbridled energy to embrace instead a more moderate ideal.

This return to his true father suggests a second biographical
interpretation of the episode at Felpham – that it may indeed have
been a crisis involving Blake's relation to his father. It may be, as
Margaret Storch has so persuasively argued, that the "spectrous
fiend" which Blake cast out at Felpham was not only the well-
intentioned yet tyrannical Hayley, but his own well-intentioned yet
(inadvertently) tyrannical father.[21] Storch suggests that Blake had
"deep and conflicting feelings" towards his father, aggravated by
personal and professional crises in 1784, which he lived with for

twenty years before casting off at Felpham. And this ambivalence towards his (now dead) father, she suggests, came to a head in the figure of Hayley, so clearly parental in his role as Blake's benefactor and as someone with the power to bestow or withdraw at will the approval Blake desperately needed. Casting off this enforced dependence marked Blake's decisive confrontation with this ambivalence at last, Storch proposes, a confrontation which allowed him to embrace not only his true spiritual father, Milton, but also the memory of his real father, now cleansed of his "spectrous" self. Blake's embrace of Milton thus suggests the return and embrace of the prodigal son; and as Damrosch tells us, the parable of the Prodigal Son was apparently one which moved Blake deeply. In Samuel Palmer's account, "I can yet recall it when, on one occasion, dwelling upon the exquisite beauty of the parable of the Prodigal, he began to repeat a part of it; but at the words, 'When he was yet a great way off, his father saw him,' could go no further; his voice faltered, and he was in tears."[22] What Blake seeks, Damrosch remarks, is "a symbol of the father that can be *elected* rather than imposed" – and in John Milton this is surely what Blake found.

Significantly, Kierkegaard's biographical crisis dramatized in *Fear and Trembling* has been similarly interpreted as a return to his father in the role of prodigal son.[23] Their relationship was by all accounts a deeply troubled one, the elder Kierkegaard a severely orthodox and melancholy Christian who, reputedly full of guilt for having once as a child cursed God, raised his children in a strict and repressive religious environment. "The anxious dread with which my father filled my soul," reports Kierkegaard, "his own frightful melancholy, the many things in that connection which I cannot record – I got such a dread of Christianity, and yet I felt myself so strongly drawn to it."[24] Like Blake, Kierkegaard's main response to his father seems to have been ambivalence; as he further reports,

in a way I loved Christianity: it was venerable in my eyes – it had, to be sure, humanly speaking, made me exceedingly unhappy. That corresponds to my relationship with my father, the man whom I loved above all. And what does this mean? Why, the point is precisely that it was he that made one unhappy – but out of love. His fault did not lie in lack of love, but he mistook a child for an old man.[25]

Once again, we are told that the worst tyranny is the well-intentioned kind; and what is also significant here is Kierkegaard's identification of his father with orthodox religion, an identification Damrosch suggests Blake made as well (269–272).

Gregor Malantschuk makes the rather interesting argument that the Abraham–Isaac story in *Fear and Trembling* is only secondarily about Kierkegaard's sacrifice of Regina; primarily, he claims, it concerns the elder Kierkegaard's sacrifice of Kierkegaard by dedicating him, while still a child, to the lifelong service of God. As the youngest of seven children Kierkegaard, like Isaac, was indeed the child of his father's old age. Writing in his journal, Kierkegaard describes Isaac as one "who understood that he was going to be sacrificed and thereby himself became an old man just like his father."[26] This is really a remark about Kierkegaard himself, claims Malantschuk: Kierkegaard's father pledged his son to God's service; Kierkegaard momentarily rebelled by pledging himself to Regina; but "his father, after all, had already 'pre-pledged' him; therefore this new engagement with Regina had to be broken off, and the suffering of separation undergone"(65). Other journal entries seem to confirm this: "Ah," exclaims Kierkegaard, "I have paid dearly for at one time misinterpreting my life and forgetting – that I was pledged!"[27] A momentary lapse – and the prodigal son returns.

To propose these alternative biographical readings of the two incidents should not alter but instead deepen and confirm my earlier ones. If indeed both incidents dramatize not only a repudiation of marriage (or its symbolic associations) but directly or indirectly the return of sons to fathers, this would seem to confirm the extent to which this "turn" is indeed a re-turn, a turning-back or retracing of steps towards a previously rejected father figure. And this figure carries the full weight of symbolic associations with reason, authority, hierarchy, and orthodox religion – all the concepts I have argued are central to the two crises.

Sons return to fathers; Oedipal and erotic passions (the former clearly evident in Blake's myth at least) are repudiated for this new, restored embrace of reason and of a form of Christianity.[28] Yet the father–son relationship is surely not the same, fundamentally because, to repeat Damrosch's phrase, it has now been "*elected* rather than imposed." By freely choosing this renewed embrace, Blake and Kierkegaard have transformed the relationship from one of necessity into one of freedom, in what we will come to see as the characteristic movement of either/or. Yet it is clear that this embrace profoundly radicalizes the relationship in potentially dangerous ways indeed.

For we may well ask in what sense a father is still a father – the authoritative origin or ground – in a relationship fully instituted by the son. And we may ask concomitantly in what sense "reason" rules when it has been similarly reconstituted by the will. Blake may embrace a Milton – and a Miltonic reason – so willfully refashioned in the image of William Blake that Milton's (and reason's) authority vanishes altogether.

The radical re-fashioning or reconstitution of fathers by sons, and of reason by will, is why it may not be enough to characterize the structure of romantic experience – for Blake and Kierkegaard at least – as simply that of "the prodigal's return." This "circular journey" is indeed, as Abrams has described it, not precisely a circle but a spiral, a return on a higher level, or a return with a differ-ence.[29] Yet for Blake and Kierkegaard this difference is exaggerated to such a degree that the extent to which it is indeed a return may be profoundly in question.

This question will prove central to my study, as we shall see. For the moment, however, the point is to see how Blake's struggles at Felpham – with division or dualism in the character of Milton and with mediation or monism in the character of Hayley, the struggles which he finally condenses into the extraordinarily dense figure of the Spectre – sum up not only his battle with the problem of the contraries throughout his career, but also his final attempted solu-tion to that problem. Blake's struggles also sum up the battle with the logic of dialectic in the romantic period as a whole. For Fichte, Schelling, Schlegel, and Hegel attempted to embody in the structure of dialectic this same dynamic unity of contraries, this same ideal of life as a "divine human," as the absolute in the heart of the contingent. They too were trying to overcome dualism – the dualism of the Kantian wound – yet they too realized the necessity of simultaneously maintaining the qualitative otherness of tran-scendence.

These idealist dialectics settled for the same solution to this problem, however – the solution Blake rejected when he rejected the Orc–Urizen dialectic. All of these dialectics reconciled life's contra-ries within a larger encompassing "both-and" system. Only Kierke-gaard, like Blake, went *beyond* this notion of dialectic to a new idea of dialectic which precisely inverted the old. Only Kierkegaard, like Blake, turned to the idea of casting off the Spectre – the Spectre not only of Kantian division but also of the Hegelian negative or mediation – as the solution to the problems of dialectic. For Kierke-gaard, as for Blake, casting off the Spectre was ideally a way of casting off both kinds of abstraction: that of dualism and that of mediation. It was a way of creating an ideal which was in between Kant's dualism and Hegel's mediation – in between yet closer to Kant, for Kierkegaard, like Blake, was philosophically reactionary in turning back to dualism as the antidote to a mediation he had come to see as more destructive than the dualism it claimed to overcome.

It is in this sense that Blake and Kierkegaard might be said to respond to a "proto-deconstructive crisis in representation," again to use Rajan's phrase – to a crisis of "dissolution" or mediation of the contraries rather than to a crisis of alienation. They realize that the dissolution or mediation of contraries designed to overcome alien-ation from life in fact formalistically abstracts from life. In their attempt to reconstitute real contraries or differences out of this dissolution into pure Becoming, they attempt to reintroduce the real difference in which life consists, the difference between Being and Becoming. And the idea of the Spectre is the key to this extra-ordinarily difficult and vital attempt.

In turning to the Spectre, Blake gave up trying to locate the fall of man in either reason or passion. And he went further than simply turning to "imagination" or Los as the redemptive, mediating faculty. In their mutual turn to the Spectre of Negation, Blake and Kierkegaard turned to the notion of *perspective* as the solution to the problem of romantic dialectics. It remains to be seen just how they hoped this new idea of perspective could capture life as these other dialectics could not.

CHAPTER 2

The Spectre as Kierkegaard's concept of dread

Around Golgonooza lies the land of death eternal; a Land of
pain and misery and despair and ever brooding melancholy.

Blake, Jerusalem

For Blake and Kierkegaard the greatest enemy of the romantic ideal
of life is spiritual passivity, a state of mental torpor. This state,
which Blake calls "jealousy" and Kierkegaard calls "dread,"
corresponds to the medieval *accidie* or spiritual despair considered to
be one of the greatest sins against God. For Blake and Kierkegaard,
it is the greatest sin against life. "Accident is the omission of act in
self & the hindering of act in another," insists Blake; "This is Vice
but all Act [from *Individual propensity*] is Virtue. To hinder Another
is not an act on the contrary it is a restraint on action both in
ourselves & in the person hinderd."[1] The man in this state of
passivity or "hindrance" suffers from melancholy, dread, fear of
futurity; he lives in a state of indolence and self-imposed repression
that hinders all action and traps him within himself, unable to
break through to true existence. "Dread ... makes the individual
impotent, and the first sin always occurs in impotence," says Kierkegaard, "melancholy is a sin, really it is a sin *instar omnium*, for not
to will deeply and sincerely is sin, and this is the mother of all sins"
(Journal III A 233: quoted from *CD*, xii; *E/O*, II, 193). And Blake
writes fervently about the evils of mental passivity and self-
thwarting repression:

if we fear to do the dictates of our Angels & tremble at the Tasks set before
us[,] if we refuse to do Spiritual Acts. because of Natural Fears of Natural
Desires! Who can describe the dismal torments of such a state! – I too well
remember the Threats I heard! – If you who are organized by Divine
Providence for Spiritual communion. Refuse & bury your Talent in the
Earth even tho you should want Natural Bread Sorrow & Desperation
pursues you thro life! (Letter to Butts, January 10, 1803; 724–5).

49

Directly experiencing it as the single greatest source of their most intense struggles, Blake and Kierkegaard suffered excessively from this condition of melancholy, repression, or "hindrance," the negation of all action in oneself. "I begin to Emerge from a Deep pit of Melancholy, Melancholy without any real reason for it, " writes Blake, "a Disease which God keep you from & all good men" (Letter to Cumberland, July 2, 1800; 706). Kierkegaard battled a chronic melancholy so intense that he claimed it as one of the reasons for breaking his engagement to Regina Olsen – that he feared to inflict it upon his wife. According to Lowrie, intense intellectual labor was his only defense against melancholy, his proliferation of writings a desperate hedge against it.[2] Neither man affected or indulged this melancholy as a "romantic" state. It was a condition of deeply felt spiritual despair which they were at great pains to conceal from others and which they battled fiercely and persistently against. Kierkegaard despised the soft, swooning melancholy of fashionable romanticism, and attacked it vigorously in his polemic against romantic irony.[3]

This melancholy of a mind turned in upon itself in too intense self-reflection resulted in no small measure from the extraordinary isolation in which Blake and Kierkegaard lived all of their lives. But their individual experience also exemplified the greatest danger to romantic philosophies of imagination generally, for once this inner spiritual power was exalted as the free and independent creator of all human meaning (and hence of life), the danger was that this imagination would sever itself totally from all sense of an external other and collapse into sterile self-absorption. It is this retreat into isolation and *abstraction* which destroys life and causes melancholy, as Blake all too painfully experienced. He lamented to Thomas Butts,

I labour incessantly & accomplish not one half of what I intend because my Abstract folly hurries me often away while I am at work, carrying me over Mountains & Valleys which are not Real in a Land of Abstraction where Spectres of the Dead wander. This I endeavour to prevent & with my whole might chain my feet to the world of Duty & Reality but in vain! the faster I bind the better is the Ballast for I so far from being bound down take the world with me in my flights & often it seems lighter than a ball of wool rolled by the wind . . . who shall deliver me from this Spirit of Abstraction & Improvidence (September 11, 1801; 716).

Kierkegaard similarly complains of living in a "spirit-world," which he again gives as his reason for not being able to marry Regina:

So I got married to her, let us suppose. What then? In the course of half a year, in less than that, she would have worn herself out. About me – and this is at once the good and the bad in me – there is something rather ghostly, which accounts for the fact that no one can put up with me who must see me in everyday intercourse and so come into real relationship with me. Of course, in the light surtout in which I commonly show myself it is different. But at home it will be observed that essentially I live in a spirit-world. I was engaged to her for a year, and still she did not really know me.[4]

Kierkegaard's apparent concern for the possible effect of his abstraction upon Regina was probably warranted; one is reminded of Catharine Blake's complaint "I have very little of Mr. Blake's company; he is always in Paradise."[5]

This "Spirit of Abstraction" is extraordinarily isolating, cutting a man off from love (as in Kierkegaard's case) and work (as in Blake's) – or in other words, from all that constitutes life. And it is this spirit of abstraction, this life-denying state resulting finally in despair, which all of Kierkegaard's writings attempt to combat and which Blake tries to master through Los's mastery of the Spectre of Urthona. As J.R. Scrimgeour has noted, Blake's Spectre is Kierkegaard's "concept of dread" personified, the "Shadow blue obscure & dismal" (FZ, IV, 49:13; 333) who stands between a man and life.[6] He binds one with mind-forged manacles, what Blake calls "the Chain of Jealousy" and Judge William "the chain of melancholy" (*E/O*, II, 208), and it is this purely mental character of the Spectre which makes him so elusive, shadowy, and dangerous a figure. He is a mental state and not an objective reality, an inner not an outer source of tyranny, not because objective reality is not "real" for Blake and Kierkegaard, but because for both this recognition that the manacles are mind-forged is the first and crucial step towards breaking out of one's passivity. Both feel that blaming something outside oneself as the cause of one's despair merely compounds the disease; one thereby adopts the stance of the helpless victim subject to an external and hence unmanageable tyrant. "A man may have sorrow and distress, yea, it may be so great that it pursues him perhaps throughout his whole life, and this may even be beautiful and true," says the Judge, "but a man becomes melancholy only by his own fault" (*E/O* II, 190). The Judge's distinction between sorrow or distress and melancholy is crucial, for it shows that he by no means denies the existence of an objective reality which inflicts very real and tangible hardships. Yet he implies that far worse than these hardships is the state of melancholy, because it is the passive attitude towards hardship that is the first and greatest obstacle to overcoming it.

Locating the cause of one's disease as "abstraction," a state of mind within oneself, however, is still only a beginning to the cure. One has to go beyond this to locate it within some faculty or quality. Does the melancholy death-in-life stem from a man's rational faculty or his passionate, willful faculty – from a failure of "reason" or a failure of "will"? As I have suggested at the end of Chapter 1, Blake and Kierkegaard conclude that the cause of spiritual inertia is neither simply reason/Urizen nor passion/Orc, but an abstract and hence passive *perspective* on life, a perspective which may result equally from either extreme of reason or of passion. Both conclude that either extreme leads finally to the same state of impotence, and that one must therefore attempt to cast off not reason or passion, but the *perspective* on reason and passion which somehow negates their dynamic interaction.

By locating the cause of the disease (or "fall") in the spectre of abstract perspective instead of in one of life's contraries, Blake and Kierkegaard hope to create a dialectic of life which avoids collapsing its contraries into either extreme of a will-philosophy (in which Orc dominates Urizen) or a reason-philosophy (in which Urizen dominates Orc). They thereby hope to go beyond, one might say (anachronistically in Blake's case), either a Schlegelian romantic irony ruled by pure *eros*, or a Hegelian mediation ruled by an abstract reason, the only two options seemingly available in idealist dialectics, and the only two options seemingly available once one conceives of life as a dialectic of reason and passion. This means that their dialectic is at once curiously moderate and intensely polemical. It is polemical in its decisive casting-off of "negation" or this passive perspective – but it is moderate in its ultimate refusal to cast off either reason or passion. It tries to cast off their *excesses* only; and this decisive casting-off paradoxically "redeems" the contraries. The complexities of this paradoxical dialectic and in particular its relation to the both-and logic of idealist dialectics in general should become clearer if we turn first to Blake's Spectre of Urthona and his actual narrative role in *The Four Zoas, Milton,* and *Jerusalem.*

The Spectre of Urthona embodies "dread" in its most literal sense, for indeed he is dreadful to behold. When Los–Urthona falls, the Spectre separates from his back with shrieks of anguish, "in temptations/And in grinding agonies in threats! stiflings! & direful strugglings" (J, I, 17:57–58; 162). He is a "dark Demon," "a black Horror ... / Howling in pain: a blackening Shadow, blackening dark & opake / Cursing the terrible Los" (J, I, 6:5–6; 149). In Blake's longest physical description of him he is a mighty armored figure, "a spectre Vast, ... feet & legs with iron scale[s];" "iron spikes instead / Of hair shoot from his orbed skull. His glowing eyes / Burn like two furnaces. He called with Voice of Thunder" (FZ, VI, 75:7–18; 352). The spectre is also dreadful in his continual howlings and shriekings, sometimes inarticulate with pain and rage, "panting like a frighted wolf, and howling," but often marvelously eloquent in his threats and temptations to insanity and despair, using "arguments of science" as well as tears and "Terrors in every Nerve" (J, I, 7:1–7; 149). He is alternately cringing and defiant, obsequiously obeying Los while plotting his revenge:

> While Los spoke, the terrible Spectre fell shuddring before him
> Watching his time with glowing eyes to leap upon his prey.
> ... He saw that Los was the sole, uncontrolld Lord of the Furnaces
> Groaning he kneeld before Los's iron-shod feet on London Stone,
> Hungring & thirsting for Los's life yet pretending obedience.
> (J, I, 8:21–28; 151)

And while he seeks to lure Los into despair, his tears are often genuine, as when he cries out in perhaps the most anguished speech in all of *Jerusalem* "Despair! I am Despair ... Life lives on my / Consuming: ... knowing / And seeing life, yet living not." Los feels genuine sympathy for the Spectre at times ("So spoke the Spectre shuddring," adds Blake, "& dark tears ran down his shadowy face/Which Los wiped off, but comfort none could give! or beam of hope"; J, I, 10:60–61; 152). But in general Los threatens and curses the Spectre as vehemently as the Spectre threatens him:

> Shuddring the Spectre howls. His howlings terrify the night
> He stamps around the Anvil, beating blows of stern despair
> He curses Heaven & Earth, Day & Night & Sun & Moon
> ... Driven to desperation by Los's terrors & threatning fears.
> (J, I, 10:23–28; 153)

All of Los's energies are devoted to furiously compelling the spectre to obey him; when he succeeds, they work together to build Golgonooza, the city of art through which Los will recover eternity.

"Ambiguity" is the most fundamental characteristic of the Los–Spectre relationship. It is intensely ambivalent, a love–hate relationship which neither one seems able to break. The Spectre hates Los and plots against him, yet also weeps with remorse and pleads continually for pity. Los rages against the Spectre yet sometimes pities him, and he cannot seem to perform his labors without him. The Spectre is somehow his indispensable tool for recreating the lost eternity; as Wayne Glausser points out, "Blake has trouble deciding what to do with the Spectre, whether to reject him or reform him or accept him as he is, but evidently Los needs him to perform the work of eternity."[7] Los and the Spectre are finally allied not only in building Golgonooza but also as the "watchmen of Eternity":

> The Spectre remains attentive
> Alternate they watch in night: alternate labour in day
> Before the Furnaces labouring, while Los all night watches
> The stars rising & setting, & the meteors and terrors of night!
> (J, IV, 83:78–81; 242)

Ambiguity is also the defining characteristic of Kierkegaard's concept of dread. Dread is a nameless fear of life and change, a fear which stops one from acting. It is ambiguous because it arises from a sense of futurity, possibility or *potential* – and "potential" is fundamentally ambiguous, arousing not fear of any definite something but fear of an indefinite (because still potential) possibility of life. Dread is therefore fear of the infinite, because the infinite is possibility; it is also fear of freedom, the freedom to realize any one of an infinite number of possibilities through decisive action. "The future, the possibility of the eternal (i.e. freedom) in the individual is dread," says Vigilius Haufniensis, and says further, "Dread is a *sympathetic antipathy* and an *antipathetic sympathy*" (CD, 81, 38), a complex mixture of fear and desire:

For dread is a desire for what one dreads, a sympathetic antipathy. Dread is an alien power which lays hold of an individual and yet one cannot tear oneself away, nor has a will to do so; for one fears, but what one fears one desires. Dread then makes the individual impotent, and the first sin always occurs in impotence. (Journal III A 233: quoted from CD, xii)

This wonderfully characterizes the way in which the Spectre, "an alien power," lays hold of Los, who cannot tear himself away, for this Spectre which he fears he also desires or at least needs. As Haufniensis also says, "He cannot flee from dread, for he loves it; really he does not love it, for he flees from it" (*CD*, 40). The Spectre himself embodies this mixture of fear and desire resulting in impotence. He is a raging lust for life, "a ravening devouring lust continually / Craving & devouring" (*FZ*, VII a, 84:37–38; 360), yet he simultaneously cringes in fear and impotence, crying out "Life lives on my / Consuming ... knowing / And seeing life, yet living not – how can I then behold / And not tremble; how can I be beheld & not abhorrd" (J, I, 10:55–59; 154). The Spectre suffers from the same sickness of dread and despair which he inflicts in turn upon Los; he is in fact its very embodiment. He is at once cause and effect, the cause of Los's despair and its effect on Los's spirit – another ambiguity which contributes to his elusiveness.

The question then becomes why Los should desire or need the Spectre, and why the Spectre is somehow indispensable to his recovery of the lost eternity. As I have suggested in Chapter 1, the answer is that the Spectre *is* in a sense that lost eternity or at least its trace. He is the memory of the unfallen Urthona, a shadowy remnant who is therefore (again ambiguously) both unfallen and fallen.[8] He is unfallen in so far as he is a trace of the eternal; but he is fallen in that he does not really exist in separate form until the fall, his separation and very existence symptomatic of it. As the vestige of the eternal in the fallen Los, the Spectre is therefore a sign of Los's immortality. He is "at once the good and the bad" in him, as Kierkegaard says, for this "something rather ghostly" is nothing other than his spirit, his eternal self. But it is also what Anti-Climacus calls "the abstractest possibility of the self," the "infinite form of the self," and "the negative self" (*SUD*, 201–2). It is the self which one wants to bring down to earth, to realize; yet this involves such a great struggle that it is easier to lose oneself in the ideal instead. As the Judge describes this struggle between the negative and the "actual" selves:

This self which the individual knows is at once the actual self and the ideal self which the individual has outside himself as the picture in likeness to which he has to form himself and which, on the other hand, he nevertheless has in him since it is the self. Only within him has the individual the goal after which he has to strive, and yet he has this goal outside of him, inasmuch as he strives after it. For if the individual believes that the universal man is situated outside him, that from without it will come to him, then he is disoriented, then he has an abstract conception and his method is always an abstract annihilation of the original self. (*E/O*, II, 263)

The Spectre is this "negative" self, the picture in likeness to which Los has to form himself, and which nevertheless Los must see as within himself. Los must struggle to sustain this extraordinary paradox which the Spectre embodies – the Spectre's radical transcendence yet radical immanence. If Los sees the unfallen Urthona as too remote, too transcendent, he will despair of being able to recapture that lost eternal self; but conversely, if he loses a sense of Urthona's radical otherness or transcendence, he will lose the ideal which he pursues. He will be evaporated or volatilized into the infinite, on the one hand, or condensed into the finite on the other. Either extreme will destroy the true self, because the true self is a synthesis of the finite and the infinite, the synthesis which Haufniensis calls the "spirit." "If a man were a beast or an angel, he would not be able to be in dread," he says, "since he is a synthesis he can be in dread, and the greater the dread, the greater the man" (*CD*, 139). But this "spirit" can ambiguously either save or damn him. It can save him by reminding him that he is fallen and divided, a self-awareness he must have if he is to strive for recovery of that lost self. But it can equally damn him if he allows this awareness of his fallenness to throw him into despair – the temptation the Spectre indeed continually holds out to Los.[9]

A. DREAD AS BEYOND INNOCENCE AND EXPERIENCE

Dread would appear to be exclusively a condition of fallenness, the state of paralysis which for Blake and Kierkegaard negates life. In this respect it seems to be the state of "experience;" yet curiously enough it can characterize both innocence and experience and thus go beyond them. Because the spectre of dread is at once unfallen and fallen, a vestige of one's eternal self yet symptomatic of one's fall away from that self, dread properly characterizes both the state of innocence from which one has fallen and the state of experience into which one falls. This rather surprising implication of the spectre's ambiguous role is paradoxical, but it is crucial to the new dialectic of "perspective" which Blake and Kierkegaard (with remarkable affinity in this instance) are attempting. Kierkegaard is very explicit that dread has both "innocent" and "experienced" forms. The unfallen state of dread is that which children exhibit; it is a state of innocence as "ignorance" in which the knowledge of the distinction between good and evil does not exist. But nonetheless, it is a sense of the future and of possibilities to be realized, a "sweet feeling of apprehension":

> The dread which is posited in innocence is, in the first place, not guilt; in the second place, it is not a heavy burden, not a suffering which cannot be brought into harmony with the felicity of innocence. If we observe children, we find this dread more definitely indicated as a seeking after adventure, a thirst for the prodigious, the mysterious...This dread belongs to the child so essentially that it cannot do without it; even though it alarms him, it captivates him nevertheless by its sweet feeling of apprehension. (*CD*, 38)

The child is a "dreaming spirit," a spirit which has not yet realized itself in what Haufniensis calls its "eternal validity." This "dread as innocence" is the world of Blake's *Songs of Innocence*, a pastoral world of peacefulness and harmony in which the antithesis of good and evil does not appear. There are presentiments of the future, of the time when "The sun does descend, / And our sports have an end: / ... / And sport no more seen / On the darkening Green,"[10] but there is nothing specifically threatening in these presentiments – they do not taint the world of innocence with experience or knowledge of good and evil. Even "The Little Boy Lost," while it may express childish dread in one of its most intense forms, cannot properly be called a vision of fallenness, evil, or experience. There is no sense of guilt or sin, no knowledge of good and evil, only the child's bewilderment and fear of an unknown future. Haufniensis uses this very image of being lost to describe innocence "brought to its last extremity," saying, "it is not guilty, and yet it is in dread, as though it were lost" (*CD*, 41).

Blake's *Book of Thel*, by contrast, provides a good example of the kind of dread which according to Kierkegaard (and also Blake) is "sin," a fall into experience or guilt which Thel brings upon herself despite (and in fact because of) her attempts to circumvent it. Thel is the epitome of dread as fear of life and futurity. She retreats into the dreamy pastoral world of innocence, a world of infinite possibility which is nonetheless stultifying because it seems she has no purpose in it. There is no role for her to play, no way to realize herself in this world of mere potential, and this sense of her uselessness is the source of Thel's dissatisfaction and longing. She desires life and yet she fears it; her soul seeks to realize itself but in order to do so must leave this world of dreamy possibility for the world of life and action. Earth, "the matron Clay," tells her to "fear nothing," "tis given thee to enter, / And to return," but in refusing this invitation to live, Thel thwarts her own growth and returns not to a state of innocence but to what has now become a fallen state of passivity and despair. The poem may seem rather more ambiguous than this in that the vision of experience or life which Blake portrays Thel as refusing is very bleak, arguably not a real option. Perhaps Thel is right, therefore, to reject this world of experience; the poem as a whole may present only two equally negative options: the world of thwarted potential removed from life, and the tragic world of life or experience which is nonetheless still a world characterized by frustrations or "hindrance," albeit of another kind. The repression in the world of experience is mater-ial, not spiritual – the "tender curb upon the youthful burning boy," the "little curtain of flesh on the bed of our desire" (IV, 6:19–20; 6). It may be then that Thel's choice is merely between two kinds of passivity or hindrance; but it would seem rather that her attempted return to innocence is mistaken, a return Blake does not endorse. The Clod of Clay seems to be the spokesman for the correct, encompassing point of view: Thel should enter the world of experience and only then return to innocence. Her spirit cries out for something more than its passive, dreamy life in the values of Har; and in thwarting that movement towards something higher, Thel falls. She falls in other words not by acting but by *refusing* to act – the "negating" act which for Blake is not an act, "but on the contrary ... a restraint on action."

This ambiguous realm of dread which can be a state of innocence at one time yet become a fallen state at another develops into the idea of Beulah in Blake's later myth. Again, "ambiguity" is the key to this state, an ambiguity metaphorically represented by Beulah's shadowy, moony atmosphere. It is a world of half-light, of "mild moony lustre":

> There is from Great Eternity a mild & pleasant rest
> Namd Beulah a Soft Moony Universe feminine lovely
> Pure mild & Gentle given in Mercy to those who sleep
> Eternally.
>
> (FZ, I, 5:29–32; 303)

Beulah is the world of maternal, brooding, protective love seen in *The Songs of Innocence* and in *Thel*, but the dangerous ambiguity of this love is much more explicit here. This world is one of suspension, a limbo, dreaming state which can be either restorative or stifling. Geographically, Blake locates it in a state of suspension between Eternity and Ulro, another metaphor for its state of psychic suspension and ambivalence. It too is a world of *potential*, out of which one can move up to Eternity, the state of higher innocence, or down to Ulro, the state of experience or fallenness. And in truth Beulah is therefore both innocence and experience – "both" because *potentially* "either." It is also "innocence" in that, like the spectre, it "preserves the Divine Vision in time of trouble:" the emanations rest there after the fall, protected from further fall, and must awake from it when the time of apocalyptic reunion is at hand. The fallen Albion is also told to "repose in Beulah's night till the Error is remov'd;" thus the eternal or "innocence" in him is preserved.

This state of suspension and repose can be restorative; but it can be equally destructive, become in itself a fall or consolidation of the fall. And just as in *Thel*, this destructiveness occurs if one stays in Beulah or this state of imaginative idleness too long. It occurs in other words through *inaction*, not through action; Beulah simply turns into or becomes Ulro if one tries to stay there. This is why Albion is confusingly spoken of as being in both Beulah and Ulro simultaneously. The frontispiece to *Jerusalem* declares that the fallen Albion rests apparently in Beulah:

> There is a Void, outside of Existence, which if enterd into
> Englobes itself & becomes a Womb, such was Albions Couch
> A pleasant Shadow of Repose calld Albions lovely Land.
> (J, frontispiece, 1–3; 144)

But chapter one opens by claiming to speak "Of the Sleep of Ulro! and of the passage through / Eternal Death! and of the awaking to Eternal Life" (J, 1, 1:1–2; 146). And the clearest example of the conflation of Beulah with Ulro is in the exhortation "Thou art in Error Albion, the Land of Ulro: / One Error not remov'd, will destroy a human Soul / Repose in Beulahs night, till the Error is remov'd" (J, II, 41:10–12; 188). Albion is already in Beulah, and it is his refusal to awaken from it that has turned it into Ulro. Yet he cannot abandon Beulah *entirely* to transform Ulro into Eternity, for Beulah holds part of Eternity too.

Beulah is "dread;" Ulro is more properly what Kierkegaard would call "despair" – the definite realization of something that is merely an indefinite possibility in Beulah. As Blake formulates it, "Thus wept they in Beulah over the Four Regions of Albion / But many doubted & despaird & imputed Sin & Righteousness / To Individuals & not to States, and these Slept in Ulro" (J, 1, 25:14–16; 171). I shall return to this distinction and in particular to "despair" presently. For now, we should examine more closely the concept of dread especially in its relation to innocence and experience.

As we have seen, the dread experienced by children is an ignorant and innocent dread, a fear not of good or evil (a distinction which does not exist for innocence), but a fear simply of "possibility." This dread is appropriate to childhood and this is also why it is "innocent." But a time comes when this dreaming spirit seeks to realize its potential in some definite way, when the child desires to grow into an adult. And if one thwarts this desire to change and grow, one "falls," a fall which transforms what was once a state of innocence into a state of experience exactly identical in terms of its *features* (being still a state of dreaming potential, etc.), but exactly reversed in terms of its *value*. The state of childish innocence is unnatural *for adults* – from their perspective, as an ideal for them, it is fallen.

This attempted retreat to childhood innocence and the womb in the face of change is only one form of dread as it is experienced by adults. Adults also experience what Kierkegaard calls "dread of the good" and "dread of the evil," because, unlike children, adults also experience a form of dread which is not ignorant of the distinction between good and evil. This distinction comes into existence whenever one *acts*, because according to Kierkegaard one can act only by acting for good or evil – that is, by realizing one or the other. So long as one does not act but remains (or tries to remain) in the realm of mere potential, the distinction does not come into being. But once one acts, one enters into either the state of evil or the state of good. And when in the state of evil one dreads the good; conversely, in the state of good one dreads the evil. In other words, what one really dreads, again, is simply "change;" this is where the affinity with the "innocent" form of dread lies.

The perspectivism of this concept of dread is clear, and its implications enormous. It profoundly alters the traditional concepts of innocence and experience – so profoundly that Blake and Kierkegaard (again with remarkable affinity) abandon them altogether for the new dialectic of contraries called truth and error. Blake and Kierkegaard might seem to use perspective simply to invert innocence and experience as we normally understand them. That is, what looks like (and indeed is, from a certain perspective) innocence – the childhood condition of ignorance – becomes from another perspective "negated," a state of fallenness or experience for the adult. And conversely, the state of experience or knowledge (knowledge of good and evil) becomes from another perspective a state of higher innocence, because such a state depends upon *action*, and action is for both redemptive. This might look at first like the familiar doctrine of *felix culpa*, but this particular version of it is so extreme that it would be repudiated by most adherents of it in its traditional form. This is because for Blake and Kierkegaard *all* action is redemptive: "all Act from *Individual propensity* is Virtue," as Blake says. For them, even action *for evil* is better than inaction. "Active Evil is better than Passive Good," declares Blake (Annotations to Lavater; 592), and "Sooner murder an infant in its cradle than nurse unacted desires" (MHH, 10:67; 38). Kierkegaard calls inaction "spiritlessness," and declares "Far rather let us sin, sin out and out, seduce maidens, murder men, commit highway robbery – " than remain in this passive state (*CUP*, 485). This is also why Blake says "Error can never be redeemd in all Eternity / But Sin Even Rahab is redeemd in blood & fury & jealousy" (FZ, IX, 120:48–49; 390). Sin – that is, *action for evil* – can be redeemed because at least it is aware of the distinction between good and evil and because it is action. Error – that is, inaction, their new name for what was formerly called evil or sin – must be utterly cast off.

This new doctrine of innocence and experience, then, essentially redefines sin as error and conversely defines redemption as truth. This would appear to approach a Socratic definition of sin. But Blake and Kierkegaard again go beyond even this doctrine, because will remains essential to their definition of error, as we shall see, whereas it is excluded from the Socratic definition. I shall return to these implications of Blake's and Kierkegaard's perspectivism, and particularly to the issues of good and evil, error, and especially will in relation to the Spectre. For now, the point is to see how they hope to use perspectivism (as illustrated in the concept of dread) to grasp their ideal of life. Clearly, perspectivism allows most for *change* in human life – for the fact that what is at one time life-denying can be at another time life-affirming and vice-versa. And these changes of perspective are in a way dictated by life itself – by the eternal or the spirit in man, the synthesis of soul and body, eternity and time, which strives to realize itself and demands that one change accordingly. What tells us that life or the eternal dictates these changes is the fact that any given state, no matter how good, inevitably *becomes* fallen if we do not continue to act. But what Blake and Kierkegaard hope will prevent this from being a deterministic idea of life is the fact that one can always *choose* whether to let inertia overcome one or whether to act. According to them, one's spirit will always rebel when its growth is being thwarted – and given this signal that change is necessary, one can always then choose whether to act or to remain in stasis – whether to battle the spectre or to give in to his temptations. This also means that one can fall repeatedly, again, that fall being always a fall not through action but through inaction. Each time one rejects or thwarts the call to life and action, one falls; each time one conquers this temptation to inertia, to a static death-in-life, one redeems oneself. But this crisis of decision and of action must be faced repeatedly as long as one lives – it is never ended until life is ended. More correctly, it *shouldn't* be ended until life is ended. One can refuse to act; but one is then spiritually dead, living only a death-in-life. One is only the spectre or shadow of one's true self.

This notion of dread, then, is in a way "*beyond* innocence and experience," since it can characterize both stages or more accurately "spheres" of life. By characterizing the prelapsarian state as dread instead of innocence as that is normally understood, Blake and Kierkegaard create a state which contains the *possibility* of a fall yet is still not itself fallen.[11] At the same time, it is also not a state to which one should want to return. The "dreaming spirit" of childhood, the pastoral blissfulness of innocence, is very different from the *decisiveness* of spirit which is necessary for its full realization. "Christianly understood, to look back – even though one were to get a sight of childhood's charming, enchanting landscape," says Johannes Climacus, "is perdition." Such a childish conception of the ideal tries "to transform the thing of becoming a Christian [i.e., realizing one's eternal spirit] into a beautiful recollection, whereas in fact it is the most decisive thing a man becomes" (*CUP*, 533).[12] Redemption therefore does not mean casting off experience and returning to innocence, but casting off a perspective on innocence and experience (dread) which allows one to redeem both. One paradoxically recovers innocence, defined as unity with life, by casting off dread and plunging into experience, defined as action and choice. Finally, because this dread is encountered by the individual repeatedly throughout life (not merely as a child), the real movement of life is not a temporal movement from childhood to adulthood but an atemporal leap from non-existence to existence. The movement is only partly dictated by temporality – the march of time by which the forms of life inevitably grow old and die; one can *master* temporality through repeatedly casting off this deadened state (dread) and recapturing innocence or life. This is why existence is more accurately described in terms of simultaneously existing spheres or states for Blake and Kierkegaard, rather than as a progression of stages.

B. THE SPECTRE AS DESPAIR

Giving in to the spectre of dread results finally in despair, what Blake calls the state of Ulro or Satan. Despair is the Spectre in his most intense form, and here Kierkegaard offers a passage wonderfully descriptive of Blake's Spectre of Urthona as both cause and effect of this condition. Despair results from a man's dread "of the highest demand made upon him, that he be spirit" (*SUD*, 155) says Anti-Climacus:

The spirit constantly desires to break through, but it cannot attain the metamorphosis; it is constantly disappointed, and he would offer it the satiety of pleasure. Then the spirit within him gathers like a dark cloud, its wrath broods over his soul, and it becomes an anguishing dread which ceases not even in the moment of pleasure ... behind the eye lies the soul as a gross darkness ... The spirit wills to break through, wills that he shall possess himself in his consciousness, but that he is unable to do, and the spirit is repressed and gathers new wrath. (*E/O*, II, 190–191)

From this description, it might seem that Los, not the spectre, causes the state of despair (i.e., through repressing the spectre). It is true that this "dark cloud" results from Los's repression of his eternal self. But it is important to remember once again that the spectre is the *embodiment* of this repression, and that as this embodiment he is both its cause (dread) and its effect, the form or shape that this dread takes in Los's soul.

When one thus represses one's spirit, the Judge says, "the spirit

will not let itself be mocked, it revenges itself upon you, it binds you
with the chain of melancholy" (*E/O*, II, 208). In its most intense
form, this melancholy becomes despair; but like dread, despair arises
from the presence of the eternal, the spirit, in man. It is (or should
be) therefore paradoxically consoling, a proof of one's immortality,
for as Anti-Climacus points out,

Socrates proved the immortality of the soul from the fact that the sickness of
the soul (sin) does not consume it as sickness of the body consumes the
body. So also we can demonstrate the eternal in man from the fact that
despair cannot consume his self, that this precisely is the torment of
contradiction in despair. (*SUD*, 153)

This "torment of contradiction" is that one dies everlastingly yet does
not die; one cannot get rid of this haunting spectre of the eternal in
oneself. "My Spectre around me night & day / Like a Wild beast
guards my way," as Blake laments (Songs & Ballads; 475). Despair is
thus "an impotent self-consumption which is not able to do what it
wills; and this impotence is a new form of self-consumption, in which
again, however, the despairer is not able to do what he wills, namely,
to consume himself" (*SUD*, 151). Los cannot rid himself of the
Spectre, no matter how much he threatens and curses and beats him
into submission. And the more he tries the more he seems to torment
himself in a fury of impotence. This state of impotent self-consumption is the "sickness unto death," and here we find the closest Blakean
parallel not in Los but in Albion: "Albion is sick! said every Valley,
every mournful Hill / And every River: our brother Albion is sick to
death" (J, II, 36:11–12; 182). Los never quite succumbs to this sickness unto death, partly because the dramatic exigencies of Blake's
myth demand that part of Albion – the part called Los – survives to
instigate Albion's resurrection. Albion is in a sense the outer man who
to all appearances has sunk totally into the passivity of death, when in
fact his hidden, inner faculties are continuing to struggle. But Los also
nearly succumbs to the sickness:

Thus Albion sat, studious of other in his pale disease;
Brooding on evil: but when Los opend the Furnaces before him:
He saw that the accursed things were his own affections,
And his own beloveds: then he turn'd sick! his soul died within him
Also Los sick & terrified beheld the Furnaces of Death
And must have died, but the Divine Saviour descended
                                        (J, II, 42:1–6; 189)

Los is saved by "the Divine Saviour" (whose role I shall examine more closely later), but he is also saved by his own continual struggle with, and refusal to yield to, the Spectre. Los quite properly never does sink into Albion's sickness unto death simply because he does resist and conquer the Spectre's temptations to despair; for him they remain temptations. Albion's despair here illustrates what Anti-Climacus calls the despair of weakness, "despair at not willing to be oneself," whereas Los manifests the despair of defiance, "despair at willing to be oneself." Together these are the two forms of despair as Anti-Climacus defines it. Albion's seems to be the despair of weakness because he has despaired over his own passivity – despaired at seeing that "the accursed things were his own affections / And his own beloveds." He cannot endure the consciousness of his own weakness: "Just as a father disinherits a son, so the self is not willing to recognize itself after it has been so weak. In its despair it cannot forget this weakness, it hates itself in a way" (*SUD*, 196). Albion's response to this self-hatred is to sink even further into passivity, to abandon the struggle. Los's despair, however – the form of despair which the Spectre most closely resembles – is more properly the defiant "despair at willing to be oneself," what Anti-Climacus also calls "demoniac despair."[13] This is characterized by the inability to lose oneself in order to gain oneself; the self "is not willing to begin by losing itself but wills to be itself." Such a self is raging, malicious, and spiteful – "with hatred for existence it wills to be itself, to be itself in terms of its misery," says Anti-Climacus, it wills "to be itself in spite" (*SUD*, 207). This demoniac self is really one's ego or pride, and indeed pride is for Anti-Climacus what underlies both the weak and the defiant forms of despair. The weak despairer thinks he is in despair over his weakness, but Anti-Climacus objects "just as if it were not pride which attached such prodigious weight to weakness, just as if it were not because he wanted to be proud of himself that he could not endure this consciousness of weakness" (*SUD*,199). The defiant despairer proudly wills to be himself without the aid of the eternal, in total independence:

The self wants to enjoy the entire satisfaction of making itself into itself, of developing itself, of being itself; it wants to have the honor of this poetical, this masterly plan according to which it has understood itself. (*SUD*, 203)

This proud despairer sees himself as an objection against the whole of existence, his own raging torment as proof that existence or the eternal is not "good" or omnipotent; his whole tormented existence is a witness against it, and he therefore clings to his misery as the only way of asserting his power against the eternal.

This pride which underlies both forms of despair is what Blake calls "selfhood," and he explicitly links this with the Spectre: "I in my Selfhood am that Satan: I am that Evil One!" exclaims Blake's Milton, "He is my Spectre!" (M, I, 14:30–31; 108). And in *Jerusalem*, Los answers his Spectre "Thou art my Pride & Self-righteousness: I have found thee out / Thou are reveald before me in all thy magnitude & power" (J, I, 8:30–31; 151). This pride or selfhood is a *false* self as opposed to the true or eternal self, "a false Body: an Incrustation over my Immortal / Spirit; a Selfhood, which must be put off & annihilated alway," as Blake says (M, II, 40:35–36; 142). It is important to see that the ideal for Blake and Kierkegaard is neither total annihilation of the self (which is in fact "despair at not willing to be oneself") nor total assertion of the self ("despair at willing to be oneself"), because both of these apparent opposites ultimately embody the same false selfhood, the same mixture of weakness and defiance, fear and desire, called pride.

What Blake and Kierkegaard finally mean by pride, however, is really will, and it is this that the Spectre ultimately represents. More correctly, he ideally represents false as opposed to true will. Because this false self or selfhood is the single state resulting from both extremes of reason and will (extremes finally identical), this raises the problem of whether we call this single state reason or will, particularly when the whole point of this new dialectic is to get beyond this opposition. It also raises the very interesting issue of what Los, as the opposite of this selfhood, should properly be called. If the Spectre is Will and Los is Reason, or conversely, if Los is Will and the Spectre is Reason, then this dialectic which has attempted to go beyond this opposition has failed. The Spectre must remain defined as a Selfhood, consisting of false will *and* false reason (or the extremes of will and reason); Los must remain defined as Imagin-ation, consisting of true will and true reason (or the moderation of will and reason) in dynamic unity.

To what extent this way of defining Los and the Spectre is indeed possible will be the central issue raised in my conclusion. For the moment, the point is to see how Blake and Kierkegaard hoped to attain this ideal. They did so primarily by making this single state called Selfhood the ground of all passivity and abstraction from life, and by claiming that this selfhood always takes two opposite forms ultimately identical. This results logically from the structure of the self as both Blake and Kierkegaard define it. For Kierkegaard, as I have mentioned, the self is a synthesis of two principles, which he calls the infinite and the finite. These would seem to correspond to the Prolific and the Devouring, or Orc and Urizen, in Blake's myth, in that Kierkegaard defines the finite as "the limiting factor" (Urizen) and the infinite as "the expanding factor" (Orc) (*SUD*, 163). Anti-Climacus defines the self, its purpose, and the despair that results from failing to achieve this purpose, as follows:

> The self is the conscious synthesis of infinitude and finitude which relates itself to itself, whose task is to become itself, a task which can be performed only by means of a relationship to God. But to become oneself is to become concrete. But to become concrete means neither to become finite nor infinite, for that which is to become concrete is a synthesis. Accordingly, the development consists in moving away from oneself infinitely by the process of infinitizing oneself, and in returning to oneself infinitely by the process of finitizing. If on the contrary the self does not become itself, it is in despair. (*SUD*, 162–3)

This is much like Blake's early formulation of his ideal in the aphorism "Reason is the bound or outward circumference of Energy" (MHH, 4; 34) – life consists of energy, the expanding factor, and reason, the limiting factor, in dynamic synthesis. Despair thus results from becoming either too finite or too infinite; one suffers from either "the despair of infinitude due to the lack of finitude," or "the despair of finitude due to the lack of infinitude," as Anti-Climacus puts it. In the despair of infinitude, the self lacks limits and thus evaporates into the infinite. "The self is simply volatilized more and more," and a man "becomes in a way infinitized, but not in such a way that he becomes more and more himself, for he loses himself more and more" (*SUD*, 164). In the despair of finitude, the self lacks a sense of possibilities; instead of expanding infinitely it contracts and becomes "desperately narrow-minded and mean-spirited." The self becomes preoccupied with temporal existence, with the trivial, and with worldly affairs – it loses itself again, but this time in the finite (*SUD*, 166).

The early Blake, the Blake who saw Urizen as the villain of his myth and Orc as the hero, could be said to have suffered from the "despair of finitude" – the repression of expanding passion by limiting reason. But when he came to see that his celebration of Orc was too extreme a reaction, he was thrown into the opposite "despair of infinitude due to lack of finitude," the despair which led him to cry out "Once Man was occupied in intellectual pleasure & energies / But now my soul is harrowd with grief & fear & love & desire / And now I hate & now I love & Intellect is no more" (J, III, 68:65–67; 222). As Judge William describes this state, "his soul is, as it were, anesthetized by despair ... his rational soul is smothered and he is transformed into a beast of prey which will shun no expedient because all is self-defense" (*E/O*, II, 226). (Again, this strikingly resembles Blake's description of the spectre as a "wild beast" guarding his way). This is how Blake came to see that both extremes, apparently such opposites, were in fact united in the same negative unity of despair, the death-in-life – that they constituted not a dialectic of life but a cycle of death and negation.

In his final attempt to correct his own extremism, Blake therefore attempts to reconstitute or redeem Urizen, the "Intellect" he had earlier rejected. This is why all three of the late prophetic works – *The Four Zoas*, *Milton*, and *Jerusalem* – are concerned each in their own way with this reconstitution of Urizen or the limiting factor. And it is no accident that his regeneration of Urizen appears simultaneously with the new character of the Spectre, for these two prominent innovations in Blake's myth are profoundly linked. As "the negation [which] must be destroyed to redeem the contraries," the Spectre is what allows Blake to redeem not only Urizen but ultimately Orc as well.

C. THE SPECTRE IN "THE FOUR ZOAS"

Although "spectres" appear in much of Blake's earlier work, the Spectre of Urthona as a distinct character does not appear until *The Four Zoas*. And as Frye has suggested, his appearance there (especially in Night VIIa, which Blake extensively revised at Felpham) probably exploded the whole Zoa scheme and led Blake to abandon the poem for *Milton* and *Jerusalem*, both of which employ the new psychological model of Los and the Spectre.[14] The Spectre is very much an evolving (and hence incomplete) conception through *The Four Zoas* and *Milton*, but he does spring forth full-blown in *Jerusalem* with great clarity and intensity. And in all three poems certain ideas (in more or less articulated form) stand out in association with him. Not only does the Spectre in each poem take on the worst of Urizen or Orc or both, he also represents various forms of false unity, the false ideal or perspective of death which threatens to usurp the true perspective of life. This repeated association of the Spectre with an idea of false unity is essential to Blake's new perspectivism, for it is how Blake represents the fact that the Spectre is not just a part of life, a contrary, but a whole: an encompassing perspective, the overarching negation which destroys the contraries.

The Spectre's role in *The Four Zoas* is somewhat confused, probably in part because it was a developing idea with which Blake was newly experimenting.[15] But as we have seen, this confusion or ambiguity is also fundamental to the Spectre's very identity as both the unfallen yet fallen form of Urthona. In this poem he is particularly interchangeable with Los in a way that he is not in the late poems, for it is Los who is referred to here as a "terrible Demon" (FZ, viia, 85:32; 368) and as "the Spectre Los" (FZ, ix, 139:5; 407). Blake at times seems to adopt the Spectre's point of view that it is Los and not himself who is the spectre or delusive phantom, the fallen form of Urthona. Blake seems sympathetic to the Spectre's exhortation:

> be assurd I am thy real Self
> Tho thus divided from thee & the Slave of Every passion
> Of thy fierce Soul Unbar the Gates of Memory look upon me
> Not as another but as thy real Self I am thy Spectre.
> (FZ, viia, 85:35–38; 368)

The Spectre appears in the fourth night, simultaneously with the division (or fall) of Los and Enitharmon. Tharmas commands the Spectre to reunite Los and Enitharmon, but the Spectre "seeing Enitharmon writhd / His cloudy form in jealous fear & muttering thunders hoarse" (FZ, iv, 49:24–25; 333). To him, Los is the fallen man while he is the eternal man who should therefore rightfully unite with Enitharmon. And indeed he does seem to be the memory of Urthona in his unfallen state, convincing even Tharmas of this by recounting how he, the last Zoa to fall, protected Tharmas in *his* fall:

> I beheld thee rotting upon the Rocks
> I pitying hoverd over thee I protected thy ghastly corse
> From Vultures of the deep then wherefore shouldst thou rage
> Against one who thee guarded in the night of death from harm.
>
> (FZ, IV, 50:24–27; 334)

The Spectre repeats this "saving" function throughout the poem, reviving Los and Enitharmon when they have fainted and guarding Orc from Urizen – all prototypes of his ultimate saving role in *Jerusalem*, where he "preserves the Divine Vision in time of trouble." He is also told by Tharmas that he must help Los to reverse the fall "& him assist to bind the fallen King / Lest he should rise again from death in all his dreary power" (FZ, IV, 51:3–4; 334). Tharmas promises Enitharmon to the Spectre as his "sweet reward," but Los, in his fury and desire for revenge upon her for her desertion, compels the Spectre to bind her as well as Urizen with molten iron:

> The Spectre wept at his dire labours when from Ladles huge
> He pourd the molten iron around the limbs of Enitharmon
> But when he pourd it round the bones of Urizen he laughd
> Hollow upon the hollow wind – his shadowy form obeying
> The voice of Los compelld he labourd round the Furnaces.
>
> (FZ, IV, 53:15–19; 326)

With this consolidation of the fall, the fixing of its limits, the fourth night ends and the Orc cycle (the cycle of fallen life and death) begins. The Spectre plays a role here as well, where (in Night V) he helps Los chain down Orc with the "chain of Jealousy" (FZ, V, 60:19–30; 341). He also stands guard over Orc, defending him against Urizen's advance (end of Night VI). But the climax of his dramatic function appears in Night VIIa, where his interaction with Los and Enitharmon unexpectedly displaces the Orc–Urizen confrontation (the Orc cycle) at its apparent climax. This curious evaporation of Orc and Urizen partway through one of the plates (FZ, VIIa, 81:7 ff.; 356) in favor of an entirely new focus seems to be where Blake's imaginative breakthrough to the Spectre suddenly began to consolidate.

The central events in this confrontation are the unity of the Spectre first with the Shadow of Enitharmon and secondly with Los. The Spectre's seduction of the Shadow of Enitharmon clearly creates a fallen unity, as a number of details seem to indicate. The

seduction occurs beneath Urizen's "Tree of Mystery" in a temptation scene clearly meant to suggest Eve's seduction by the serpent in
Paradise Lost (FZ, viia, 84:1–42; 359–60). And this union gives birth
to "a wonder horrible": Vala, Rahab, or "Error." The union of Los
and the Spectre however is much more ambiguous. The Spectre
promises Los, as he promised Enitharmon, a recovery of the lost
Eternity if Los will unite with him; indeed, he threatens that his
recovery is totally impossible unless Los obeys him:

> Thou never canst embrace sweet Enitharmon terrible Demon. Till
> Thou art united with thy Spectre . . .
> If we unite in one[,] another better world will be
> Opend within your heart & loins & wondrous brain.
>
> (FZ, viia, 85:32–45; 368)

Frye suggests that these two unities provide the poem with a
"double crisis" – that the unity of the Spectre with the Shadow of
Enitharmon and the subsequent birth of Rahab from this union
symbolizes "a consolidation of error," while the unity of the Spectre
with Los symbolizes "an imaginative advance."[16] Yet Los's unity
with the Spectre here may be a false or delusive unity as well. The
eternity the Spectre promises Los seems to be not the real eternity
but Beulah, the Eden or false eternity which Blake ultimately
rejects. For the Spectre repeatedly describes the "better world" as
"threefold," and despite their mingling, he still seeks to destroy Los:

> But mingling together with his Spectre the Spectre of Urthona
> Wondering beheld the Center opend by Divine Mercy inspired
> He in his turn Gave Tasks to Los Enormous to destroy
> That body he created but in vain for Los performed Wonders of
>   labour
>
> (FZ, viia, 87:2–5; 368)

The Eternity which the Spectre promised Enitharmon was similarly
Beulah, or the "married Land," "those mild fields of happy Eternity
/ Where thou & I in undivided Essence walkd about / Imbodied.
Thou my garden of delight & I the spirit in the garden" (FZ, viia,
84:4–6; 359). And as we have seen by the birth of the "wonder
horrible" from Enitharmon's surrendering to this vision of the lost
unity, the result was not Eternity or Truth but a state of Error. The
Spectre's seduction of Enitharmon is indeed probably not an act
separate from his attempt to unite with Los, but the same act. His

seduction of Enitharmon is part of an attempt to unite with and hence destroy Los through Enitharmon, not to unite fruitfully with him, as Urizen's command to his daughter (also in Night VIIa) seems to verify:

> bring the shadow of Enitharmon beneath our wondrous tree
> That Los may Evaporate like smoke & be no more
> Draw down Enitharmon to the Spectre of Urthona
> And let him have dominion over Los the terrible shade.
>
> (FZ, VIIa, 80:5–8; 355)

The delusive unity of the Spectre with Enitharmon, then, is merely the first step in uniting with Los in a similarly delusive unity, one which will "evaporate" him into the Spectre's shadowy parody of life, the unity not of life but of death.

It is significant that this unity of death which tries to "evaporate" Los is instigated by Urizen, for it demonstrates a fundamental alliance of the Spectre with Urizen – or with Urizen's most negative qualities. The Spectre is Urizenic most notably in his cold, shadowy abstraction from life, an abstraction which threatens to be as tyrannical over and destructive of Los as was Urizen's earlier tyranny over Orc. Urizen also tries to tempt Los into the Spectre's point of view by exclaiming "The Spectre is the Man the rest is only delusion & fancy" (FZ, I, 12:29; 307). And the Spectre is most notably in league with Urizen or with Urizenic functions in that he takes on himself the blame for the divisive activity which caused the fall, weeping and exclaiming "I am the cause / That this dire state commences – I began the dreadful state / Of Separation & on my dark head the curse & punishment / Must fall … " (FZ, VIIa, 87:32–34; 369). This admission is the most explicit indication in the poem of how the presence of the spectre will allow Blake eventually to absolve Urizen and Orc – or at least, the best of Urizen and Orc – from culpability.

With typical ambiguity, the Spectre is not only aligned with Urizen but also at times opposed to him. For while he is often himself Urizenic, he also helps Los against Urizen, by binding Urizen and by protecting Orc against Urizen's advance. This doubleness may have two possible explanations. The first is that where Los controls the Spectre he is able to thwart the Spectre's own Urizenic tendencies or alliances with Urizen. The second is that the Spectre's antagonism is to the "good" Urizen – the redeemable portion which Blake has realized he wants to rehabilitate. The Spectre naturally wants to thwart this healthy restored unity of the Zoas and substitute his own unhealthy parody of it, a unity in which "false reason" would dominate instead of the true reason which Blake has newly decided that Urizen can be.[17] Again, we see how Blake is beginning to reformulate life's dialectic more moderately as involving not the confrontation of reason with passion, but that of false reason versus true reason, or of two perspectives on reason and passion.

Urizen is indeed redeemed as "true reason" in *The Four Zoas*, in a narrative innovation as striking as the introduction of the Spectre. In Nights I through VI Urizen is, as in Blake's earlier myth, responsible for the initial fall of the four Zoas into disunity. But significantly, Orc–Luvah is equally responsible: Luvah and Vala have flown up from their proper place in the loins to usurp Urizen's horses of light. Urizen's sin is now not his desire to dominate (as in the early myth), but his voluntary relinquishing of the reins of reason to the anarchy of the passions. This means that not division but *false unity* – the mistaken alliance of Urizen and Luvah – is the cause of the fall. And Blake's new ideal of recovered unity, therefore, is one in which Urizen will separate himself again and resume his rightful place of dominion over the passions. This is why Albion sends Urizen forth to begin the process of regeneration (Night II), and why Blake has Urizen voice perhaps the most lyrical vision of Eternity in the entire poem (FZ, V, 64; 343–4), in a piercing lament for its loss. Urizen's unexpected redemption occurs at the end of Night VIIa:

> Startled was Los he found his Enemy Urizen now
> In his hands. he wonderd that he felt love & not hate
> His whole soul loved him he beheld him an infant
> Lovely breathd from Enitharmon he trembled within himself.
> (FZ, VIIa, 90:64–67; 371)

This redemption is repeated from a more cosmic perspective in the apocalyptic Ninth Night, when Urizen repents his error, shakes off the "snows from his Shoulders," and rises "into the heavens in naked majesty / In radiant Youth" (FZ, IX, 121:1–32; 390–1). And this redemption of Urizen is explicitly associated with the spectre and with Blake–Los's new sense of moderation in the poem. Enitharmon suggests to Los "if thou my Los / Wilt in sweet moderated fury fabricate forms sublime / Such as the piteous spectres may assimilate themselves into / They shall be ransoms for our Souls that we may live" (FZ, viia, 90:21–24; 370). In obedience "Los his hands divine inspired began / To modulate his fires," and the direct result of this is Urizen's redemption (FZ, viia, 90:25–26; 370).

Blake–Los is able to redeem Urizen as true reason by displacing false reason onto the Spectre, redefining life as the struggle of false versus true reason. Concomitantly, he also tries to redefine life as the battle of true versus false passion. For if the Spectre contains all the worst of Urizen's rational qualities – his cold abstraction, his divisiveness – he also contains Orc's corollary excesses of passion. The Spectre is not only a repressive Urizen but a repressed Orc, the raging passion chained down by Urizenic repression. He is a thwarted lust for life, as his uncontrollable passion for Enitharmon symbolizes, self-thwarted and tormented by his impotence:

> Thou knowest that the Spectre is in Every Man insane brutish
> Deformd that I am thus a ravening devouring lust continually
> Craving & devouring but my Eyes are always upon thee O lovely
> Delusion & I cannot crave for any thing but thee.
>
> (FZ, viia, 84:36–39; 360)

This is also why his unity with Enitharmon produces Vala or the female will – the fallen form of passion or will. Their unity demonstrates Blake's recognition that either excess of reason or passion produces the same state. It is the Spectre's Urizenic, rational evaporation of the Shadow of Enitharmon up into himself, as well as his "ravening devouring lust," which has produced this extreme of will represented by Vala. This displacement of "evil" will onto the Spectre's unity with Enitharmon will allow Blake to redeem Orc–Luvah just as it allowed him to redeem Urizen; indeed, Orc–Luvah will become the Christ-figure in *Jerusalem*. Blake is not here concerned with the eventual redemption or resurrection of Luvah, however, because it is the imbalance *towards* Orc-Luvah and away from Urizen which he is trying to correct at this point.

D. THE SPECTRE IN "MILTON"

Despite the embryonic state of the Spectre in *The Four Zoas*, his association with a more moderate perspective on life which will allow Blake to redeem Urizen is very clear, as is his association with the notion of false unity, a false ideal. These ideas become progressively more explicit through *Milton* and *Jerusalem*. *Milton* in particular makes clear (as we have seen in part already) the way in which the Spectre represents false unity, divisiveness, and especially false as opposed to true reason. To begin with, battle with the Spectre is the central dynamic of *Milton*, as opposed to its peripheral role in *The Four Zoas*. Blake's battle with his spectre Hayley–Satan, as we have seen, is a battle primarily against the false unity of mediation. Blake's numerous names for this spectre of false unity make much clearer the sense in which it is both false and a unity. The spectre is a unity in that it is a "pretense of pity and love," "officious brotherhood," "soft dissimilation of friendship," and "corporeal friendship." It is a *false* unity because it is in truth profoundly divisive: the alliance of Blake–Los with Satan–Hayley divides him radically from the true poetic vision which he seeks. Blake also much more explicitly associates this state of false mediation with the landscape of Beulah, the geographic location of the entire poem, as he makes clear from its very beginning, where he calls on the Daughters of Beulah to "Record the journey of immortal Milton thro' your Realms / Of terror & mild moony lustre, in soft sexual delusions / Of varied beauty" (M, 1, 2:2–4; 96). The second book similarly begins by placing us firmly in the landscape of Beulah, which he defines as "a place where Contrarieties are equally True, / ... a pleasant lovely Shadow / Where no disputes can come" (M, 11, 30:1–3; 129).

As commentators have often noted, in rejecting the soft delusions, the false mediations of Beulah, Blake is rejecting the Eden of *Paradise Lost* for a higher ideal of eternity, a higher strife of contraries which are not equally true.[18] The spectre which Blake battles in "The Bard's Song" may look very different from the spectre which Milton battles in the rest of the poem, a spectre defined as Urizen and as Satan. But as I have suggested earlier, these battles are the same battle, halves of a whole. Beulah is an excessively naturalistic ideal, a land of generation and nature which leads ultimately to death: "the Natural power continually seeks & tends to Destruction / Ending in Death," as Blake says in Book 1 (M, 1, 26:41–42; 124). Hayley–Satan's appeal is to the "natural man" instead of the poet, the man who must make money and eat to live, the man who fears bodily death. Such a man when controlled by this sense of necessity becomes preoccupied with the vegetable world of the body, the soft, swoony sleep of spiritual torpor which in its unity with nature is ultimately a unity with death. Milton's spectre Urizen, by contrast, is hard, divisive, and cold, a masculine god of division who appears to be the opposite of the soft feminine mediations of Beulah. But his excessive rationalism is simply another kind of death, not the feminine "natural power," but the masculine rational power which in its apparently contrasting sterility is equally deathly. Beulah is really concomitant with or the result of Urizen's excessive rationalism, which has split the world into the two extremes of body and mind.

The association of the Spectre with Beulah and with Urizen, an association merely begun in *The Four Zoas*, is much clearer here. Blake's explicit identification of Milton's spectre with Urizen as false reason is even further developed by Milton's catalogue of exactly what rationalistic qualities he is casting off in the figure of his Satanic-Urizenic spectre; he comes, he says,

> To cast off Rational Demonstration by Faith in the Saviour
> To cast off the rotten rags of Memory by Inspiration
> To cast off Bacon, Locke & Newton from Albions covering
> To take off his filthy garments, & clothe him with Imagination
> To cast aside from Poetry, all that is not Inspiration . . .
> To cast off the idiot Questioner who is always questioning,
> But never capable of answering; who sits with a sly grin
> Silent plotting when to question, like a thief in a cave;
> Who publishes doubt & calls it knowledge; whose Science is Despair,
> Whose pretence to knowledge is Envy, whose whole Science is
> To destroy the wisdom of ages to gratify ravenous Envy
> That rages round him like a Wolf day & night without rest
> (M, II, 41:3–18, 142)

It is clear that the spectre, as "the reasoning power in man," a "selfhood," is the time-bound ego as opposed to the vital imagination. He is the demand for rational proof instead of faith, the insistence that the only truth is that which can be proven with absolute rational certainty. As memory instead of inspiration, he is the passive dependence of the mind on external reality instead of on its own creative powers, a mind which creates only "by imitation of Natures Images drawn from Remembrance" (M, II, 41:24; 142). Worst of all, perhaps, as "the idiot questioner" the Spectre is the intellectual skeptic, who sees history only as civilization's negation of itself.

As we have seen, Milton decisively casts off these Urizenic excesses of reason to embrace not only Albion but also Blake. As in *The Four*

Zoas, this casting-off is paradoxically extreme and moderate, an embrace. For the poem is not finally about the *rejection* of Urizen or reason; on the contrary, it is about Blake's embrace of reason in the form of Milton himself. Just as casting off the spectre paved the way for the redemption of a modified Urizen in *The Four Zoas*, the fact that Milton and Blake cast off their spectres paves the way for their embrace of each other and especially for Blake's embrace of Miltonic reason. But it is crucial that this is a reconstituted and hence *moderated* Miltonic reason – just as Blake-Los had to "modulate his fires" of passion/Orc in *The Four Zoas*, Milton here has had to modulate his fires of reason/Urizen. To use a more accurate metaphor, he has had to "melt" Urizen's snows of reason in a neat inversion of Los's modulation of his fires, remaking Urizen in the image of man.

Battle with the Spectre thus leads, in *Milton* as in *The Four Zoas*, to the redemption of reason not to its casting-off. It excludes the excesses of reason, the false reason symbolized by Hayley, to embrace a more moderate ideal of reason, the "true" reason which attempts to fall into neither extreme of Beulah-like mediation or of Urizenic division. This is how "the negation must be destroyed to redeem the contraries," – the false forms of reason and passion must be cast off for the true.

E. THE SPECTRE IN JERUSALEM

In *Jerusalem* the Spectre of Urthona springs forth full-blown at last. The poem opens with a thundering confrontation between Los and the Spectre which is sustained for a full seven plates, a confrontation which reveals with great clarity the Spectre's full symbolic value. Its climax is the Spectre's own culminating outburst:

> O that I could cease to be! Despair! I am Despair
> Created to be the great example of horror & agony ...
> ... Life lives on my
> Consuming: & the Almighty hath made me his Contrary
> To be all evil, all reversed & for ever dead: knowing
> And seeing life, yet living not; how can I then behold
> And not tremble; how can I be beheld & not abhorrd
> (J, I, 10:51–59; 153–4)

Once again, the Spectre is very closely associated with a false ideal, the delusive unity of mediation or Beulah. The fallen Albion sleeps

in Beulah, "a Void, outside of Existence, which if enterd into /
Englobes itself & becomes a Womb" (J, I, 1:1–2; 144). Los immediately perceives that this state of mediation or false unity is the enemy
which he must combat: "Half Friendship is the bitterest Enmity said
Los" (J, I, 1:8; 144). Blake later in the poem identifies this false unity
not only with false friendship, but with what he calls "soft Family-
Love," exclaiming, "A mans worst enemies are those / Of his own
house & family" (J, II, 27:77, 81–2; 173). The Spectre repeatedly
tries to substitute his false brotherhood for the true, arguing that
Los's brotherhood with Albion – the true unity or ideal – is the
delusory one:

> And thus the Spectre spoke: Wilt thou still go on to destruction?
> Till thy life is all taken away by this deceitful Friendship?
> He drinks thee up like water! ... thy stolen Emanation
> Is his garden of pleasure! all the Spectres of his Sons mock thee
> Look how they scorn thy once admired palaces! Now in ruins
> Because of Albion! because of deceit and friendship!
>
> (J, I, 7:9–17; 149)

Another form of false unity besides "brotherhood" which the
Spectre represents is again the false unity of "marriage," union with
Enitharmon, as Los clearly recognizes:

> Tho my Spectre is divided: as I am a Living Man
> I must compell him to obey me wholly: that Enitharmon may not
> Be lost: & lest he should devour Enitharmon: Ah me!
>
> (J, I, 17:16–18; 161)

The Spectre tries to undermine the true unity of Los and Enitharmon as rigorously as he tries to destroy the unity of Los with Albion;
when Los and Enitharmon quarrel,

> A sullen smile broke from the Spectre in mockery & scorn
> Knowing himself the author of their divisions & shrinkings, gratified
> At their contentions, he wiped his tears he washed his visage.
>
> (J, IV, 88:34–36; 247)

The last form of false unity which the Spectre represents is that of
memory – as in *The Four Zoas*, he is a memory of the unity-that-was,
the abstract eternity from which Albion and his Zoas have fallen.
"Listen, I will tell thee what is done in moments to thee unknown,"
he commands Los, and proceeds to tell the whole story of the Zoas'
fall (J, I, 7:29–50; 149–50).

Fundamentally, the Spectre is Los's abstract self, but as we have seen through all three of these prophecies, this abstract self takes two forms: the natural and the rational. The dominance of the natural or vegetable man, the "corporeal" self or ego associated with bodily desires and the temporal world, is what Blake calls "corporeal friendship" as opposed to "spiritual friendship." This distinction first arose in *Milton*, where Los exclaimed "Mark well my words! Corporeal Friends are Spiritual Enemies," and where it became the basis for Blake's crucial differentiation between Hayley and Milton (M, I, 4:26; 98). (As Blake wrote in a letter to Butts from Felpham in 1803, "if a Man is the Enemy of my Spiritual Life while he pretends to be the friend of my Corporeal, he is a Real Enemy"; April 25, 1803, 728.) In *Jerusalem* Blake–Los exclaims "I have tried to make friends by corporeal gifts but have only / Made enemies: I never made friends but by spiritual gifts; / By severe contentions of friendship & the burning fire of thought" (J, IV, 91:15–17; 251). This corporeal Spectre of the natural man attempts to drag man toward death by means of "Turning his Eyes outward to Self," Blake's description of Albion's disease (FZ, II, 23:2; 313).

It is excessive reason which tries to convince a man that he is only corporeal, his existence merely material or vegetable. This again is how the excessively rational self is in fact the same as or leads to the natural or corporeal self. Blake is explicit about the Spectre's role as false reason here, as even the frontispiece proclaims; the fallen Albion's "Sublime & Pathos become Two Rocks fixd in the Earth / His Reason, his Spectrous Power, covers them above / Jerusalem his Emanation is a Stone laying beneath" (J, frontispiece, 1:4–6; 144). And as Blake later defines the Spectre:

> The Spectre is the Reasoning Power in Man, & when separated
> From Imagination, and closing itself as in steel, is a Ratio
> Of the Things of Memory. It thence frames Laws & Moralities
> To destroy Imagination! The Divine Body, by Martyrdoms & Wars.
> (J, III, 74:10–13; 229)

As "the Reasoning Power in Man," the Spectre tries to undermine all faith in life, to dissolve life within the fictions of skeptical reasoning. Los cries out to him not to tempt his "children" to despair – "Reason not against their dear approach / Nor them obstruct with thy temptations of doubt & despair" (J, I, 10:32–33; 153) – but the Spectre obstinately replies:

... the joys of God advance
For he is Righteous: he is not a Being of Pity & Compassion
He cannot feel Distress: he feeds on Sacrifice & Offering:
Delighting in cries & tears & clothed in holiness & solitude.
                                        (J, I, 10:46–49; 153)

Albion's Spectre similarly represents skepticism and the temptation
to despair, presenting Albion with a chilling version of the rise and
fall of civilizations, the march of history toward oblivion:

I am your Rational Power O Albion & that Human Form
You call Divine is but a Worm seventy inches long
That creeps forth in a night & is dried in the morning sun
In fortuitous concourse of memorys accumulated & lost
It plows the Earth in its own conceit ...
... London & Canterbury tremble
Their place shall not be found as the wind passes over[.]
The ancient Cities of Earth remove as a traveller.
                                        (J, II, 29:5–14; 175)

If the Spectre is so clearly the Rational Power in *Jerusalem*, in what
sense is he not Reason but *false* reason – an embodiment merely of
reason's *excesses*? No obvious redemption of Urizen or reason occurs in
the plot of this poem as it did in *The Four Zoas* and in *Milton*. But other
details suggest even more powerfully that indeed Blake means to cast
off the false reason for the true. As I have been suggesting, the first
evidence for this is that here as in the other two poems the Spectre
takes on the naturalistic and rationalistic extremes formerly associated with Orc–Luvah and Urizen. And Blake's rejection of these
extremes for a more moderate ideal is most strongly supported by two
narrative details: a new description of the Zoas' fall, and the introduction of a separate spectre for Albion. Blake now sums up the fall thus:

The Four Zoa's clouded rage; ...
And the Four Zoa's are Urizen & Luvah & Tharmas & Urthona
In opposition deadly, and their Wheels in poisonous
And deadly stupor turn'd against each other loud & fierce
Entering into the Reasoning Power, forsaking Imagination
They became Spectres; & their Human Bodies were reposed
In Beulah, by the Daughters of Beulah with tears & lamentations.
                                        (J, III, 74:1–9; 229)

The significance of this new description of the fall is that *all* the Zoas
fall by "entering into the Reasoning Power, forsaking Imagin-

ation." Urizen is now no longer alone symbolic of the Reasoning Power; that power has become a state into which all the Zoas enter equally when they fall. Although in their fallen state the Zoas are divided against each other, in a true sense they are not really divided against each other because none of them specifically has caused the others to fall. *All* have fallen by the "Spectrous Power," a power which cannot be identified with any one Zoa. The real division then is not among the Zoas, but between a true and a false form of the Zoas: the spectrous fallen form and the imaginative eternal form. And both of these forms are unities: the fall is in a sense not from unity into division but from true unity, the unity of life, into false unity, the unity of death. This point is crucial to understanding just how Blake can claim paradoxically both to cast off and to embrace Orc and Urizen (and indeed all the Zoas). Only their spectral forms are cast off; their true forms can be embraced. It is also critical for seeing just how Blake hopes to use the idea of perspective to attain his ideal: one does not cast off division for unity (although in a sense this remains true), but one kind of unity for another – or more accurately, one perspective on the unity of the Zoas (the Spectre's) for another perspective on that same unity (Los's).

This new way of conceptualizing the fall is also why Albion now has a Spectre as well, a Spectre who plays a role in the poem separate from that of the Spectre of Urthona. Again, neither Urizen nor Orc is responsible for Albion's fall, but rather his spectre, a spectre who combines the excesses of both. Blake calls Albion's Spectre "his Spectrous Chaos," his "Rational Power," and describes him in terms formerly associated with Urizen and Orc. When Albion falls, his spectral form duplicates the Urizen of Blake's early myth:

> Cold snows drifted around him: ice covered his loins around
> He sat by Tyburns brook and underneath his heel, shot up
> A deadly Tree, he nam'd it Moral Virtue, and the Law
> Of God who dwells in Chaos hidden from the human sight.
> The Tree spread over him its cold shadows.
>
> (J, II, 28:12–17; 174)

The fallen spectre is also described with imagery associated with the Orc of Blake's early myth,

There to eternity chain'd down, and issuing in red flames
And curses, with his mighty arms brandish'd against the heavens
Breathing cruelty blood & vengeance, gnashing his teeth with pain
Torn with black storms, & ceaseless torrents of his own consuming
    fire.

(J, II, 36:36–39; 182)

The presence of this Spectre of Albion again "redeems" the four Zoas from individual culpability in Albion's fall. Like the Zoas, Albion has fallen by succumbing to his spectrous power, a power which is not merely some single part or faculty but somehow a separate whole. By giving Albion this Spectre, Blake again makes it clear how he is reconceiving life as a struggle not between parts within a whole, but between two wholes. And one is the "shadow" or false form of the other, which is to say, they are the false and true perspectives on the single unity of life.

All of these narrative details point to a new dialectic of perspective. Blake's strategy of putting the worst of Orc and Urizen into the Spectre in order to cast it off, yet still redeem Orc and Urizen, demonstrates how he is trying to redefine life's contraries in an entirely different way. By trying to cast off the excesses or false forms of reason and passion in order to save what is best in them, their true forms, essentially he is redividing life's contraries into truth (true reason and passion) and error (false reason and passion) instead of into reason and passion. In other words, life is now the struggle not between two contraries within a single systematic dialectic (two parts within a larger whole) but between two entire dialectics (or two wholes). Again, this is why the spectre is so repeatedly linked with the idea of false *unity*; he is not a mere part which can be reconciled within a larger whole, but an entire encompassing perspective on life, a whole in himself. Life is the struggle between two mutually exclusive perspectives: truth vs. error, Los vs. the Spectre, Life vs. Death. It is a dialectic of *exclusive perspectives* rather than of *inclusive contraries*. We can see how this idea of life as a battle between two irreconcilable absolutes (i.e., one of which must be cast off) which nonetheless casts off neither reason nor passion would seem to approach Blake's lifelong ideal of life as a struggle of dynamic, *unsystematic* contraries. And we can see how it would seem to create a new, unsystematic definition of dialectic which in its lack of system might seem inherently truer to life. We should now turn to Kierkegaard to see more clearly the struggle of this new, unsystematic "either/or" dialectic with the systematic "both-and" logic of idealist dialectics in general. For it is Kierkegaard's attack on, yet assimilation of, both Schlegelian romantic irony and Hegelian mediation that allows us to situate Blake relative to these discourses of romanticism and in turn perhaps to other discourses of undecidability.

CHAPTER 3

The Spectre and the line of life

The great and golden rule of art, as well as of life, is this: That the more distinct, sharp, and wirey the bounding line, the more perfect the work of art; . . . Leave out this line and you leave out life itself . . .

Blake's Exhibition and Catalogue of 1809

. . . what the ancients regarded as positive, the passion for distinctions, has now become a childish folly.

Johannes Climacus, Philosophical Fragments

My argument has been that at Felpham Blake came to see the true enemy of life not as division / Urizen but as mediation / the Spectre of Urthona, who is really a *disguised* form of division. This is why the Spectre is identified with Beulah, the delusive paradise "Where Contrarieties are equally True" (M, II, 30:1; 129). It is significant that this "married land" of mediation disguises at once truth or eternity where contraries are absolute and not equally true, and error or Ulro, where contraries again are absolute. Ulro is the *negative* state of true division, the profound alienation from life which really underlies Beulah's (and the Spectre's) appearances of mediation.

Blake ultimately calls Beulah the land of negation, where "the Contraries of Beulah War beneath Negations Banner" (M, II, 34:23; 134). He also explicitly calls the Spectre the spirit of negation, in one of his clearest and most forceful descriptions:

And this is the manner of the Sons of Albion in their strength
They take the Two Contraries which are calld Qualities, with which
Every Substance is clothed, they name them Good & Evil
From them they make an Abstract, which is a Negation
Not only of the Substance from which it is derived
A murderer of its own Body: but also a murderer

84

Of every Divine Member: it is the Reasoning Power
An Abstract objecting power, that Negatives every thing
This is the Spectre of Man: the Holy Reasoning Power.
(J, 1, 10:7–15; 152–3)

These lines make it clear that Blake associates negation or this passive perspective on life with a certain logic of contraries in which both are subsumed within a larger whole which negates them. This logic of negation is for Kierkegaard the logic of all the post-Kantian idealist dialectics, the both-and logic which negates life's contraries by mediating them in a reconciliation which destroys existence. Negation, "the abstract objecting power," is for him the spectre not only of the Hegelian negative but also of Schlegel's romantic irony. According to Kierkegaard, both dialectics ultimately share the same logic of contraries, the same perspective on life which he sees as the source of the nineteenth century's melancholy and despair.

A. KIERKEGAARD'S ASSESSMENT OF HIS TIMES

"The age of distinctions is past and gone," laments Vigilius Haufniensis in the epigraph to *The Concept of Dread*, "the System has overcome it. He who loves distinctions is regarded as an eccentric man, who longs for that which has long vanished." All qualitative distinctions, all real differences, have been annihilated by the Hegelian negative pervading German life and thought. God has been collapsed into man and nature in one vast pantheism. Good and evil, truth and error, reason and passion, subjectivity and objectivity – all the distinctions which give life value and energy – have been collapsed within the system. Even language has lost its potency and degenerated into that ambiguous word at the heart of the Hegelian system, the self-contradictory "*Aufhebung*" which both preserves and annuls in vacillating indeterminacy (*CUP*, 199). Spiritual inertia and apathy are widespread: people either sit in stolid complacency, convinced that they know the truth or have been saved simply by being born into the "theocentric" nineteenth century (*CUP*, 354); or they languish in listlessness and romantic melancholy, with brief frenzied spurts of illusory and primarily erotic passion. Men are afraid or cannot be bothered to act, since one cannot act without choosing among alternatives, alternatives which have been negated within the system. The age indulges in "a fantastic ethical weakness," Johannes Climacus declares. Distinctions have no significance, so that men scramble vainly to be "different":

Men have perceived that it avails nothing to be ever so distinguished an individual man, since no difference avails anything. A new difference has consequently been hit upon: the difference of being born in the nineteenth century. Everyone tries to determine his bit of existence in relation to the age as quickly as possible and so consoles himself. But it avails nothing, being only a higher and more glittering illusion. (*CUP*, 318)

People are afraid, Climacus says, "that if they were to become particular existing human beings, they would vanish tracelessly, so that not even the daily press would be able to discover them, still less critical journals, to say nothing at all of speculative philosophers immersed in world-history;" they fear that "if a man lets go of Hegel he will not even be in a position to have a letter addressed to him" (*CUP*, 317–18). Such fear is legitimate, he acknowledges, in that insofar as a man lacks ethical and religious passion he may well vanish tracelessly: "it cannot be denied that when a man lacks ethical and religious enthusiasm, being an individual is a matter for despair – but not otherwise" (*CUP*, 318). People do not act because they are afraid to make the decisions necessary for action – or because they assume that these decisions have already been made for them by the system. They are paralyzed by living in a realm of abstraction – the realm defined by not only the Hegelian mediation but also the romantic irony pervading the age. This realm is "the fantasy-medium of possibility," "the realm of abstract thought with its shadow-boxing," a realm which fictionalizes existence within the sphere of pure thought (*CUP*, 514, 316).

The Hegelian dwells in the world of infinite retrospect or what Climacus calls "recollection;" the romantic ironist dwells in the realm of infinite prospect or possibility. Both are at once everything and nothing: the Hegelian is the sum of all that has gone before, the romantic ironist is the sum of all future possibilities. And both therefore cannot act, because for both life is contemplation. Both are spectators "outside the game," spectators for whom there is no either/or. "You mediate contradictions in a higher madness," Judge William tells the romantic ironist, "philosophy mediates them in a higher unity. You turn towards the future ... You say 'I can either do this or do that, but whichever of the two I do is equally mad, *ergo* I do nothing at all'" (*E/O*, II, 174). "What unites you is that life comes to a stop," the Judge says:

Philosophy turns towards the past, towards the whole enacted history of the world, it shows how the discrete factors are fused in a higher unity. It mediates and mediates ... the philosopher hastens back into the past to such a degree that, as a poet says of an antiquarian, 'only his coat tails are left behind in the present.' (*E/O*, II, 174–5)

The philosopher is "outside, he is not in the game, he sits and grows old listening to the songs of long ago, harkening to the harmonies of mediation" (*E/O*, II, 176). The romantic ironist finally mediates contradictions within the negative unity of "boredom," for his poetry is merely "poetry about poetry in the infinite." "The fact that this poetry vacillates between opposites shows that in a deeper sense it is not true poetry" (*CI*, 321, 320); and "As there must always be a bond uniting these oppositions, a unity into which these intense dissonances of feeling resolve themselves, so upon close examination one will even find such a unity in the ironist," Kierkegaard claims:

Boredom is the only continuity the ironist has. Yes, boredom: this eternity void of content, this bliss without enjoyment, this superficial profundity, this hungry satiety. But boredom is the negative unity ... the negative unity in which opposites disappear. That both Germany and France at this moment have only too great a number of such ironists, and no longer need to be initiated into the secrets of boredom by some English lord, the travelling member of a spleen club; and furthermore, that one or another youthful ward of the Young Germany or France would long ago have died of boredom had not their respective governments been so fatherly as to arrest them in order to give them something to think about – all this would scarcely be denied by anyone. (*CI*, 302)

The infinite striving or becoming of the romantic ironist turns out to be a kind of death-in-life, a "habit of vacillation" within a realm of infinite possibility (*CUP*, 444). (Notice again the appeal to something "fatherly" to "arrest" this dissolution, by introducing actuality or life into the ironist's abstracted state.) "And is it not painful and sad to let life go past one thus without ever gaining a firm position," asks the Judge, "Is it not sad, my young friend, that for you life never acquires content?" (*E/O*, II, 88). Life is always absent for such an individual; and he is not merely sad but comic, because he is comically absent-minded (or absence-minded, as one might say of the deconstructionist version of the romantic ironist): he has forgotten that he must exist. It is indeed true that "there is no special difficulty connected with being an idealist in the imagination," acknowledges Climacus, "but to *exist* as an idealist is an extremely strenuous task, because existence itself constitutes a hindrance and an objection" (*CUP*, 315).

While the Hegelian and the romantic ironist are very alike in some respects, they are also very different. The Hegelian is too dogmatic, complacent, and systematic – the epitome of a stolid, apathetic complacency which looks on life as mere "result," as something already finished. He is paralyzed (albeit unknowingly) by Kierkegaard's "despair of finitude" or necessity due to lack of infinitude or possibility (*SUD*, 162–175). No possibilities exist for the Hegelian because possibility belongs to the realm of the future which Hegelianism excludes. The Hegelian individual lives under the yoke of necessity and result, confined in the routine of domestic everyday life and in a state of quiet, invisible despair unnoticed by all around him, who see him as a solid citizen and family man. The romantic ironist is the aesthete and seducer who lives in a state of infinite, tortured, restless striving after the infinite (defined for him as the interesting) which will save him from his melancholy and his boredom. His despair is the opposite of the Hegelian's (despite the fact that both conditions of despair result from living abstracted from life): he suffers from the despair of infinitude or possibility. Where the Hegelian suffers from too many limits and the lack of possibility, the romantic ironist suffers from limitlessness and too much possibility. For such an individual "possibility ... appears to the self ever greater and greater, more and more things become possible, because nothing becomes actual. At last it is as if everything were possible – but this is precisely when the abyss has swallowed up the self" (*SUD*, 69). This self lacks reality because it lacks limits; the Hegelian self lacks reality because it lacks possibility. Either extreme of Hegelian system or Schlegelian striving results equally in unreality and the despair of the self that cannot break through to existence. Hegelian thesis and Schlegelian antithesis, result, finally, in death-in-life, reconciled within this negative unity.

We can see how these two dialectics manifest the two forms of despair as Kierkegaard has defined them. Further, they demonstrate the two extremes into which all of the post-Kantian idealist dialectics ultimately fall. All collapse into either a reason-philosophy (here represented by Hegelian mediation) or a will-philosophy (here represented by Schlegel's romantic irony) – the extremes of rationality and irrationality which Kierkegaard, like Blake, wants to avoid and go beyond. Kierkegaard's analysis clearly demonstrates how these two extremes are not really opposed, not real contraries, but the reason and will poles of the same dialectic. Mediation is the dialectic of pure transcendence, Being, Reason, or Absolute spirit; romantic irony is the dialectic of pure immanence, Becoming, passion, or life. Mediation emphasizes the reconciliation of contraries within the system; romantic irony emphasizes infinite process not final reconciliation or resolution. Mediation stresses objectivity, romantic irony subjectivity. Yet according to Kierkegaard, both dialectics are equally undialectical, equally static and dogmatic system on the one hand, equally vacillating and indeterminate process on the other. Both are equally rational because equally abstracted from life into the realm of pure thought; and both are equally irrational because both are dialectics of pure will. Both are equally dialectics of pure transcendence in which existence and passion are swallowed by pure thought, and dialectics of pure immanence in which thought is swallowed by life and passion. They are not really then two different dialectics but the two poles of the single dialectic of both-and logic.

Both dialectics offer in other words the same abstract *perspective* on life. The key to Kierkegaard's criticism of the Hegelian and the romantic ironist is his complaint that both are "spectators," for this not only emphasizes the idea of perspective so crucial to his dialectic, but also underscores the aptness of Blake's choice of the word "spectre" for this state of abstraction and inertia. This state is spectral – i.e., shadowy and elusive – because it *is* only a perspective. Yet it is also spectral because it is a passive frame of mind which "spectates" on life instead of participating in it, a "*spectator ab extra*," as Nelson Hilton calls it.[1] This perspective is spectral too because its effect is such a shadowy, negative one; its potency lies in its impotence, its indefinite hindering of all action, rather than in any active, defined evil. Finally, this perspective is spectral because as a way of seeing, a perspective, it is potentially everywhere, an all-pervading, ghostly shadow haunting all of life and coloring it "blue obscure & dismal."

The Spectre is thus a vast illusion or error, a veil over man's vision which blurs all distinctions into confusion and indeterminacy. He is the illusion of life, the fiction that one is living when one is really not existing in any truly dynamic sense. And "illusion" is the most difficult enemy to fight, for obvious reasons – because it is so elusive, something which appears and disappears with the wink of an eye, but mostly because its central strategy is to masquerade as the truth, to cultivate a resemblance to it. As Climacus says, "the most dangerous form of skepticism is always that which looks least like it" (*CUP*, 275). And as we have seen, in Blake's spiritual crisis at Felpham he was apparently most threatened by Hayley's resemblance to him, his "seeming a brother" but "being a tyrant," his corporeal friendship but spiritual enmity. The greatest difficulty is to convince people that they must change into something which they think they already are – for Blake to convince Hayley that he must become his friend when Hayley is convinced that this is what he already is, or in the more general terms of the romantic ideal, to convince people to live when they take it for granted or insist that this is what they are always already doing. Climacus gives as an example of this the difficulty in convincing the Hegelian "Christian" that he is in fact a false Christian who must convert to the true:

everyone knows that the most difficult leap, even in the physical realm, is when a man leaps into the air from a standing position and comes down again on the same spot. The leap becomes easier in the degree to which some distance intervenes between the initial position and the place where the leap takes off. And so it is with respect to a decisive movement in the realm of the spirit. The most difficult decisive action is not that in which the individual is far removed from the decision (as when a non-Christian is about to decide to become one), but when it is as if the matter were already decided. . . . In brief, *it is easier to become a Christian when I am not a Christian than to become a Christian when I am one*; (*CUP*, 327, Kierkegaard's emphasis)

The spectre of Hegelian Christendom asserts that one is always already a Christian by virtue of being born into Protestant nineteenth-century Germany. And Climacus's point is that this illusion is the first and greatest obstacle to be overcome, for until it has been dispelled there will be no motivation to change, no incentive for movement: only complacency and spiritual stasis.

Illusion or error must be expelled; this is the first step in Blake's and Kierkegaard's dialectic. It must be expelled by being forced to reveal itself as it really is – as illusion not truth, as death not life. As Blake says of the Spectre "he who will not defend Truth, [must] be compelled to defend / A Lie: that he may be snared and caught and snared and taken / That Enthusiasm and Life may not cease" (M, 1, 8:47–48; 102 and J, 1, 9:29–31; 152). The demon can be exorcised only after he has been forced to appear in his true shape. Traditional lore has it that one does this by reciting the Lord's Prayer backwards (Frye's description of *Jerusalem*)[2]; or to repeat Judge William's injunction, one must "play the same piece of music backwards without making a single mistake" (*E/O*, II, 169). In other words, one makes first a *negative* movement; the revelation and hence destruction of error must precede revelation of the truth.

Blake and Kierkegaard both use the metaphor of corrosion to describe the initially negative activity of their dialectic. Blake speaks of his activity as "printing in the infernal method, by corrosives, which in Hell are salutary and medicinal, melting apparent surfaces away, and displaying the infinite which was hid" (MHH, 14; 39). His other equally corrosive, negative, and medicinal image for this (in *Jerusalem*) is circumcision, the stripping away of a veil of flesh: "Establishment of Truth depends upon destruction of Falshood continually / On Circumcision: not on Virginity, O Reasoner of Albion" (J, III, 55:65–66; 205). Kierkegaard describes the negative strategy of stripping away illusion thus:

there is an immense difference, a dialectical difference, between these two cases: the case of a man who is ignorant and is to have a piece of knowledge imparted to him, so that he is like an empty vessel which is to be filled or a blank sheet of paper upon which something is to be written; and the case of a man who is under an illusion and must first be delivered from that. Likewise there is a difference between writing on a blank sheet of paper and bringing to light by the application of a caustic fluid a text which is hidden under another text. Assuming then that a person is the victim of an illusion, and that in order to communicate the truth to him the first task, rightly understood, is to remove the illusion ... one must first of all use the caustic fluid. But this caustic means is *negativity*. (*PV*, 39–40)

Kierkegaard is careful to distinguish this caustic negativity, however, from the infinite negativity or destruction of illusion characteristic of the romantic ironist; as Judge William in *Either/Or* tells the romantic ironist:

You are absolutely indefatigable in ferreting out illusions in order to smash them. ... However, you have not reached the truth, you have come to a stop with the destruction of illusions, and inasmuch as you have wrought that destruction in all possible and imaginable directions, you have really worked yourself into a new illusion: the illusion that one can stop there. Yes, my friend, you are living in an illusion, and you accomplish nothing. (*E/O*, II, 80)

Blake similarly castigates the illusion that the destruction of illusions can in itself be a kind of truth or knowledge when he rants against the Spectre "Who publishes doubt & calls it knowledge; whose Science is Despair, / Whose pretence to knowledge is Envy, whose whole Science is / To destroy the wisdom of ages to gratify ravenous Envy" (M, II, 41:15–17; 142). Both Blake and Kierkegaard would insist that the destruction of illusion or error is only one half of their dialectic, the other (crucial) half being the subsequent leap to truth – the truth of life that ideally stands revealed in sharp opposition.

By forcing the Spectre to "defend a Lie," or as Blake also says, to "be reveald in his System" (J, II, 43:10; 191), Blake and Kierkegaard hope to reintroduce the qualitative distinction between truth and error which the Spectre has tried to negate. They hope in other words to re-introduce *the principle of contradiction* which he has tried to abolish – and whose abolition is according to Climacus the root cause of the spiritual stasis of his age. *This* is the lie or fiction which the Spectre must defend: that contradiction can be abrogated for the existing individual.

B. THE PRINCIPLE OF CONTRADICTION

at bottom it is an immovable firmness with respect to the absolute, and with respect to absolute distinctions, that makes a man a good dialectician. This is something that our age has altogether overlooked, in and by its repudiation of the principle of contradiction.

Johannes Climacus, *Philosophical Fragments*

In Eternity one thing never Changes into another thing Each Identity is Eternal.... A Man can never become Ass nor Horse some are born with shapes of Men who may be both but Eternal Identity is one thing & Corporeal Vegetation is another thing

Blake, *A Vision of the Last Judgment*

"Wherever there is life, there is contradiction," declares Climacus. This is why life has escaped idealist dialectics: "in our philosophical nineteenth century ... dialectics has lost its passion," because "it has become so easy and light-hearted a thing to think contradictions" (*CUP*, 345). All contradictions have become mediated and finally abrogated within the system of pure thought. This is because all of the post-Kantian idealist dialectics took as their first principle the abolition of Kant's claim that the phenomenal, finite world of Becoming or A exists over against the noumenal, infinite world of Being or Not-A, and that the two cannot therefore be reconciled (A cannot be Not-A). Instead of accepting Being as the ground of life, they made Becoming the ground, and Being a merely phenomenal appearance within Becoming – an illusory stability thrown up by this underlying Becoming. And in making Becoming the underlying substance of reality they abolished the principle of contradiction because as A becomes Not-A there must be a point at which A is both A and Not-A. A and Not-A are one in the process of Becoming – and yet their difference is at the same time supposedly preserved.[3]

Climacus bluntly responds that "to answer Kant within the fantastic shadow-play of pure thought is precisely not to answer him" (*CUP*, 292). All this "becoming" and unifying of the finite and the infinite is illusory, for if all disjunctions are only apparent, reconciled at bottom in the principle of becoming, the passionate striving or becoming which is life is reduced to a feeble, illusory struggle for something which is always already mediated. Climacus insists that "the abrogation of the principle of contradiction, if it really means anything ... means for an existing individual that he has ceased to exist" (*CUP*, 310). The existing individual can never see life as a system or unity in which all contradictions have been reconciled, either in the positive unity of Hegel's Absolute Spirit or in the negative unity of Schlegel's romantic irony, for "anyone who is himself an existing individual cannot gain this finality outside existence," this abstract perspective on life (*CUP*, 108).

In abolishing the principle of contradiction, claims Climacus, these dialectics have reduced the true negative of life to a mere relativity – they have substituted a faint, shadowy negation, a merely systematic difference, for the absolute difference (between what Blake would call the "contraries") in which life consists. "The higher an individual stands, the more differences he has annihilated or despaired over, but he always has one difference left which he is not willing to annihilate, that, namely, in which his life consists" (Judge William, *E/O*, II, 233). This absolute difference is the distinction between the finite and the infinite, the qualitative value of transcendence whose mediation or compromise Kierkegaard and Blake so fiercely resist. "The negativity that pervades existence," says Climacus, "or rather, the negativity of the existing subject ... has its ground in the subject's synthesis: that he is an existing infinite spirit" (*CUP*, 75). It is an irreducible *paradox* that the existing individual should be this synthesis of the finite and the infinite; it is an irreducible, incomprehensible paradox that the eternal should enter time at all. For Climacus, this paradox defies reason and

demands faith, in absolute contrast to the contradiction which mediation and reason are able to resolve and hence abolish. Contraries
may be unified in *thought*, Climacus acknowledges, but in *life* they are
always separated: "The systematic Idea is the identity of subject and
object, the unity of thought and being. Existence, on the other hand,
is their separation" (*CUP*, 112). The truly existing individual

> is conscious of the negativity of the infinite in existence, and he constantly
> keeps the wound of the negative open, which in the bodily realm is
> sometimes the condition for a cure. The others let the wound heal over and
> become positive; that is to say, they are deceived. (*CUP*, 78)

One is reminded here of Los's binding of Urizen in Blake's early
myth, a binding which cauterizes or seals open the wound of their
separation rather than closes it over. And his later fiercely antagonistic struggle against the Spectre who has been similarly wrenched
apart from him also serves to maintain their separation rather than
to heal it. This cauterizing image, like the metaphor of corrosion,
again emphasizes the paradoxically healing negativity of this dialectic.

Everything Kierkegaard says through the pseudonyms about his
ideal of life sounds almost exactly like what all the romantics and
idealist dialecticians claim to be their ideal of life: his emphasis on
life as the paradox of contraries kept apart yet also unified (preserved and annulled?), his attacks on system, his emphasis on striving or becoming. And indeed this is the heart of the difficulty of his
enterprise (and of Blake's): they share the same ideal of life as do all
the romantics, but differ from them in advocating what appears to
be the opposite way of arriving at this ideal. Because Blake and
Kierkegaard work through differentiating instead of through
mediating, they make idealist dialectics appear to be shadowy,
inverted parodies of the true dialectic of life. Their shared passion
for absolute distinctions is at least as strong if not stronger than their
desire for unity; the deliberate making of distinctions, rather than an
emphasis on their mediation or abrogation, becomes increasingly for
them the central activity of life, the negative way of uniting *with* life.
Again, as Blake puts it, "whenever any Individual Rejects Error &
Embraces Truth a Last Judgement passes upon that Individual"
(VLJ, 562). Rejecting error means rejecting vacillation, compromise, blurred distinctions, and indeterminacy for clarity – the clarity
of sharp distinctions and decisiveness. The task of the existing

individual is to become "clear" or "transparent," the Judge says, and "it is a mistake to think that the abstract is the transparent. The abstract is the turbid, the foggy" (*E/O*, II, 252). This making of distinctions, this "becoming transparent," is what Blake calls "drawing the line of life":

The great and golden rule of art, as well as of life, is this: that the more distinct, sharp, and wirey the bounding line, the more perfect the work of art; and the less keen and sharp, the greater is the evidence of weak imitation, plagiarism, and bungling. ... The want of this determinate and bounding form evidences the want of idea in the artist's mind, and the pretence of plagiary in all its branches. How do we distinguish the oak from the beech, the horse from the ox, but by the bounding outline? How do we distinguish one face or countenance from another, but by the bounding line and its infinite inflexions and movements? What is it that builds a house and plants a garden but the definite and determinate? What is it that distinguishes honesty from knavery, but the hard and wiry line of rectitude and certainty in the actions and intentions. Leave out this l[i]ne and you leave out life itself; all is chaos again, and the line of the almighty must be drawn out upon it before man or beast can exist. (Blake's "Exhibition and Catalogue of 1809"; 550)

Here again Blake demonstrates not only his passion for distinctions, but also his conviction that the real enemy of life is false resemblance or illusion, here called "weak imitation" and "pretence of pla-giary." And he clearly identifies the line of life as "the line of the almighty" – which is to say, the absolute line or negative of the infinite *in* existence, the qualitative distinction which only the quali-tative difference of the eternal can introduce into time. This decisive black line, the line of either/or, is for Blake and Kierkegaard the true line of life; the both-and line of merely relative differentiation is a pale and wavering inverted reflection of it, a weak imitation.[4]

Blake and Kierkegaard want to re-introduce this true negativity of the infinite into existence, the absolute difference in which life consists. As Climacus puts it, he wants to reintroduce the "diffi-culty" of life, "not to make it more difficult than it is" (*CUP*, 495), but to be true to the individual's experience of life:

Out of love for mankind, ... seeing that I had accomplished nothing and was unable to make anything easier than it had already been made, and moved by a genuine interest in those who make everything easy, I con-ceived it as my task to create difficulties everywhere. (*CUP*, 166)

Kierkegaard and Blake try to "create difficulties everywhere" by reintroducing this negativity which has been falsely expelled from life. And they try to reintroduce this negativity not in order to negate life but to affirm it, for as Climacus says, "existing individuals must be represented in their distress, when existence presents itself to them as a confusion, which is something different from sitting safely in the chimney corner and reciting *de omnibus dubitandum*" (*CUP*, 236). In keeping open the wound of the negative in existence they attempt to re-open something very like the Kantian wound between the finite and the infinite; and the principle of contradiction is their surgeon's knife. But they are re-opening the wound in order to heal it; they are re-introducing distinctions for the sake of *uniting* with life. The principle of contradiction which they introduce is the contra-diction of warring *perspectives*, and the "difficulty" of life becomes casting off one perspective absolutely and embracing the other absolutely. As Climacus puts it, "the difficulty consists . . . in holding fast the qualitative dialectic of the absolute paradox and bidding defiance to the illusions" (*CUP*, 498). We shall see whether this paradox of mutually exclusive perspectives, the paradox of either/or, can indeed escape the relativism of both-and logic and manage to capture life. Is this dualism of perspectives a real dualism, an either/or, or a merely apparent dualism, a both–and?

C. LIFE AND THE SYSTEM

Existence must be revoked in the eternal before the system can round itself out: there must be no existing remainder, not even such a little minikin as the existing Herr Professor who writes the system.

Johannes Climacus, *Concluding Unscientific Postscript*

Negation, transition, mediation, are three masked men of suspicious appearance, the secret agents which provoke all movements.

Vigilius Haufniensis, *The Concept of Dread*

By its abrogation of the principle of contradiction, both-and logic has dissolved the qualitative distinctions in every sphere of life: those between thought and reality (or logic and life), system and striving, Being and Becoming, good and evil, reason and passion, truth and error. These are the distinctions which Blake and Kierkegaard undertake to revitalize – to re-introduce, but again, with a preca-rious difference. Because Blake and Kierkegaard reconstitute these distinctions or contraries to impose decidability onto undecidability and flux, the contraries are ideally both determinate and indeterminate: determinately redeemed from their dissolution within Becoming, but nonetheless neither so stable that they annihilate the flux of life, nor so unstable that they dissolve back into it. The method for sustaining this difficult paradox consistently follows the pattern we have seen in Chapter 2 – that of casting off not one of the contraries, but the perspective which negates them – so that (as we have seen) they attempt to cast off neither reason nor passion, Being nor Becoming, good nor evil, etc., but the perspective which collapses them into each other. At the same time, they would claim that their sustaining of both contraries in this unity of life escapes being both-and logic. We need to look more closely at just how they can make this remarkable claim.

Like all the romantics, Blake and Kierkegaard use the word system to signify any abstract form of life. Life becomes systematized when it loses its energy and becomes passively instead of actively lived. For Blake and Kierkegaard, this means lived either purely retrospectively as memory and result (the despair of finitude) or purely prospectively as infinite possibility (the despair of infinitude). These are the spectral parodies of life, its empty forms, superficially resembling it but profoundly opposed to it. Separating the forms of life from its informing energy and elevating these empty forms to laws which dictate over life is the worst form of tyranny for Blake and Kierkegaard because it encourages passive obedience to laws abstracted from the changing realities of circumstances. Yet conversely, they equally abhor chaos or pure striving, the antithesis of system and the total lack of any laws or stabilities in life. One cannot overemphasize the extent to which there can be no true action or life for Blake and Kierkegaard without fulfillment – without a breakthrough from potentiality or striving to actuality, from nonexistence (in a spiritual sense) to existence. This is why all conditions of pure striving (i.e., towards an unattainable goal, as for instance in romantic irony) are in fact static for them, the cause of spiritual impotence and despair. "Invention depends Altogether upon Execution," declares Blake (Annotations to Reynolds; 637). They "must create a system," as Los says, must break out of the cycle of Becoming into the fulfillment of Being. "If we want a single word for the view of life as an Orc cycle," Frye remarks, "we may call it a vision of 'Becoming,' the totality of change within an immutable framework of time and space. ... The words 'Becoming' and 'Being' are not Blake's, but may be used to approximate the meaning of the

words he does use, which are Orc and Los."[5] Again, this is why
Blake's and Kierkegaard's entire effort is towards re-introducing the
Being which has been mediated within the idealist principle of
Becoming. But it is critical to remember that they are re-introducing
Being for the sake of true Becoming or Life. They seek to re-
introduce the *distinction between* Being and Becoming for the sake of
both. This is why Los says "I must Create a System, or be enslav'd
by another Mans. / I will not Reason & Compare, my business is to
Create" (J, I, 10:20–21; 153). Los rejects the immanential system of
reason or negation, within which one can only "reason and
compare" since all its contraries are merely comparative differences
of degree. But he does not reject the whole notion of system. His task
is to create his own, individual, dynamic system of life – to create.
For him, creation is not an endless striving towards something
already created, a "reasoning and comparing," but the making of
something *new*, the fulfillment of striving in a new stability, whole, or
system.

Here again it is difficult to see how Blake and Kierkegaard differ
from other romantics. They too shared this ideal of striving and
system, the dynamic system. Schlegel's succinct formulation of this
ideal would be endorsed not only by other romantics, but by Blake
and Kierkegaard as well. As Schlegel puts it, "It is equally destructive for the mind to have a system and to have none. It will simply
have to combine the two."[6] That this is a fairly precise formulation
of the romantic ideal is true enough. But again, the *way* in which
they are combined is the crucial differentiating factor for Blake and
Kierkegaard. For both would add a slight qualifier – a qualifier
which makes all the difference; both would reply that the only way
"to have a system and to have none" is to *separate* the two.

D. BEING AND BECOMING

The terms Being or system and Becoming or striving are confusing
because, like all such terms in Blake's and Kierkegaard's dialectic,
they have a true and a false form. The idealist systems of Becoming,
for example, are really static systems of pure Being, Kierkegaard
argues, because in them nothing really becomes or is created –
everything just *is*. And he argues that his own dialectic which seeks
to re-introduce absolute Being, on the other hand, is really a
dynamic dialectic of true Becoming. This confusion is again due to

both-and logic. Because this logic has abrogated the distinction between Being and Becoming, the terms become interchangeable, and the choice of one rather than the other a matter of emphasis. But this confusion can perhaps be clarified if we abandon the terms Being and Becoming for the moment and introduce instead the word movement. Movement or life is what Kierkegaard feels has fundamentally been lost by the idealist systems; movement is the transcendence which has escaped them. Whether we say it has escaped because they have collapsed Being into Becoming or vice-versa is less important (at this point at least) than the recognition that it has escaped because the two poles have been collapsed into each other. And what we *call* this movement which Kierkegaard tries to re-introduce is similarly for the moment at least less important than the recognition that according to Blake and Kierkegaard it can be re-introduced only by re-introducing their separation. This indeed is Kierkegaard's goal: to re-introduce movement in such a way that his dialectic cannot be called one of either Being or Becoming, cannot collapse into either extreme.

Kierkegaard's attack on the lack of movement in the idealist systems takes the form of an attack on the negative. As always, his focus is the false negative or negation, the relative difference. As Vigilius Haufniensis complains, the idealist systems turn life into pure thought or logic:

in logic, they use *the negative* as the motive power which brings movement into everything. And movement in logic they must have, any way they can get it, by fair means or foul. The negative helps them, and if the negative cannot, then quibbles and phrases can, just as the negative itself has become a play on words. In logic no movement can *come about*, for logic *is*, and everything logical simply is ... In logic every movement (if for an instant one would use this expression) is an immanent movement, which in a deeper sense is no movement, as one will easily convince oneself if one reflects that the very concept of movement is a transcendence which can find no place in logic. The negative then is the immanence of movement, it is the vanishing factor, the thing that is annulled (*aufgehoben*). If everything comes to pass in that way, then nothing comes to pass, and the negative becomes a phantom. (*CD*, 11–12)

"The negative becomes a phantom," the ubiquitous spectre once more. True movement is a *transcendence*, Climacus insists, "the immanent transition of speculative philosophy is ... a chimera, an illusion ... ; for the category of transition is itself a breach of immanence, a *leap"* (*CUP*, 262). Movement is "decisiveness," it is "repetition." Movement consists in making absolute distinctions, thereby bringing the eternal, the qualitative difference or absolute negative, into time:

Existence is in this respect something like walking. When everything is, and is at rest, it seems plausible enough to say that everything is equally important, provided I can acquire a view of it which is equally calm. But as soon as movement is introduced, and I am myself also in motion, my program in walking consists in constantly making distinctions. (*CUP*, 370)

As Climacus also puts it, "the goal of movement for an existing individual is to arrive at a decision, and to renew it" (*CUP*, 277). Until the individual has introduced or realized the qualitative difference in time, he is not really existing. And the only way to introduce this qualitative other is by "arriving at a decision" – which is to say, by casting off one alternative and embracing another. This must be repeated as long as the individual lives – it is the task of life.

But what are these distinctions, what is this decision which one must make and constantly renew? It is the decision "between existing finitely and existing infinitely," Climacus responds. I quote the following passage at length because it is one of the clearest and most central expressions of Kierkegaard's philosophy:

On paper the proposal to mediate looks plausible enough. First we posit the finite and then the infinite; thereupon we set it down on paper that there must be a mediation. And it is incontrovertible that here has been found a secure foothold outside of existence where an existing individual may mediate – on paper. The Archimedean point has been discovered; only it does not yet appear that the world has been moved. But when the scene is in existence and not on paper, the mediating individual being an existing individual (and thereby prevented from mediating), then any individual who becomes conscious of what it means to exist (that *he* exists) will instantly become an individual who distinguishes absolutely, not between the finite and the infinite, but between existing finitely and existing infinitely. For the finite and the infinite are put together in existence, in the existing individual; the existing individual therefore has no need to trouble himself to create existence, or to imitate existence in thought, but needs all the more to concentrate upon existing. Nowadays existence is even produced, on paper, with the assistance of mediation. In existence, where the individual finds himself, the task is simpler, namely, whether he will be so good as to exist. As an existing individual he is not called upon to create existence out of the finite and the infinite; but as one who is himself composed of finite and infinite it is his task to *become* one of the two existentially. It is impossible to *become* both at the same time, as one *is* both by *being* an existing individual. For this is precisely the difference between being and becoming. (*CUP*, 375–6)

The critical phrase here is Climacus's stipulation that the individual "distinguishes absolutely, not between the finite and the infinite, but between existing finitely and existing infinitely." For what he means is that the individual "distinguishes absolutely," not between the *contraries* of life ("the finite and the infinite") but between *two perspectives on the contraries* ("existing finitely and existing infinitely"). One perspective is that of Being: the individual *is* both the finite and the infinite as the "given" of his being. But this is not really life or existence; it is the state of *potential* with which all individuals are endowed as the condition of their creation. Existence is not just a given but also a *task*, Kierkegaard insists – the task of *becoming* oneself; for "actuality (the historical actuality) relates itself in a twofold way to the subject: partly as a gift which will not admit of being rejected, and partly as a task to be realized" (*CI*, 293).[7] And as Climacus says, "it is impossible to *become* both [contraries] at the same time, as one *is* both by *being* an existing individual." One cannot become all possibilities simultaneously in reality (however possible this may be in thought, as he readily acknowledges); one must become some one thing in particular. Otherwise, one remains abstract.

One must therefore realize or become one of the possibilities within oneself: either the finite or the infinite. One must choose one and cast off the other. But paradoxically, this does not mean that the absolute choice is indeed "between the finite and the infinite" (the contraries) after all, and that Climacus's added qualification of "existing finitely and existing infinitely" is redundant. It is true that the only way to cast off the passive *perspective* of mere potential or being is to choose one *contrary* and cast off the other. But the point is that casting off *either* contrary constitutes the leap, the qualitative decision which expels error and brings the eternal into time. One brings the eternal or infinite into time *even if one chooses to become the finite*. This is how *both* contraries are in a way paradoxically redeemed despite the fact that one is absolutely cast off. One does not have to cast off specifically the finite contrary to bring the eternal or infinite into time; casting off the infinite contrary equally brings the eternal into time. Failure to bring the eternal into time is traceable not to either contrary in particular but to the failure to choose between them – to negation, the failure to *act*.

This raises the new question of whether in fact the contraries are not therefore relativized despite the supposedly absolute casting-off of one and embrace of the other. For if it does not matter so much *which* contrary is cast off as *that* one of them is cast off, they would seem to lose their qualitative distinction. I shall return to this issue in chapter 4; it becomes particularly interesting when the contraries are good and evil, as we shall see.

For now, the point is to see how Kierkegaard (and Blake) hoped that this dialectic would work. In casting off one of the contraries to embrace fully the other, the existing individual brings the eternal into time, into unity with himself, by virtue of making the qualitative distinction or leap. This means that time and eternity are united in time – or in other words, that the finite and the infinite have united in the unity of life or existence. Yet this is a very different kind of unity from their unity in the realm of mere potential or being, and the contraries seem to be much greater and more vital here as well. The synthesis of the finite and the infinite in the realm of potential was passive, a given, a state of possibility. This new synthesis of the finite (the individual in time) and the infinite (the qualitative other which he has brought into time through leaping out of potentiality into actuality) is a dynamic synthesis, one which has required decision, action, and great energy. We can see how this new synthesis also appears to be a new kind of dialectic. It has reduced the systematic both-and dialectic of contraries to just one pole – existing finitely – of an entirely new dialectic; and the other pole – existing infinitely – indeed seems to be a transcendence beyond system, outside "both-and." The new dialectic of life is between these two mutually exclusive perspectives, which is why the Spectre of Urthona moans in *Jerusalem* that "the Almighty hath made me his Contrary / To be all evil, all reversed & for ever dead" (J, 1, 10:56–57; 154). It is a higher notion of "Contraries" as well, an apparently unsystematic dialectic in that these perspectives cannot be reconciled, cannot be held simultaneously in existence. One must choose one and cast off the other. As Climacus puts it:

Two ways, in general, are open for an existing individual. *Either* he can do his utmost to forget that he is an existing individual, by which he becomes a comic figure ... *Or* he can concentrate his entire energy upon the fact that he is an existing individual. (*CUP*, 109)

We can see, then, how one kind of synthesis seems to be a pale and spectral reflection of the other, how they superficially resemble each other yet may be profoundly different. One is pale because it exists only in the realm of potential; the other is darker, more vivid, because it is that potential realized. This true as opposed to false synthesis is what Constantine Constantius calls repetition – it is the repetition of what one already is (a synthesis of the finite and the infinite in the realm of potential) in a dynamic, higher, truer form (the same synthesis in the realm of actuality). This again is why repetition is a leap, and why it is so difficult – because, as Climacus says, "the most difficult leap, even in the physical realm, is when a man leaps into the air from a standing position and comes down again on the same spot." And this is why it is so difficult to convince men of the necessity for repetition – of why they should try to become a synthesis of the finite and the infinite when they always already are this synthesis. They should do so, Kierkegaard would reply, because there is a qualitative distinction between the two syntheses – the difference between potential and actual, non-existence and existence, the difference between spiritual death and life.

Life is the opposite of death; this is the sense in which through repetition the individual becomes the opposite of what he was before. "Man is born a Spectre or Satan & is altogether an Evil, & requires a New Selfhood continually & must continually be changed into his direct Contrary," says Blake (J, III, 52; 200). Yet he does not really become his "direct Contrary" in the sense of becoming, for example, reason instead of passion (or vice-versa); he is the contrary synthesis of reason and passion, the dynamic as opposed to the static synthesis. He is "the same and yet not the same," in Kierkegaard's favorite phrase, "the whole of life and existence begins afresh, not through an immanent continuity with the foregoing (which is a contradiction), but by a transcendent fact which separates the repetition from the first existence by such a cleft that it is only a figure of speech to say that the foregoing and the subsequent states are related to one another" (Vigilius Haufniensis, *CD*, 16 n.). This repetition through which one becomes one's direct contrary (alive instead of dead) is what Climacus means by existing infinitely, and mediation, through which one stays what one is (dead instead of alive) is what it means to exist finitely. Mediation is the opposite of repetition, its usurper:

In our days they have even gone so far as to want to have motion introduced into logic. There they have called repetition 'mediation.' Motion, however, is a concept which logic cannot endure. Hence mediation must be understood in relation to immanence. Thus understood, mediation cannot be employed at all in the sphere of freedom, where the next thing constantly emerges, not by virtue of immanence, but of transcendence ... To prevent ... this ambiguous agreement between logic and freedom, I thought that in the sphere of freedom one might use repetition. (Constantine Constantius, *R*, 19–20)

Mediation is the play of relative differences; repetition is the leap of absolute differences. Repetition is total, radical change, not gradual, evolutionary change – a rupture not a continuity. This is because the change is one of absolute value – from false to true, or from existing finitely to existing infinitely. This repetition happens "continually," as Blake says, but he does not mean that it continually approaches but never reaches its goal. For Blake, as Frye says, "immortality cannot mean the indefinite survival of a 'Becoming' life arrested at some point in its development ... What is immortal about the man is the total form of his creative acts," his Being.[8] Repetition is the opposite of such an indefinitely extended or arbitrarily arrested process – it is the repeated embrace of the infinite or the truth in all its fullness, a "Last Judgment." Each repetition is a complete, not partial, breakthrough to transcendence; the continuing struggle or task of life is that this breakthrough must be fought for over and over again. One can never break through once and for all in a "chimerical mediation", as Climacus says; and indeed, one should not want to do so, for that would mean the end of life. And "to be finished with life before life has finished with one, is precisely not to have finished the task" (*CUP*, 147).

Repetition rather than mediation is thus Los's task in *Milton* and *Jerusalem*. Blake's repeated use of the word task (as in "my task is not to reason and compare") and his emphasis on Los's great struggles and labor at his task indicate the extent to which he, like Kierkegaard, feels that life is not just a given but also a task, something the individual must labor to create. That Blake considered the greatest struggle in life to be the task of realizing one's potential or given is clear too from his repeated references to the parable of the talents in letters written to Thomas Butts from Felpham. "That I cannot live without doing my duty to lay up treasures in heaven is Certain & Determined & to this I have long made up my mind," he declares, exhorting, "if we ... tremble at the Tasks set before us ... if you who are organised by Divine Providence for Spiritual communion. Refuse & bury your Talent in the Earth ... Sorrow & Desperation pursues you thro life!" (January 10, 180[3]; 724–5). And in a second letter (also to Butts, and also from Felpham), he says "I know that you see certain merits in me which by Gods Grace shall be made fully apparent & perfect in Eternity. in the mean time I must not bury the Talents in the Earth but do my endeavour to live to the Glory of our Lord & Saviour" (April 25, 1803; 728). It is no coincidence that the parable of the talents should be so persistent a reference during his time at Felpham, by all accounts the worst crisis in his spiritual development and the time he came closest to succumbing to the spectre which tempted him to bury his talents.

Leaping out of the realm of potential and non-existence into the realm of actuality and life, then, is Los's great task, his struggle against the Spectre to attain his own repetition. In *Jerusalem* he attains this repetition in Christ (the form of the eternal in time for Kierkegaard as well); as Albion says to Christ, "I see thee in the likeness & similitude of Los my Friend" (J, IV, 96:22; 256). This divine likeness, similitude, or *repetition* of Los is true "Friendship & Brotherhood," as Christ tells Albion – the true unity of contraries which is life. I shall deal more fully with this Christ figure in Blake's and Kierkegaard's thought presently; for the moment we should look more closely at the nature of Los's task and why it is repetition rather than mediation.

Los's task is repetition because deliberate acts of decision and differentiation – acts of judgment – are a critical prelude to the desired state of unity. We have already seen this in terms of the narrative structure of *Milton*, where the expulsion of Hayley–Satan had to precede Blake–Los's embrace of Milton. But Blake also simply says that Los must differentiate in order to unite; as Los cries out,

Fellow Labourers! The Great Vintage & Harvest is now upon Earth
... Therefore you must bind the Sheaves not by Nations or Families
You shall bind them in Three Classes; according to their Classes
So shall you bind them. Separating What has been Mixed
... When under pretence to benevolence the Elect Subdud All
From the Foundation of the World.

(M, I, 25:17–32; 121–2)

Los and his fellow-laborers must separate what has been mixed under the "pretence of benevolence," the false unity; thus "the three

Classes of Men take their fix'd destinations," says Blake, adding "they are the Two Contraries & the Reasoning Negative" (M, 1, 5:13–14; 98). Los's critical task is in other words to divide life according to contraries and negations, to create the "qualitative dialectic" of life. In this poem, the contraries are Blake and Milton, as I have suggested, and the negation is Hayley; and this critical differentiation is what saves Blake–Los from his state of inertia and despair. The poem as a whole gives us the clearest case of repetition in the three prophecies – clearest perhaps because it was Blake's great moment of crisis and illumination when he discovered the idea.

Repetition is thus a complex act, for Blake's Los: it is an act of remembrance, in which Los recalls, in the character of the Spectre, the vestige of his lost immortal self, the "abstractest possibility of the self;" it is an act of judgment, in which Los differentiates between the true and the false, the spiritual and the corporeal man; and it is, finally, an act of creation, in which Los creates or realizes his actual self through the enormous exercise and labor of mastering the Spectre. In all these respects, repetition is the opposite of its spectral parody, the static repetition of Freudian neurosis. As Wayne Glausser has remarked, Los's remembering through the Spectre is the opposite of psychoanalytic remembering, because, while "reductive psychoanalysis succeeds only in making the patient aware of a secret debt to the past, over which he can have little or no control," the Blakean individual "is not enslaved to an inert set of primal conditions. The act of remembering as re-membering does not passively reproduce what has come before. It constitutes a creative judgment, happening now, in which the past and present mutually inform each other: it makes as much sense to say that the present determines the past as that the past determines the present."[9] In thus determining the past, Los once again masters temporality, escaping the static Orc cycle to which the purely corporeal or temporal man is enslaved. Freud indeed explains obsessional neurosis, the compulsion to repeat past events and patterns of behavior, as a death instinct, "an urge inherent in organic life to restore an earlier state of things ... the expression of the inertia inherent in organic life."[10] The task of true Kierkegaardian repetition, as George Stack points out, is to transform this negative, "erroneous" form of repetition into its positive, true form, "a form of willed repetition which is central to the becoming of the self in an ethical or religious existence."[11] "In effect," Stack argues, "existential repetition is a recovery of our original freedom, the very freedom which eludes the individual caught in a cycle of neurotic, compulsive repetition"[11] (259). To master the Spectre, to make the Spectre one's slave instead of one's master, is to transform necessity into freedom, in the characteristic movement of either/or.

By putting the static Orc–Urizen, infinite-finite, dialectic into the Spectre, and by re-locating the struggle of life in the conflict between the Spectre and Los, Blake performs essentially the same logical move to perspectivism which we have seen Kierkegaard perform. Blake–Los, the existing individual, now "distinguishes absolutely, not between the finite [Urizen] and the infinite [Orc], but between existing finitely [the Spectre] and existing infinitely [Los]." He distinguishes absolutely, not between the contraries of life, but between two mutually exclusive perspectives on the contraries.

Here again we are faced with the puzzling resemblance of either/ or to both-and, a resemblance which Blake and Kierkegaard would claim masks profound opposition. For the both-and logic of mediation looks moderate insofar as it mediates the contraries, whereas either/or looks extreme because of its claim to differentiate them absolutely and to cast off negation. Yet Blake and Kierkegaard would argue that both-and logic is in fact extreme or one-sided, because by refusing to differentiate life's contraries absolutely, it inadvertently collapses them into each other, so that they no longer can be said to exist. The existing individual who lives according to mediation finds himself one-sidedly abstracted from existence, in either the despair of finitude or the despair of infinitude. His one-sidedness comes from the fact that one contrary is always mediated within the other, and no matter which contrary has been mediated within which, his state of abstraction and despair remains the same. The either/or individual, by decisively differentiating life's contraries, ideally brings the absolute or qualitative *distinction* into existence – that is, he brings true "two-sidedness" into existence. The choice brings the absolute difference into being, the difference which is the only way of preserving *both* contraries. The paradox of this resemblance yet opposition could be summed up thus: the passive two-sidedness of both-and results paradoxically in one-sided abstraction from life. The active one-sidedness of either/or results paradoxically in two-sidedness (involvement in life). In other words, the paradox of either/or is that the only way not to be one-sided is to be one-sided, i.e., to choose, because by choosing one brings both contraries into being. One battles the one-sidedness of abstraction by the one-sidedness of commitment – false one-sidedness with true. As Climacus explains this difference between kinds of one-sidedness:

... the misfortune of the present age is not that it is one-sided, but that it is abstractly all-sided. A one-sided individual rejects, clearly and definitely, what he does not wish to include; but the abstractly all-sided individual imagines that he has everything through the one-sidedness of the intellectual ... the one-sidedness of the intellectual creates the illusion of having everything. (*CUP*, 312)

The one-sidedness of intellectual mediation lives under the delusion that by refusing to differentiate the contraries, by being all-inclusive, it has grasped the whole of life. But in fact it precisely thereby loses life. We should now turn to the sexual contraries of male and female and to the ethical contraries of good and evil to see the consequences of this abstract one-sidedness for the life of human community.

CHAPTER 4

Mastered irony as the ground of human community

Altho' our Human Power can sustain the severe contentions
Of Friendship, our Sexual cannot: but flies into the Ulro
Blake, *Milton*

By reason of the infiltration of the State and social groups and
the congregation and society, God can no longer get a hold on
the individual. ...So let us rather sin, sin out and out, seduce
maidens, murder men, commit highway robbery – after all,
that can be repented of, and such a criminal God can still get a
hold on.
Johannes Climacus, *Concluding Unscientific Postscript*

The tension between the extremes of reason and will, the two forms
of unmastered irony which can for Blake and Kierkegaard equally
negate life, in the realm of human community takes the form of an
extreme tension between "the public" and "the private." Indeed,
this tension between public and private is for many the central
difficulty or problem with Blake's and Kierkegaard's ideal of life, for
their radical individualism threatens to undermine any public realm
– political, social, or ethical – whatsoever, and may in fact underlie
the profoundly vexed question of their politics (that is, the question
of what politics their radical individualism entails). This individualism is why despite their resistance to the perspectivisms of radical
Nietzschean irony Blake and Kierkegaard belong finally more
within the tradition of Nietzschean philosopher-poets concerned
with the project of self-creation than within any tradition of sociopolitical philosophers of community or human "solidarity."[1] Nonetheless, both celebrate an ideal of human "brotherhood" which they
hope can in a sense reconcile the public and the private, an ideal
which tries to resist dissolving into the extreme individualism of the
radical ironist whose autonomous project is absolutely incommensurable with any communal, public ideal. Once again, it is this

109

resistance to radical perspectivism or irony which makes Blake and
Kierkegaard so particularly interesting and complex, for their resistance attempts to use perspectivism or irony against itself, to master
irony for the sake of life. Their ideal of brotherhood which attempts
to reconcile the public and the private is itself a perspective, a
private "point of view." Yet it is also a point of view that masters
individual points of view in what Blake and Kierkegaard hope can
be a communal ideal.

We can see this most clearly in two social realms of human life
which Blake and Kierkegaard directly address in their works: the
sexual and the ethical. Both want to celebrate sexuality, passion, or
eros as central to their ideal of life, as in some sense the ground of life.
Yet both lament the negation of this ground of vital passion and
energy by two extremes of reason and will, or two extremes of the
public and the private. Kierkegaard blames Hegelian reason for
negating sexual passion by destroying the separation or incommensurability of private and public, the individual and community,
through mediating them within the Hegelian *Aufhebung*. For him,
the aesthetic, erotic energy of the sexes is stultified by the "stuffy
reek" of the Hegelian marriage bed, where a man finds himself in
bed with not only his wife but his wife's family and beyond this the
Hegelian state itself. According to Kierkegaard, for Hegel the inner
man is the outer and vice versa (again, the abolition of contradiction); the private, erotic, individual man has hardened into a
purely conventional outer shell, a spectre of his living self.[2] This
disappearance of the private within the public is one way in which
for Kierkegaard the private-public tension essential to human life
can be destroyed. But it can equally be destroyed when the private
appropriates the public within itself. The Schlegelian romantic
ironist, seducer, or aesthete who lives for erotic passion equally
destroys the private-public tension by flouting conventions – particularly the convention of marriage – at will. Yet by living purely
for erotic passion or will he actually destroys what is for Kierkegaard
the true form of passion, which consists precisely in the tension
between private and public the Schlegelian aesthete ignores.

Blake similarly attacks both the social institutions or conventions
– especially the convention of marriage – that destroy erotic passion,
and (in his later poems) the opposite extreme of pure passion
without restraint. He attacks in other words the bourgeois public
morality that negates sexual energy (in *The Marriage of Heaven and*

Hell and in the *Songs of Experience*) but also the private "torments of love & jealousy" that so contort the relations between the sexes in *The Four Zoas*. Like Kierkegaard, he seeks in *Milton* and *Jerusalem* to find a middle way between these two extremes of a negating public reason on the one hand and an ironizing private will or eros on the other – a way that will redeem the sexual contraries and sexual energy for human life.

This public–private tension is also critical to the ethics of human community as Blake and Kierkegaard define it. For Kierkegaard, the energy of the ethical contraries of good and evil is dissolved by either extreme of private, abstract aestheticism or the public, bourgeois morality that makes of good and evil a "moral abstract," in Blake's phrase, removed from life. The aesthete negates the contraries of good and evil by living in a private realm removed from public morality; the Hegelian more hypocritically negates good and evil by pretending to live within them, making them into universal public moral laws requiring no difficult moral choices or decisions. Blake tries in his last prophecies to reject two similar extremes of public and private morality: the bourgeois system of moral virtue that fixes good and evil into a universal law abstracted from the realities of changing circumstances, and his own early individualistic lawlessness (again in *The Marriage* and in the *Songs of Experience*), where he rejected – by more or less simply inverting – the orthodox categories of good and evil.

Casting off or mastering these spectrous extremes which negate the fundamental sexual and ethical distinctions or contraries essential to the life of human community is therefore Blake's and Kierkegaard's attempted solution to the problem of human community as they define it: its tendency to collapse the essential public–private tension into purely private eros or lawlessness on the one hand, or to let it ossify into purely public convention on the other. And again, their strategy of casting off the Spectre of Negation attempts to take them beyond the usual ways of looking at or perceiving the contraries – to a new and vital perspective that redeems them. This new perspective, which both describe using masculine metaphors of brotherhood (Blake) and knights of faith (Kierkegaard), takes them in some sense then beyond the contraries themselves: beyond sexual difference and beyond good and evil to a new ideal of human community.

But the fact that Blake and Kierkegaard attempt to go beyond

sexual difference and beyond good and evil as they are usually
conceived is precisely where the precariousness and difficulty of
their ideal community lies. For it has been argued of both that their
final ideal of life is an exclusively masculine one that in its rejection
of the feminine repudiates or transcends sexuality altogether, in a
mystical repudiation of this life understood either as a kind of
gnosticism or as a state of "sexual indifference" that covertly destroys the feminine within a tyrannically patriarchal ideal.[3] And
their attempt to transcend good and evil in a higher dialectic of
truth and error is similarly open to the charge that it is singularly
anti-moral or amoral (and anti-religious). After all, Blake's Los
exclaims, "I care not whether a Man is Good or Evil; all that I care /
Is whether he is a Wise Man or a Fool" (J, IV, 91:54–55, 252). And
as Blake exclaims in *A Vision of the Last Judgment*, "The Combats of
Good & Evil is Eating of the Tree of Knowledge The Combats of
Truth & Error is Eating of the Tree of Life" (563). There is no
question which of these trees is for Blake the right one from which to
eat. If these charges are correct – that Blake and Kierkegaard
repudiate sexual and ethical difference for an ideal of truth and
error that is somehow beyond both sexual and ethical contraries,
then their claim to create a dialectic of human life is surely under-
mined if not destroyed. Any community that repudiates sexuality
and ethics seems far removed from any community – possible or
actual – in this life. Their ideal threatens to be either an otherworldly "Christian brotherhood" or the willful private world of the
radical ironist ceaselessly engaged in his own self-destruction and
self-creation. The challenge becomes then how to differentiate their
ideal from the private, ironic visions of the mystic and the aesthete,
both of which in their own way spectrally abstract from life.

A. COMMUNITY, BROTHERHOOD, AND THE SEXES

As we have seen, both *Fear and Trembling* and *Milton* repudiate
marriage for a restored embrace of "father and son;" and beginning
with Night VIIb) of *The Four Zoas* and continuing in both *Milton* and
Jerusalem, Blake seems to dramatize increasingly the embrace of
males rather than of males and females, in an ideal of community
which seems wholly masculine – a community of men who are at
once brothers, fathers, and sons. This transformed ideal of community, a turn from marriage to brotherhood which Leonard Deen has

recently characterized as a transformation from *eros* to *agape*,[4] results for both Blake and Kierkegaard from very similar attempts to formulate an ideal of human community which far from being sexually defined is rather in some sense beyond sexuality altogether.

This issue of Blake's attitude to sexuality has always been a vexed one in Blake studies. Does Blake celebrate sexuality continuously (albeit differently) throughout his myth? Or does he repudiate it altogether in his last three prophecies for a private, otherworldly ideal? Blake has also come under increasing attack lately for his supposed demotion of the feminine or female principle in his later myth and corresponding elevation of the masculine. Blake's emanations are either pale, watery shadows of their male counterparts, completely lacking in independent volition, runs the argument, or the opposite extreme of aggressive willfulness, the castrating Female Will summed up in the figure of Vala.[5] Despite Blake's theoretical commitment to what is often referred to (incorrectly) as an androgynous Human Form Divine and to a consistently liberationist philosophy, it is argued, he exercises a "residual male supremacism" because "in [his] metaphoric system, the masculine is both logically and physically prior to the feminine."[6] Blake classifies as female everything which he wants to expel from his eternity: passivity, narcissism, bodies (woven by the looms of the emanations in Beulah), nature, and generation or fecundity.

Even his critics, however, acknowledge Blake's commitment theoretically at least to an ideal state in which the sexes are equal because essentially non-existent. The very existence of differentiated sexes in Blake's myth after the *Songs of Experience* is clearly a product of the fall; in *Milton* and *Jerusalem* in particular Blake becomes increasingly careful to distinguish what he calls "the Human" from "the Sexual." "The Sexual is Threefold: the Human is Fourfold," he declares in *Milton* (M, I, 4:5; 97), and relegates the Threefold to the lower realm of Beulah. Milton's emanation, Ololon, casts off her sexual or "Feminine Portion" in order to unite with Milton, saying "Altho' our Human Power can sustain the severe contentions / Of Friendship, our Sexual cannot: but flies into the Ulro" (M, II, 41:32–33; 143). "Humanity knows not of Sex," declares Los in *Jerusalem*, "wherefore are Sexes in Beulah?" (M, II, 44:33; 193), a declaration echoed by *Jerusalem*: "O Vala! Humanity is far above / Sexual organization & the Visions of the Night of Beulah / Where Sexes wander in dreams of bliss among the Emanations" (M, IV,

79:73–75; 236). Further, as Los tells Enitharmon, "Sexes must vanish & cease / To be, when Albion rises from his dread repose" (J, IV, 92:13–14; 252). And because sexes must vanish and cease to be, "In Eternity they neither marry nor are given in marriage" (J, II, 30:15; 176) – marriage must cease to be also.

Nonetheless, Blake still maintains the metaphor of marriage – a metaphor hence necessarily sexual – in envisioning eternity as the reunion of Zoa with emanation, Albion with Jerusalem, and Jerusalem in turn with Christ. Blake's problem, as we have seen before, is that he wants a marriage animated by the energy of sexual contraries, yet at the same time he seems to want a marriage that transcends sexuality. Hence "the spousal imagery here," suggests Damrosch (referring to the marriage of Jerusalem with Christ) "symbolizes a union not between male and female but between mankind and the Savior"(230). Indeed, by "man" Blake clearly does mean mankind or humanity: "I see the Four-fold Man," says Los, adding "The Humanity in deadly sleep / And its fallen Emanation" (J, I, 15:6–7; 159). And similarly, "all are Men in Eternity. Rivers Mountains Cities Villages, / All are Human" (J, III, 71,15–16; 225).

It is for this reason – because he wants a marriage that is not a marriage exclusively of the sexes – that Blake arguably rejects or at least de-emphasizes marriage as the central metaphor for his ideal of community, choosing instead the metaphors of friendship and brotherhood. The lost eternity is pictured by the fallen Albion and the fallen Zoas not only as a happy marriage where, as the Spectre of Urthona tells Enitharmon, "thou & I in undivided Essence walkd about / Imbodied. thou my garden of delight & I the spirit in the garden" (FZ, VIIa, 84:5–6; 359), but more significantly as a state of brotherhood: "Rent from the Eternal Brotherhood we die & are no more," laments Albion (FZ, III, 41:9; 328). As Christ reminds him in *Jerusalem*, there is hope for redemption in the friendship and brotherhood of Christ: "I am not a God afar off, I am a brother and friend; / Within your bosoms I reside, and you reside in me" (J, I, 4:18–19; 146). But again, in emphasizing brotherhood, Blake seems to expel the female – and hence perhaps sexuality or eros – from his final ideal.[7] By *Jerusalem*, many have argued, the emanations exist only for the purpose of uniting the male Zoas, and are ultimately simply absorbed by the males in Blake's final definitive exclusion of real otherness. And Deen's proposal that Blake's later myth dramatizes a shift from *eros* to *agape* suggests that Blake virtually abandons narratives of erotic conflict between zoas and emanations for "redemption" plots concerning Los's "conversion" to an ideal of Christian brotherhood.[8]

These arguments are not in fact wrong, but rather only partially right. For they overlook once again the extent to which Blake's notion of community and the role of eros within that community is complicated by the perspectivism that centrally complicates all the ideas in his later myth. The struggle of the sexes is a continuing theme in all of Blake's poetry, early and late, from the *Songs of Experience* through *Jerusalem*. And with the exception of the *Songs of Innocence*, I would argue, sexuality is always central to Blake's myth in the sense that he remains consistently concerned with preserving its vitality, as he does about all spheres of life. What changes is not Blake's acceptance of sexuality, but rather his conception of how one preserves its essential energy and life. Blake's turn to perspectivism and brotherhood during his crisis at Felpham marks his solution not only to the problem of jealousy as that is generally defined (as all passivity or "hindrance") but to the problem of specifically *sexual* jealousy as well.

Clearly, jealousy is perhaps most vividly experienced in the realm of sexual relations, as the "torments of love & jealousy" in *The Four Zoas* make plain. Jealousy also dominates the early relations of the sexes in the *Songs of Experience*: the sick rose, whose "dark secret love" or repression destroys her like a worm from within; the "maiden Queen" who similarly "hid from him [her] hearts delight;" the Rose-tree who "turned away with jealousy" from her lover's attentions; the rose with her thorn and the sheep with his horn, both repelling love's advances. What is significant, however, is that Blake does not here see sexuality as inherently fallen or "jealous;" rather, he places the source of jealousy outside sexuality or nature in the public, Urizenic forces of convention and social institutions. In these poems, characters of both sexes find themselves bound by "Priests in black gowns, ... walking their rounds, / And binding with briars, [their] joys and desires;" by marriage contracts "chartering" their freedoms; and most ironically of all, by their own conventionality, a conventionality nonetheless imposed upon them from without. As the life-giving liberator from these restrictions, Orc, the power of energy which is "the only life and is from the Body" (MHH), will stamp these stony laws to dust (as he threatens Urizen in *America*):

nature, erotic energy, and the body will overthrow convention and reason as the source of all that jealously manacles their vitality.

That Blake celebrates what is often called "free love" in these poems, where his ideal is that "the Lilly white, shall in love delight / Nor a thorn nor a threat stain her beauty bright," and that he attacks external, "public" institutional hindrances (however "mind-forg'd") to that freedom, is generally recognized. What is recognized as well is his change – in the minor and major prophecies and the poems from the Pickering manuscript – to seeing sexuality as *inherently* fallen, that is, as a product of man's fall. Now, when the female separates from the male, "All Eternity shudder[s] at sight / Of the first female now separate" (BU, 18:9–10; 78), and when she in turn divides to bring forth a child, Eternity "shudders" again to see "Man begetting his own Likeness, / On his own divided image" (BU, 19:15–16; 79).

Here is where the argument begins over whether Blake henceforth rejects sexuality from his vision of ideal human life. For from now on, the sexes are portrayed not as warring against an external public tyrant, but as waging a private war between themselves, in what Milton would call (referring to the fallen Adam and Eve) "mutual accusation," "neither self-condemning, / And of thir vain contest appear[s] no end" (*Paradise Lost*, IX, 1187–1189). Urizen's emanation Ahania voices the plight of all the fallen emanations newly divided from their zoas:

> But now alone over rocks, mountains
> Cast out from thy lovely bosom:
> Cruel jealousy! selfish fear!
> Self-destroying: how can delight
> Renew in these chains of darkness
>   (BA, 5:39–43; 90)

How *can* delight renew in these chains of darkness or jealousy? Ahania's question is significant, for it indicates that indeed Blake does still hold that "delight" – meaning among other things sexual delight – can somehow be renewed. And it shows us that despite the apparent change in attitude towards sexuality, Blake is still asking the same question: how can sexuality be redeemed from its fallenness? The question has merely become more complicated because it would seem that Blake has recognized the answer is not so simple as casting off the public institutions that supposedly tyrannize over sexual freedom. It may be that those institutions cannot realistically be cast off; or it may be that even if they were cast off, one would not be free because the problem of sexual jealousy is a private one inherent in sexuality itself – hence its self-destroying nature.

This recasting of the conflict as a private one confined to the erotic sphere of life would seem to be why the struggle between the sexes increasingly dominates Blake's myth, resulting in the torments of love and jealousy in *The Four Zoas*, where, rather than the early strife of both sexes against external social convention, the private, sexual strife of zoas against emanations dominates the narrative. What is significant about his portrayal of this strife, however, is Blake's insistence that although sexuality may be fallen, neither sex is alone responsible for their mutual fall into sexual division. The cause of Albion's division is that "Luvah and Vala woke & flew up from the Human Heart / Into the Brain ... / And Luvah siez'd the Horses of Light" (FZ, I, 10:11–13; 305) – that is, the passions (here defined as male and female) usurped the place of reason (Urizen's Horses of Light). Further, Urizen willingly handed over the reins, as Ahania reproaches him: "Why didst thou listen to the voice of Luvah that dread morn / To give the immortal steeds of light to his deceitful hands" (FZ, III, 39:2–3; 326). As Blake portrays it, one might say that the problem of freeing sexuality has become a problem of preventing the private, erotic passions from imposing a new tyranny that is just as oppressive as the Urizenic tyranny of public institutions and reason.

These two features – the mutual implication not merely of Orc–Luvah and Urizen but of both sexes in the fall – are highly significant, for in this restructuring of the fall lies the key not only to Blake's treatment of reason and will (as we have already seen), but also to his treatment of male and female or of sexuality. To implicate Luvah or passion in the fall suggests that the origin of the fall cannot be in the public sphere of reason and social convention alone; private passion and sexuality in league with reason and convention are somehow responsible for the fall into sexual jealousy. Sexuality is no longer inherently innocent, as it was in the *Songs of Experience*, but now somehow implicated in its own fall. The further implication of the female Vala in this fall – her implication with Luvah, her male counterpart, who is in turn implicated with Urizen – would seem to be Blake's way of emphasizing the sexual symbolism which Orc–Luvah has always carried, but which Blake now deliberately wants to reinforce. Further, the mutual implication of male and female also reinforces his insistence that neither sex can be held responsible as the origin of this fall; it originates in both of them, together with Urizen.

If the sexes are thus mutually implicated in their fall, this would seem to make the strife between them less significant. For if they are equals – equally guilty and hence also equally innocent – their strife cannot be resolved, at least not in the terms on which it has been proposed, terms that are here specifically sexual ones. This is precisely the pattern of conflict or non-conflict we have seen before in the characters of Orc and Urizen once mutually implicated in the static Orc cycle, a cycle within which there can be no progression. Blake once again rejects the terms of the conflict as embodying somehow a false opposition, whether of reason and passion or of male and female; and their strife is consequently a far less significant one.

The question becomes, of course, less significant than what? And here again, I would propose, it is less significant than the real conflict, a conflict not between sexual contraries but between contraries and negations. This is why Vala's arguments with Jerusalem become more important than her (Vala's) arguments with Luvah; why (in *The Four Zoas* and *Jerusalem*) Los's arguments with the Spectre of Urthona become more important than his arguments with Enitharmon; why (in *Milton*) Milton's and Ololon's conflicts with their respective spectres become more important than their conflict with each other; and finally, (in *Jerusalem*) why Albion's conflict with his spectre becomes more important than his conflict with Jerusalem. It is also why Blake probably abandoned *The Four Zoas* – in which, with the exception of the remarkable Night VIIa, the conflict is cast almost exclusively in the static terms of Orc against Urizen and zoa against emanation – for *Milton* and *Jerusalem*.

To recast the conflict as being with the spectre signifies that whatever is causing sexual strife is something outside of or beyond the sexes themselves. Yet this something is no longer simply public institutions or conventions, nor is it reason, as in Blake's early myth; the tyrant here is also sexuality itself, which by usurping reason's "horses of light" and trying to rule over life has reduced life to endless struggles for sexual domination. Both sexes are equally victims of this tyranny of unrestrained eros, a world dominated by struggles for power and conquest, which is why Blake treats the sexes (I shall argue) equally. Male does not tyrannize over female (or vice versa); unrestrained sexuality tyrannizes over both.

Strife with this spectre of rational and erotic extremes thus becomes the necessary prelude not only to the reunion of reason with passion, as we have seen, but to that of zoa with emanation – to the reunion of the sexes. The spectre indeed confesses to Los his responsibility for sexual division in Night vııa of *The Four Zoas*, when, "Being a medium between him & Enitharmon," he weeps before Los, saying "I am the cause / That this dire state commences I began the dreadful state / Of Separation" (FZ, vıı, 87:26, 31–33; 369). And seeing the strife of Los with Enitharmon in *Jerusalem*, "a sullen smile broke from the Spectre in mockery and scorn / Knowing himself the author of their divisions & shrinkings" (J, ıv, 88:34–35; 247). In *Milton*, Milton confesses "I am that Satan! He is my Spectre!" before embarking on his quest to redeem his emanation – a confession that in essence locates the cause of Milton's error not so much in Milton himself as in his spectral self. Milton's error is also defined in part as an explicitly sexual one: he is sent to redeem a "six-fold emanation" who is reputedly his three wives and three daughters; he is sent to the specifically female realm of Beulah to undertake this mission; and both he and his emanation are required to discard their "sexual portions" in order to embrace. All of this suggests that Blake is indeed most concerned here with correcting not only Milton's erroneous ideas of reason, but also and concomitantly his ideas of sexuality. By correcting his spectrous reason, Blake's Milton not only modifies his hierarchy of reason and will, but modifies his hierarchy of male over female. He casts off his superior masculinity as Ololon casts off her "sexual body," and the result is their union or marriage at the end of the poem.

In contrast to Milton, Blake always sees the sexes as equal, not hierarchical, and in this respect he consistently avoids Milton's error throughout his myth. Blake does not blame women for the fall, nor identify women alone with sexuality; nor does he blame sexuality but "false sexuality" for the fall. It is admittedly somewhat misleading to say that because both Luvah and Vala are implicated in the fall both sexes must therefore be equal; for, after all, the Divine Human is ideally of neither sex, so that theoretically Luvah and Vala are not even differentiated until "they" (meaning really "s/he") fall. But my point is that Blake seems to go out of his way to equallize the sexes throughout his myth, both in their unfallen state (where neither theoretically exists as such) and in their fallen state (in which they are mutually implicated). To the argument that

Blake's emanations are either passively dependent or aggressively domineering one could reply, I think, that so are the zoas. The nature of the fall is at once an act of willfulness or self-assertion and an "act" of passivity, in the same paradoxical way that Milton's Satan is curiously impotent in his titanic self-assertion. Urizen (in *The Book of Urizen*) and Albion (in the later myth) fall by withdrawing; again, the essentially fallen act for Blake is passivity, the hindering of either oneself or of others. When it takes the form of self-hindrance, this act is obviously passive; when it takes the form of hindering others, it looks active but in essence is not. "He drave the Male Spirits all away from Ahania," says Blake of the fallen Urizen; of the equally fallen Ahania, "And she drave all the Females from him away" (FZ, II, 30:51–52; 320). Hindrance and jealousy are fundamentally passive–aggressive for Blake – the trait traditionally associated with females but which Blake clearly also associates with the male zoas. It is true that Blake speaks of the "feminine indolent bliss" against the "active masculine virtue;" but it is also true that, as the context of the passage makes clear, both of these traits in their differentiation are fallen ones. Here again, neither sex as such but the figure of the Spectre – a figure clearly fallen and if anything masculine rather than feminine – best exemplifies the combination of power yet impotence, willful self-assertion yet abject, often whimpering self-denial, and aggressive independence which Blake regards as the quintessentially fallen self.

It is also argued that Blake adopts the traditional hierarchical division of the male as (higher) culture or intellect, and the female as (lower) nature or will, the latter qualities condensed in the figure of Vala, so newly potent and threatening in *Jerusalem*.[9] Vala, as the "Female Will," would seem to be a particularly sinister version of Milton's Eve, whose "willful" independence from Adam seems to bring about his fall. But one has to question whether this supposed locus of Blake's anti-feminism is really so potently charged. Despite the fact that "Vala" is Blake's subtitle in *The Four Zoas*, Vala plays no larger part than do any of the other emanations. Granted, it is she who, with her male counterpart Luvah, is partly responsible for Albion's fall. But if Blake wanted to make the female will responsible for the fall, why did he so carefully implicate a masculine counterpart? Why not stick to Milton's (and the Bible's) version of the fall, which makes the origin of man's fall so unambiguously woman? Further, why implicate not one but two masculine figures in the fall

– not only Luvah, but Urizen? Not only does Blake refuse to say that the female will brought about the fall, he refuses to say either that will is exclusively female, or that will alone brought about the fall. Vala does play a more significant role in *Jerusalem*, but so does Jerusalem, her unfallen feminine counterpart. And while the sexual strife between Luvah and Vala provides part of the narrative conflict, by far the more significant conflict (and proportion of the conflict) occurs between Vala and Jerusalem – in other words, between two females. This again suggests that Blake does not want to locate the origin of the fall in a woman who brings about the fall of mankind, but rather in the false form of woman – and in the false form of man, the spectre. Again, he locates it in the false forms of sexuality itself, in an eroticism which attempts to take over the whole of life as Luvah and Vala attempt to take over Urizen (and thereby Albion). Albion's spectre is clearly the masculine equivalent of Vala; and this together with Los's Spectre of Urthona demonstrates that there is a destructively "Male Will" as well. It is well to remember here too that Luvah is after all Orc – a decidedly masculine figure of energy, passion, or will. Blake always, in other words, associates the traditionally feminine quality of passion or will with a male character; even when he turns from Orc to the more moderately passionate figure of Los, it is clear that passion remains central – and centrally embodied in this masculine figure. (My argument about Blake's – and Los's – return to an ideal of reason or intellect does not contradict Los's fundamental identification with passion, as I hope is or will become clear.) One could even say that insofar as passion or will is assumed to be traditionally feminine, Blake always retains a feminine ideal, for his ideal is consistently passion or life.

Vala is not only the female will, but also nature; and it is usually acknowledged even by those attempting to defend Blake from charges of sexism that indeed he does associate the female most fundamentally with nature. Vala embodies our fallen sense of nature as an alien force, a teasing yet intractable otherness that will not yield to our attempts to bring it under control in a fruitful marriage of man and nature, spirit and matter. In this role, Vala simply sums up what all the female emanations represent: the separateness of nature from the alienated man. The emanations, unlike Vala, however, are also engaged in the potentially redemptive activity of weaving bodies for the fallen males in the generative – but potentially regenerative – realm of Beulah.

It is true that Blake does identify femininity with nature, and that in doing so he adheres to the patriarchal tradition of associating women with nature and with generation simply because they are child-bearers as men are not. But does he not also come to associate nature and the cycle of generation with masculinity, again in the symbolism of the Orc cycle? It is Orc–Luvah, Vala's counterpart, who represents the crucified body on the Tree of Mystery, a crucifixion of the physical body which, as in traditional Christianity, redeems what Blake calls the spiritual body from death. Orc–Luvah, as the consolidation of error, is the natural as opposed to the spiritual man, whose preoccupation with the body, with nature, and with sexuality embodies a kind of death-wish of the spirit. Yet this death-wish must reveal itself as such in order to be cast off; it must take on the shape of the serpent Orc, which is simply the shape of the natural or vegetable or corporeal human body that will die as opposed to the spiritual body that for Blake will not.

As the incarnation and crucifixion of the spiritual body in the physical, Orc–Luvah is not only Blake's Satan but also his Christ; as Blake tells us repeatedly, Christ dons Luvah's "robes of blood," meaning the human body, in order to redeem the spirit. By voluntarily taking on this body of death, he paradoxically casts it off, so that incarnation becomes at once the fall of the spirit and its potential redemption. This Christ-like activity is to some extent imitated by Blake's emanations, who weave bodies for the fallen males, consolidating their fall in an incarnation that makes possible their redemption. Further, the emanations also imitate Christ insofar as they symbolize not only the fall into alienation from nature, but also the fall into alienation from the spiritual ideal. Like Christ, they represent the visionary spiritual ideal which each male zoa pursues, Blake's vision of the perfection of life. The emanations thus represent not merely nature but also the traditionally male opposite of culture or intellect; Jerusalem is, after all, not only a woman but also a *city*. If "Man cannot be redeemd but by Christ alone," as Blake says, he also declares that "Man cannot unite with Man but by their Emanations" (J, IV, 88:10; 246). The emanations perform almost identical functions to those of Blake's Christ in some respects, a figure who, as many have suggested, is, like Los, a combination of male and female in a unity transcending both. Christ thus stands beyond sexuality, for Blake, and the fact that Blake is forced to use "gendered language" for "an essentially genderless ideal," as Diana

Hume George has pointed out,[10] should not blind us to the fact that he does virtually everything possible to dramatize the equality of the sexes throughout his myth. To ignore the full weight of his symbolism because his Christ is a "he" is to trivialize the content of his myth. It ignores Blake's consistent refusal to locate the fall of man in the female alone; and his refusal to locate it in will, traditionally female, divorced from reason, traditionally male – a division that Blake also deliberately rejects, by locating will and reason, nature and culture, not in either sex alone but in both.

As in all three of the late prophecies, then, Blake casts off the spectre of negation to redeem the contraries, in this case the sexual contraries. Our evidence for this is his deliberately equal treatment of the sexes; his careful implication of both sexes in the fall; his clear statements that the spectre is the cause of sexual strife; and finally, his overlaying of what Deen calls the "eros plot" of sexual strife with a higher plot of conversion or redemption in which zoas and emanations battle not each other but their spectres as the prelude to their unity. All of these points are not really separable: it is because the sexes are equal that their strife (the eros plot) cannot progress, so that Blake is forced to look for some higher solution to their conflict – the conversion plot. And it is because they are equal that he will not cast either of them off as the cause of the fall, but looks instead for a third thing which, by being cast off, will allow him to redeem them.[11]

We still do not really know, however, just what it means to say that sexuality is redeemed by casting off the spectre and subsequently embracing friendship and brotherhood. What does it mean for sexuality to cast off the spectre? And who is to say that sexuality itself is not simply cast off *for* friendship and brotherhood, a state of sexual indifference in which sexuality is not in fact redeemed at all? Alicia Ostriker has persuasively argued that this is so, remarking that not only does Blake's attitude towards the sexes change significantly over the course of his career, it changes in ways consistent with "other ideological and doctrinal transformations" in his myth: "from an essentially sociopolitical to an essentially mythic base;" from a pastoral poet's love of nature to an apparently total rejection of it as a merely "vegetable glass" of eternity; and "from an immanent to a transcendent God."[12] The early believer in what Hirsch has called "revolutionary naturalism" and in a fully immanent God thus celebrates sexuality and sexual equality, according to

Ostriker, whereas the later anti-naturalistic Blake rejects sexuality as symptomatic of an inherently fallen nature, reverting as well to a Miltonic hierarchy of the sexes. This reiterates the widely-held view of Blake's myth as having moved from an overtly political to a more mythic or psychological and finally to a radically Christian vision – a view that, as this study should make clear, I in turn would largely endorse. But Blake's final vision does not I think reject sexuality but master it, through the perspectivism that so profoundly radicalizes the "Christianity" of his Jerusalem.

To insist on the importance of this perspectivism is nothing new; in fact, it is the perspectivism of Blake's eternity which often arouses the greatest skepticism among his critics. If Blake's eternity is not so much a place as a state of mind, a perspective on life, it is, accordingly, a perspective which makes them "the same as," yet radically different from, marriage and sexuality as we know them. In Blake's most oft-quoted description of this conversion through perspective, in eternity "Embraces are Comminglings: from the Head even to the Feet; / And not a pompous High Priest entering by a Secret Place" (J, III, 69:44–45; 223). Yet as Damrosch questions, voicing indeed a representative complaint, "Who can say what that mysterious 'commingling' would be in which Blakean man escapes what Frosch calls the 'tyranny' of genital sexuality? For non-Blakeans, nongenital sexuality is nonhuman sexuality" (238). Further, he remarks, "the regenerated body is so different from the fallen one that they might as well be altogether distinct" (238). In other words, runs the charge, Blake's perspectivism means that far from embracing he abandons all that we call reality in the material sense.

But far from abandoning sexuality – and hence the reality of the physical body – Blake is simply insisting that sexuality is *part* of life yet not the *whole*. As he elsewhere describes fallen perception, it is "in ignorance to view a small portion & think that All / And call it Demonstration blind to all the simple rules of life" (FZ, VIIa, 92:32–33; 364). This is, finally, the essence of Blake's perspectivism: in terms of sexuality, it is to see sexuality as something lower than the highest ideal of life. In more general terms, this perspectivism simply means that one should not make the relative (the "small portion") into the absolute (the "All") and vice-versa. Life is something beyond mere sexuality; it is something beyond the strife of reason and passion and male and female. To make the erotic the whole of life destroys life; what kills life is to reduce it to physical eros, for by doing so one closes oneself up from the infinite "till [one] sees all things thro' narrow chinks of [one's] cavern" (MHH, 14; 39).

Blake thus hopes his higher ideal of friendship and brotherhood – an ideal potentially accessible to all humans, male and female – will liberate sexuality from its chains of jealousy. The erotic man is the slave of sexuality; because he sees it as the whole of life he makes it into his master. "I am drunk with unsatiated love," is his cry, "I must rush again to War: for the Virgin has frownd & refusd ... There is no time for any thing but the torments of love & desire" (J, III, 68:62–68; 222). Because he cannot see beyond erotic love, he is completely trapped within it; lacking the objectivity of intellect, he is lost in a welter of chaotic emotions which given continuing rule will destroy his spirit. Far from enjoying his submersion in eros he is tormented by it because he is *unfree*. And what will free him, claims Blake – free him not from eros but to enjoy it fully – will be to master eros instead of being its slave. Blake thus hopes to convert sexuality from necessity to freedom – and this conversion from necessity to freedom and from death to life is the essence of his either/or. By casting off sexuality as the whole of life, one can embrace it as a part of life; it is "excluded as the absolute, but relatively it is still left," in Judge William's phrase (E/O, II, 181–2). Further, one has excluded it absolutely, in one sense, because one has cast it off *as* the absolute, and this qualitative distinction not between things but between the absolute and the relative is paramount to Blake and Kierkegaard. Paradoxically, casting it off absolutely allows one to embrace it absolutely, despite the fact that it is now a merely relative value. For by correctly realizing that it is part and not the whole of life, one can now embrace it freely – which is to say, absolutely – and for the very first time. After all, Blake and Kierkegaard would ask, in what sense does one embrace something absolutely when that embrace is dictated by necessity not freedom?

This means that it is all rather absurd to complain that, given Blake's description of sexuality and the body in Eternity, they will be so totally unlike sexuality and the body as we know them that they cannot properly be labelled such at all. For Blake is describing not sexuality *per se*, but different perspectives on sexuality. One is the passive perspective of entrapment, in which sexuality is experienced either as negated by reason and public convention (one extreme) or as endless torments of love and jealousy (the other extreme). The other is the active perspective of freedom, in which sexuality is experienced as "comminglings from head to foot" – that is, as "unhindered" not by being freed of the body and sexuality altogether, but by being freed of the negating perspective *on* these things. The mistake is to reify or take too literally Blake's geographical realms of Ulro, Generation, Beulah, and Eternity, instead of remembering that they are merely Blake's attempt to render metaphorically four different perspectives on the same reality. It is true that a change of perspective involves a change in value which is absolute for Blake, and which therefore in some sense changes the reality seen through that perspective absolutely. But Blake is nonetheless representing the same reality, the reality of human existence, lived passively on the one hand and actively on the other. Whether one lives one's life actively or passively, in each case one is still eating, sleeping, walking, and making love, not casting off any one of these activities by casting off one of the perspectives on them. All the activities of human life are retained – the inclusiveness of Blake's dialectic; but they are lived either actively or passively (which is to say, not at all) – its exclusiveness. Again, the movement of the dialectic is not from sexuality to non-sexuality or from x to y, but from a passive to an active perspective *on* x and y: from necessity to freedom, and from death to life.

The Blakean individual then (male or female), does not necessarily live divorced from marriage and other social institutions, but on the contrary lives within them in a way that preserves the incommensurability or tension between private eros and public institutions (in the sexual sphere, marriage). Indeed, preserving the incommensurability between private and public constitutes the true passion or eros of life. Mastering eros means wanting to live in such a way that this tension is not resolved, either by the private wholly usurping the public (where the relations between male and female are ones of conquest and domination), or by the public subsuming the private (where the relations between the sexes are dictated by convention). To allow one's sexuality to be mastered either by private passion without restraint or by public laws and institutions which threaten too much restraint is to submit to a view of sexuality, indeed of life, which is dictated by these forms of necessity instead of making this necessity the ground of human freedom.

Blake's *Jerusalem* takes us up to the apocalyptic moment when the transformation of human community might be said to occur; but his vision does not tell us how we are to live beyond that moment.

Kierkegaard is much more interested in describing how real communities and institutions – particularly the institution of marriage – are to sustain this vision of reformed community, and in this sense he is able to extend and make more explicit what may be implicit in Blake's visionary city. Like Blake, Kierkegaard conceives of human life in terms of simultaneously existing spheres or perspectives, in his case, the familiar spheres of erotic love (the aesthetic), marriage and family love (the ethical), and religious love (the religious).[13] All of these spheres involve not merely individuals but individuals within human communities of different kinds. And as always, Kierkegaard's definition of these spheres and the dynamic of their interaction is more explicit than Blake's in ways which may usefully explicate Blake's myth, demonstrating clearly how the paradox of exclusion yet embrace so characteristic of either/or functions within the realm of human community. Kierkegaard's erotic man, his aesthete, for example, is urged by his ethical man, Judge William, not to renounce his aestheticism for marriage but to discover "the *aesthetic* validity of marriage" (my emphasis) – not to "exclude" eros but to master it in a higher ideal of life and human community.

Kierkegaard, like Blake, sees the erotic man as the slave of eros, enslaved not only by sexual passion but by time, as indeed are all whose master is the body and hence death. He is obsessed by the immediacy and intensity of "first love," and in his attempt to recapture that intensity involves himself in an endless chain of amorous liaisons, each one ironically a first love because each one a new love. He therefore in a sense has no memory; love has no continuity in time for him. What marriage bestows, according to Judge William, is precisely continuity in time, a continuity which also allows him to truly possess his love as well. The aesthete, by contrast, is "bent upon conquest but is able to possess nothing," for unlike the ethical man he does not understand that "possession ... is a steady acquisition" (*E/O*, II, 134). The married man, claims the Judge, "has not fought with lions and ogres, but with the most dangerous enemy: with time. ... The married man ... solves the great riddle of living in eternity and yet hearing the hall clock strike" (*E/O*, II, 141). The ethical man masters time without abrogating it, and he is thus the opposite of the aesthete, who is mastered by time, and the mystic, who attempts to transcend time altogether. The mystic regards time as at best a period of probation when God "tests" men; but, the Judge argues, the temporal ... does not exist for God's sake, in order that in it, speaking mystically, He may test and try the loved one, but it exists for man's sake and is the greatest of all the gifts of grace. For man's eternal dignity consists in the fact that he can have a history, the divine element in him consists in the fact that he himself, if he will, can impart to this history continuity, for this it acquires only when it is not the sum of all that has happened to me or befallen me but is my own work in such a way that even what has befallen me is by me transformed and translated from necessity to freedom. (*E/O*, II, 254–255)

That time should be "the greatest of all the gifts of grace" should call to mind Blake's remark that "Time is the Mercy of Eternity" (MHH). Time – meaning implicitly death – is the fundamental necessity of human existence which the Kierkegaardian and Blakean individual labors to transform into freedom; again, as Frye reminds us, although "Orc brings life into time, the shaper of Orc [Los] brings life in time into eternity" (251).

As the slave of time, then, the aesthetic or erotic man is in chains. And the way to cast off these chains is not to seek to transcend time but to master it – to master the Spectre who as the Chain of Jealousy or necessity is also, as Frye has called him, "the time-bound ego" (112). Only marriage, by preserving love in time, thus masters both time and eros, according to Judge William. At his urging, the aesthete should cast off the erotic for the ethical precisely to preserve the erotic, in the characteristically paradoxical movement of either/ or: "nothing is destroyed, all of the aesthetical remains in a man, only it is reduced to a ministering role" (*E/O*, II, 233).

Kierkegaard, like Blake, thus dethrones private, erotic love from its status as the absolute or whole of life to a merely relative part of life; he makes sexual love a part embraced nonetheless fully or absolutely only by virtue of that very dethronement. For as we have seen before, by its dethronement it can be fully – which is to say, absolutely – embraced as it could not be when it was master. By casting off purely erotic love for the ethical, and by informing the ethical with the erotic, the truly erotic individual (male or female) increases the oppositional tension between the two; she sharpens the difference, we might say, between private, erotic passion and the public institution of married love. This is why the renunciation or choice ideally revitalizes both the private and the public; the choice actualizes the difference between them and thus the true oppositional tension that is life. Nonetheless, to say that the purely erotic

love can be mastered by choosing marriage does not explain why
marriage does not remain merely marriage instead of a new understanding of marriage informed by erotic love. How is the aesthete's
private passion preserved by the public institution of marriage? Why
is the private tyranny of sexuality not simply replaced by a new,
more public tyranny?

First of all, Kierkegaard would claim again, because the choice
actualizes most of all the difference between public and private, thus
revitalizing the tension between them. The essence of the erotic is its
hiddenness; if there is no public realm behind or beneath which the
erotic is hidden, the hiddenness vital to its very essence will die of
exposure. But more than this, Kierkegaard would reply, marriage
will not be a new tyranny because it too must like the aesthetic be
mastered; it must also be understood in light of a more comprehensive ideal of life which holds in tension both extremes of wholly
private (aesthetic) and wholly public (ethical) experience. This is
where the higher opposition or collision between the ethical and the
religious occurs; and this is where we see the greatest challenge not
only to Kierkegaard's ideal oppositional tension of private and
public, but to his ideal of a human community that includes sexuality. For while women and erotic love remain explicitly central to his
conversion of the aesthetic into the ethical sphere of life, in the
higher conversion of the ethical into the religious sphere their role
would seem to come into question, as indeed does any notion of
specifically human community at all. As we shall see, Abraham
renounces the ethical to sacrifice his son Isaac at the command of
God. And even though he receives Isaac back again – a reinstatement of the ethical bond of father and son he had earlier
renounced – it is not clear how such a reinstatement has any place
for women. It is surely significant that Kierkegaard should choose
for his model of this highest sphere or perspective on life not a
marriage of the sexes (relegated to a lower realm much as Blake
relegates marriage to Beulah), but an embrace of father and son in
what appears to be, like Blake's, an exclusively masculine ideal.
Because Abraham receives only Isaac back, it is unclear how marriage or the relation of the sexes can be redeemed or recovered
through their embrace. More than this, it is unclear how Abraham's
act is in any way ethical or publicly justifiable, for ethically
speaking it is an act of attempted murder. Abraham seems to
renounce public institutions and laws (the ethical) for a private,

willful act of murder based on a mystical higher law, a private passion (the passion of faith) just as dangerous – in fact, more dangerous – than the aesthete's private passion. Kierkegaard's greatest challenge is therefore to distinguish Abraham's passionate act of faith from the aesthete's willful acts of seduction, for both appear to be equally acts of private, willful, destructive – even murderous – passion. How can Abraham's attempted murder of Isaac in any way be a public act of brotherhood, one that could be understood to redeem both sexuality and human ethical community?

What Abraham renounces and recovers in Isaac is in symbolic terms the ethical and the finite; in other words, it is also marriage (the category of the ethical) and woman. Isaac in a certain sense is (or is also) woman; the fact that Abraham's sacrifice is widely held to symbolize Kierkegaard's sacrifice or renunciation of marriage and Regina strongly argues for this fundamental identification as well. Kierkegaard's Judge William also explicitly identifies woman with the finite, earnestly explaining to the aesthete that

in general woman has an innate talent, a primitive gift and an absolute virtuosity for explaining finiteness. When man was created he stood there as master and lord of all nature . . . but he did not comprehend what he was to do with it all. . . . Then was woman created. She was in no embarassment, she knew at once how to handle this affair. . . . Woman explains finiteness, man is in chase of infinitude. So it should be, and each has one's own pain; for woman bears children with pain, but man conceives ideas with pain. . . . But because woman thus explains finiteness she is man's deepest life, but a life which should always be concealed and hidden as the root of life always is. (*E/O*, II, 315–316)

As the finite, woman for the Judge thus would seem to represent temptation – the temptation to embrace the finite, the temporal, and the erotic as all of life. (Unlike Blake, Kierkegaard's Judge does identify one sex – woman – with sexuality itself.) By embracing woman one embraces this world; yet here again, it is only when one embraces her (and her symbolic associations of finiteness, nature, temporality, and eros) from a certain perspective, as the whole of life – that one thereby loses life. Woman must be not be seen as the whole of life, as something to be pursued and conquered (as for instance the aesthete sees her); yet by this change of perception, the Judge claims, one paradoxically receives her back again. She is merely dethroned, not expelled; the knight of faith is not celibate any more than he is a mystic. In fact to avoid woman's embrace is to live abstractly and hence not at all.

In this respect, the Abraham–Isaac parable retells the story of the renunciation and recovery of sexuality (here called the finite) we have already seen in the collision of the aesthetic and the ethical. It indirectly reiterates the point that in theory Kierkegaard's ideal community need not exclude anyone, not even women; in other words, it need not exclude sexuality. This is so in part because, as we have seen, woman or the female principle of life (temporality, etc.) is not expelled but transformed, by the conversion of perspective typical of either/or. Indeed, women can themselves become members of this community, "knights of faith," through the movement of "resignation" by which all knights of faith resign themselves to loss of the finite:

She will introduce herself into that order of knighthood into which one is not received by balloting, but of which everyone is a member who has the courage to introduce himself, that order of knighthood which proves its immortality by the fact that it makes no distinction between man and woman. (*FT*, 55)

In the highest sphere of life, then, for Kierkegaard as for Blake, in a certain sense "sexes must vanish and cease to be:" sexual domination with its corollary conflicts and reconciliations belongs only to the lower spheres of life, spheres or perspectives that mistakenly exalt the relative into the absolute, making a part of life the whole. In his treatment of women, Kierkegaard thus in a sense tries to have it both ways: he continues to associate women metaphorically with their traditional symbolic values of finitude, temporality, and eros (a traditional association I have argued Blake much more successfully resists), yet insists that the highest sphere of life exposes and transcends such differentiations as merely metaphorical or illusory ones. It has been suggested that Kierkegaard "resists the attempts to establish sexual equality in the external, secular sense;" yet "his conception is mainly based on Christianity's perception of the two sexes as essentially equal without thereby denying that there are sexual differences, which pose particular tasks in life for each of the sexes."[14] But we should ask whether such an explanation is true to Kierkegaard's ideal of life. For to say that Kierkegaard resists sexual equality in the external, secular sense suggests that equality is possible only in some purely private or otherworldly realm, which surely is not Kierkegaard's ideal. The fact that it is Judge William, not Kierkegaard, who prescribes these "particular tasks in life for each of the sexes" should give us some pause; for despite his superiority to the aesthete or erotic man, his perspective is clearly satirized by Kierkegaard as a limited one.

Kierkegaard's perspectivism, like Blake's, ideally allows him to cast off not sexuality but a certain perspective on sexuality, the perspective which sees sexuality in terms of conquest and power, as the whole of life, either to be embraced (by the aesthete) or to be repressed (by the ethical individual). In this respect, the relation between the sexes remains a vital part of his and Blake's final vision of human community; but it is, critically, only a part and not the whole. This results logically from their analysis of tyranny (or jealousy) – for tyranny is always for them the tyranny of the relative perspective claiming to be the absolute. We should be able then to see once more the essential moderation of their ideal, for they seek not to cast off the passions (including sexual passions) but to moderate them. Again, their perspectivism is what enables them to do this; for by realizing that a passion should properly be just part of life and not the whole, one should accept the merely partial nature or perspectivism of that passion which should in turn prevent it from becoming an all-consuming or totalizing will-to-power.

The metaphors of brotherhood and family (including father and son) attempt fundamentally to suggest this moderation, for they are metaphors in which the extremity of passion – sexual passion – is absent (although indeed it may be present in Oedipal form).[15] Such metaphors also invoke the paradoxical combination of equality yet hierarchy which characterizes Blake's and Kierkegaard's ideal of life, for if "brothers" suggests equality, "fathers and sons" does not.[16] All men (and women) can be brothers or equals; but only those who master the potentially dissolving irony of pure *eros*, making it a part of life yet not the whole, can participate in this community of men and women.

The metaphor of brotherhood, while one that need not then exclude sexuality, is nonetheless deliberately chosen for the way in which it can supplement or go beyond Kierkegaard's identification of the ethical with marriage in *Either/Or*. The ethical in conflict with the religious in *Fear and Trembling* invokes not merely (and indirectly, through Isaac) the public institution of marriage, but beyond this the orthodox public morality of good and evil. Abraham's intended murder of Isaac violates public laws far more profoundly than does the aesthete's violation of the laws of marriage. Because of this, Abraham's act raises to a correspondingly higher degree the conflict between private and public the aesthete experiences in his choice between erotic and married love. If the aesthete has difficulty justifying his private passions to the ethical Judge William, how much the more difficult is it for Abraham to justify his act of murder to society. How can this apparent ironist's private act of murder be reconciled with – and indeed redeem – the public ethics of human community? This question brings the conflict between private irony and public community fundamental to Kierkegaard (and, I shall argue, Blake) to its highest pitch, in what may well be the central difficulty of their ideal brotherhood of life.

B. BEYOND GOOD AND EVIL: THE IRONIC BROTHERHOOD

And now the Spectres of the Dead awake in Beulah: all
The Jealousies become Murderous: uniting together in Rahab
With Moral Law, an Equal Balance, not going down with decision
                                                    Blake, *Jerusalem*

Paine is either a Devil or an Inspired man. Men who give themselves to their Energetic Genius in the manner that Paine does are no *modest Enquirers* Examiners. If they are not determinately wrong they must be Right or the Bible is false. as to *modest Enquirers* Examiners in these points they will *always be found to be neither cold nor hot & will* be spewed out.
                              Blake, Annotations to *An Apology for the Bible*

The absolute duty may cause one to do what ethics would forbid, but by no means can it cause the knight of faith to cease to love. This is shown by Abraham. The instant he is ready to sacrifice Isaac the ethical expression for what he does is: he hates Isaac. But if he really hates Isaac he can be sure that God does not require this, for Abraham and Cain are not identical.
                              Johannes de Silentio, *Fear and Trembling*

If the idea of brotherhood is supposed to redeem or transform the sexual contraries, as we have seen, it is also supposed to redeem the orthodox ethical and religious contraries of good and evil – that is, to go beyond them and yet at the same time to revitalize them. Such an ideal which celebrates breaking public laws in the name of life is clearly a dangerous one, for it threatens to destroy the very foundations of human community. Blake and Kierkegaard manifest a

particular interest in this problem in their exploration of two biblical tales of murder: Abraham's sacrifice of Isaac and Cain's
murder of Abel. Kierkegaard's *Fear and Trembling* celebrates Abraham's act as one justified in the name of life; similarly, I shall argue,
Blake's poetic drama "The Ghost of Abel" celebrates Cain as a man
of action and life. Abraham and Cain heroically cast off the spectre
of inaction, error, and dread to *act* – indeed, to commit (or nearly
commit) murder. Yet "Abraham and Cain are not identical," as
Kierkegaard's Johannes de Silentio points out: Abraham acts "for
good" while Cain acts "for evil," as we shall see. This critical
distinction between acting for good and acting for evil is what
Kierkegaard – and Blake – hope will prevent their celebration of
action and life from being a Nietzschean celebration of purely
individual action or private will. Their celebration of "All Act from
Individual Propensity [as] Virtue" yet ultimate refusal to endorse
the act of murder is the precarious limit they set on action, a limit
that ideally reconstitutes a ground for human community. This limit
again serves to "master irony" – to master the ironist's private,
willful project of self-creation and autonomy that threatens to
undermine communal human life.

Kierkegaard's attack on the spectre of negation that dissolves the
ethical contraries once again focuses on the "phantom" of the
Hegelian negative:

Leaving logic to go on to ethics, one encounters here again the negative,
which is indefatigably active in the whole Hegelian philosophy. Here too a
man discovers to his amazement that the negative is the evil. Now the
confusion is in full swing; there is no bound to brilliancy ... One sees how
illogical movements must be in logic since the negative is the evil, and how
unethical they must be in ethics since the evil is the negative. In logic this is
too much, in ethics too little; it fits nowhere if it has to fit both places. If
ethics has no other transcendence, it is essentially logic; if logic is to have so
much transcendence as after all has been left in ethics out of a sense of
shame, then it is no longer logic. (Vigilius Haufniensis, *CD*, 12–13)

Just as movement has supposedly been imported into logic by the
system, so ethics, the moral distinction between good and evil, has
supposedly been captured within the idealist system. But once again
Haufniensis invokes the principle of contradiction, insisting that the
negative "fits nowhere if it has to fit both places;" it is only a *phantom*
once more. If the negative is logic then it cannot also be evil, a
category of ethics, and vice-versa; ethics, the realm of freedom, and

logic, the realm of necessity, are fundamentally opposed and cannot be reconciled. Just as logic *is not* life and being *is not* becoming, logic is not ethics; nor can either become the other through any mediated transition. And Climacus further invokes, in relation to this principle of contradiction, the individual's perspective on life, the perspective to which his philosophy is trying to adhere: "If a man occupied himself, all his life through, solely with logic, he would nonetheless not become logic; he must therefore himself exist in different categories" (*CUP*, 86).

Good and evil have become systematized into an "Abstract" or "system of moral virtue," terms Blake explicitly associates with the Spectre, who is the negation or "Reasoning Power" made from "the Two Contraries which are calld Qualities, with which / Every Substance is clothed" (J, 1, 10:7–14; 152–3). This abstract or system abstracted from particular circumstances and made into a universal law is for both Blake and Kierkegaard the good and evil of conventional morality. And again, both perceive this mediation of good and evil, their false alliance, as the real enemy of life. The struggle of life is once more not between the contraries of good and evil, but against this false mediation which effectively negates them.

Blake and Kierkegaard therefore propose to go beyond good and evil, to cast off this abstract systematic perspective on them. But again, they want to go beyond good and evil in order to redeem them as true contraries; they do not want to cast off good or evil per se, but what we might call good-and-evil. They want to bring good and evil under the rubric of life – under life's control – instead of having life under the rubric and control of conventional good and evil. Climacus states his position on good and evil in phrases almost identical to his statements about the finite and the infinite. Again, one must choose good *or* evil in the interests of true becoming or life; good and evil belong only to the static realm of being:

It is possible to *be both* good and bad, as we say quite simply, that a man has tendencies to both good and evil. But it is impossible *at one and the same time to become both good and bad* ... take the individual out of the medium of the imagination, the medium of being, and place him in existence: Ethics will at once demand that he be pleased to become, and then he becomes – either good or bad. ... This *summa summarum*, that all men *are* both good and bad, does not concern Ethics in the least. For Ethics does not have the medium of *being*, but the medium of *becoming*, and consequently rejects every explanation of becoming which deceptively explains becoming within being, whereby the absolute decision that is rooted in becoming is

essentially revoked, and all talk about it rendered essentially nothing but a
false alarm. (*CUP*, 376–77)

This same distinction between *being* both good and bad versus
becoming one or the other seems to be implicit in Blake's statement
"Good & Evil are Qualities in Every Man whether a Good or Evil
Man" (VLJ, 86; 563). The distinction is latent and in this sense
non-existent until one chooses to become either good or evil; as
Judge William puts it, "only when I have absolutely chosen myself
have I posited an absolute difference, the difference, that is to say,
between good and evil" (*E/O*, ɪɪ, 228). Yet at the same time, the
distinction is not between good and evil but between whether to live
according to the absolute distinction (the "true" perspective) or
whether to exclude it (the false perspective):

> What is it, then, that I distinguish in my either/or? Is it good or evil? No,
> ... my either/or does not in the first instance denote the choice between
> good and evil; it denotes the choice whereby one chooses good and evil/or
> excludes them. Here the question is under what determinants one would
> contemplate the whole of existence and would himself live. (*E/O*, ɪɪ, 172–3)

Here again, the either/or does not "in the first instance" denote the
choice between the contraries, but the choice between two perspectives on the contraries. And even though choosing the right perspective involves choosing one of the contraries, this latter choice
remains in a sense secondary in importance. The question that
further arises once more then is in what sense these contraries are
truly absolutes. If it matters more that one chooses to live according
to good or evil than whether one chooses to live according to good
instead of evil, are the contraries not equallized?

   Again, this is the question raised by Kierkegaard's Abraham and
Blake's Cain, for because Abraham acts for good while Cain acts for
evil, both are therefore redeemed as the true contraries of life. Both
commit – or nearly commit – what society calls murder; yet "Sooner
murder an infant in its cradle than nurse unacted desires," exclaims
Blake (MHH, 10:67; 38), in what may well be more than mere
hyperbole. And similarly, rather than languish in spiritless inaction,
exhorts Climacus, "far rather let us sin, sin out and out, seduce
maidens, murder men, commit highway robbery – after all, that can
be repented of, and such a criminal God can still get a hold on"
(*CUP*, 485). Anything – it seems – is better than the state of inaction
or error, an ethos that obviously threatens to destroy rather than to

revitalize human community. What are the limits to this potentially murderous passion or will?

Blake and Kierkegaard appeal to limits that are precarious indeed, as we shall see, but both do nonetheless appeal to such limits and therein lies their attempted moderation of sheer passion or will. There is a vital, however tenuous, distinction between Abraham – who after all does *not* end up murdering Isaac – and Cain, who does follow through on the act of murder. This vital distinction is between "the knight of faith" and "the sinner," or between what Blake calls the "Inspired Man" and "the Devil," a difference that for Blake and Kierkegaard constitutes life itself.

Abraham's passion, according to Silentio, is that he lived according to the tension between the finite and the infinite – the tension between love for Isaac (the finite) and love for God, or between the public, ethical demands of fatherhood and the private, religious demands of his relation to God. Like the aesthete, Abraham in a sense lives according to a private passion – in his case, his passion for God – that sharply conflicts with his public duty. Public morality would call his intended sacrifice of Isaac evil, and Abraham a murderer. Yet Silentio's Abraham knows privately within himself (as conventional morality cannot know) that he has been told to sacrifice Isaac by God. Abraham is breaking the public law of conventional morality to obey God's law, a law that appears to be a wholly private and mystical one. The public laws of society are suddenly transformed by this private law into a temptation – the temptation to disobey God's command and follow the lower, ethical duty of father to son. Conversely, one might say that the private, inner law has become the temptation – in this case, to break public laws and commit murder. These temptations are the greater for the fact that Abraham must face them totally alone, unable to speak even to his wife of what he has been told to do.

Abraham is therefore at the highest pitch of dread, in fear and trembling at the decision before him. He is faced with the realization (characteristic of dread) that what was once a positive state, his protective and fatherly relation to his son, has now become a negative state which he must repudiate. Dread attempts to hold him back, but as a knight of faith Abraham conquers this spectre of dread by making the leap of faith. He moves to sacrifice Isaac – and receives Isaac back again, saved by God's substitution of a lamb even as he draws the knife. He and Isaac are reunited as father and son in a luminous instance of repetition – their relationship transformed or infinitized by the test of faith. Isaac is in a sense no longer merely a given but something Abraham has earned; hence their relationship is no longer static but dynamic, as is Abraham's relation to God. His relationship to both the public or ethical laws (Isaac) and to his private law (God) has been transformed.

Here again we see the peculiar logic of contraries governing Kierkegaard's dialectic. Conventional morality, he would claim (and Abraham, in so far as he is a conventional father), has blurred or mediated the distinction between the ethical and the religious, the public and the private. God's command forces Abraham to confront the opposition between his love for Isaac and his love for God – to sharpen that opposition or in a sense bring it into being by being forced to choose between them. But the ultimate choice turns out to be not the choice between Isaac and God (since Isaac is in fact returned to Abraham), but between existing without any awareness of the distinction between love of Isaac and love of God, and existing with the awareness of that distinction. And again, the only way Abraham can attain such awareness is through the decision.

Once again, despite the apparent casting-off of one of the contraries (Isaac), the contrary is nonetheless paradoxically redeemed. It is redeemed in two senses – literally, one might say, in the fact that Isaac is saved at the last minute. But it is also redeemed in the sense that it is not merely Abraham's willingness to sacrifice Isaac which brings the absolute distinction into being, but his great love for Isaac. Only because his love for Isaac is absolute does the conflict between the two loves become so intense; his decision is not an easy one but excruciatingly difficult. In other words, his love for or "embrace" of Isaac is as decisive for the choice as is his "casting-off." This is why one cannot say that one contrary – love for Isaac and for one's public, ethical duty – is "at fault" or "wrong" and to be cast off, while the other contrary is therefore good and to be embraced. Once again, the perspective which does not differentiate between the contraries is more properly what is at fault.

A similar logic of contraries seems to operate in Blake's "The Ghost of Abel". Written in response to Byron's *Cain*, Blake's work corrects – significantly, by moderating – Byron's nihilistic celebration of Cain, in the attempted moderation so typical of his and Kierkegaard's dialectic. Like Abraham, Byron's Cain is confronted with a tension between the private and the public: a private, mystical encounter not indeed with God but with Lucifer, a Lucifer who similarly in a sense commands him to murder not a son but a brother. The savagery of Byron's satire lies in its implicit equation of Lucifer with God; Byron would see no difference between God's command to Abraham and Lucifer's implicit command to Cain.

This equation of God with Lucifer is where Blake vehemently disagrees. Blake does agree with Byron that Cain is a visionary of sorts, whose quest for a knowledge beyond the limits of orthodox morality is in some sense heroic. But Cain's heroism is qualified for Blake by being the heroism of what Kierkegaard calls the sinner – that is, an act of heroism that is nonetheless profoundly wrong. Like Kierkegaard, Blake stops short of endorsing the act of murder – for it is surely significant that Abraham does not in the end murder Isaac, and that Cain's murder of Abel is in Blake's eyes a great "sin" instigated by the devil.

Byron's version of the Cain–Abel story in *Cain* clearly holds up Cain as having a great intellectual curiosity and spiritedness that the insipid Abel entirely lacks. Byron admires Cain's quest for ultimate knowledge as a spirited defiance of God's prohibition, and implies that Cain's murder of Abel is simply the logical consequence of that quest. For in seeking ultimate knowledge, Cain seeks (wittingly or unwittingly) death, in what is for Byron a heroic rather than a misguided quest. Cain's murder of Abel is therefore not evil but a sign of his superiority to orthodox good and evil and of the success of his quest; and Byron laments that Cain should be exiled for this superiority.[17]

Blake's response in "The Ghost of Abel" seems to be that, on the contrary, Byron is wrong, or at least only partially right – hence his address to "Lord Byron in the Wilderness" (to Byron as a prophet rather than an embodiment of the truth) and his remonstrance "can a Poet doubt the Visions of Jehovah?" Byron's Cain is indeed a visionary or poetic genius of sorts who does go (or see) beyond good and evil. But Blake objects that Cain has misinterpreted his vision, making his response, the murder of Abel, deeply wrong. Byron's Cain has been taken on a visionary journey by Lucifer, a journey which essentially shows Cain man's insignificance in the universe, and the universe itself as a vast conglomerate of whirling spheres of dead matter. It is this materialism of Cain's vision that Blake seems to find most objectionable, for it has blurred the outlines of Cain's (and Byron's) vision, the determinate black line of life. As Blake objects in his short prologue addressed to Byron:

... Nature has no Outline: but Imagination has. Nature has no Tune: but Imagination has! Nature has no Supernatural & dissolves: Imagination is Eternity (1; 270)

Cain has correctly seen that nature is merely dead matter; he has correctly seen the Orc cycle of generation and death to which nature is subject.[18] This is why he is a visionary – because he *has* seen the cycle clearly from a perspective outside it. But his mistake is in then succumbing to that vision as representing the whole of life instead of seeing that it is only part of life – the cycle of nature. This vision of life as ultimately ending only in death is what leads him to murder Abel, in an attempt to murder not only Abel but the God who has made such a world. Cain refuses to see the immortality of the spirit which transcends this cycle of nature (rather ironically, since his own vision of this cycle is itself a perspective beyond it). Further, by murdering Abel, Cain introduces an entire cycle of self-destructive vengeance into the world – the vengeful good-and-evil of orthodox morality. In Blake's coda to Byron's drama, the ghost of Abel appears to Adam and Eve as they mourn over Abel's body, and cries out savagely for vengeance, that Cain in turn be killed in retribution. But "Jehovah" replies "He who shall take Cains life must also Die O Abel / And who is he? Adam wilt thou, or Eve thou do this? (1:15–16; 271). The vengeful "Life for life! / ... Sacrifice on Sacrifice Blood on Blood" which Abel demands is no better than Cain's original murder, not least because Abel in turn shows Adam and Eve the same chilling vision of death and nothingness that Lucifer once showed Cain (and Cain all too vividly "showed" Abel). "Abel is dead & Cain slew him! We shall also Die a Death / And then! what then?" cries Adam, "be as poor Abel a Thought: or as / This!" (referring apparently to Abel's corpse lying before them; (1:19–21; 271). The victim and the murderer with their respective visions of death have become equallized in a static law of action and reaction, a cycle of sin and moral retribution which Blake represents by Satan. When Jehovah offers a way out of the cycle by replying "Lo I have given you a Lamb for an Atonement instead / Of the Transgres[s]or, or no Flesh or Spirit could ever Live" (II:10–11; 272), Satan appears, insisting "I will have Human Blood & not the blood of Bulls or Goats / And no Atonement ... Thou shalt Thyself be Sacrificed to Me thy God on Calvary" (II:13–18; 272). But Jehovah appears to have the last word, replying "Such is my Will. That Thou Thyself go to Eternal Death," and the drama ends with a chorus of angels celebrating "the Forgiveness of Sin," "Peace / Brotherhood and Love."

This forgiveness, atonement, or "love" appears to be the central way through which Blake and Kierkegaard hope to break out of the static cycle of good and evil, for as we saw in *Fear and Trembling*, Abraham is similarly saved from committing murder by God's loving substitution of the lamb for Isaac. This suggests that Blake and Kierkegaard simply appeal to an orthodox notion of divine intervention, grace, or atonement to redeem one's passionate and potentially murderous actions. Both also seem to appeal to revelation by claiming that one cannot sin *unknowingly*: "sin is, after having been informed by a revelation from God what sin is, then before God in despair not to will to be oneself, or before God in despair to will to be oneself," declares Anti-Climacus (*SUD*, 227). And Blake insists "no man can do a Vicious action & think it to be Virtuous. no man can take darkness for light. he may pretend to do so & may pretend to be a modest Enquirer, but he is a Knave" (Annotations to *An Apology for the Bible*; 614). "Do or Act to Do Good or to Do Evil who Dare to Judge but God alone," he also declares (619).

But where Blake and Kierkegaard radicalize this seemingly orthodox conception is in their equal and opposite – perhaps more than equal and opposite – emphasis on the existing individual's passion or faith which in essence calls this power of grace into being (or more accurately, into being in time). Cain is a sinner because he has acted not merely with passion, but with the wrong passion, that of hatred instead of love. This is why his God is appropriately Lucifer; it is almost as though Cain's hatred for Abel and for God *produced* this God, just as Abraham's love for Isaac and for God produces the God of love who similarly manifests himself to him. Similarly, Blake's Adam and Eve seem to produce the God of atonement or love who appears to them by choosing to believe in "the Visions of Jehovah." They see death before them in Abel's corpse, "yet Jehovah sees him / Alive & not Dead," says Eve, and urges further (as Blake is undoubtedly urging Byron) "were it not better to believe Vision / With all our might & strength tho we are fallen & lost" (GA, II:1–2; 271). They do choose to believe with great passion – "with all [their] might & strength," and it is clear too that the struggles of Blake's

Los in the prophecies emphasize the role that human love or passion must play in escaping from the static cycle. Significantly, this also seems to have been an option for Byron's Cain, who realizes that his capacity for love is what fundamentally differentiates him from Lucifer – and yet who rejects this apparent escape from the cycle offered by his wife and sister Adah (II, ii, 305–338).[19]

This means, critically, that Blake and Kierkegaard appeal not to some transcendent authority to ground or justify murderous actions, but to the private passion of the existing individual who brings that power of grace into existence. In other words, Abraham is justified in his action not by God's command, but by his own great love for Isaac – by his private, individual passion and not by a transcendent authority. The nature of one's private passion is what wholly justifies one's actions: if one loves one is an Inspired Man, a knight of faith; if one hates one is a Devil, a sinner whose actions are admirable (since after all passionate) but profoundly wrong. This qualitative difference between two kinds of passion for Blake and Kierkegaard decisively differentiates Abraham from Cain, for again, "the Absolute duty" can never "cause the knight of faith to cease to love," declares Silentio; "If he (Abraham) really hates Isaac, he can be sure that God does not require this, for Abraham and Cain are not identical." The bottom line for Blake and Kierkegaard seems to be that love can never culminate in murder – that "love," a private passion or eros, can therefore "ground" human, public community.

What this means, however, is that one must always "know" – through a saving remnant of *reason* – the qualitative difference between love and hate. Those who "devote themselves to their Energetic Genius," as Blake puts it, will always be either Right in their passionate love or determinately Wrong in their equally passionate hate. One can always master irony, in other words – master or understand passion or eros, rationally distinguishing between kinds of passion. Unmastered passion, which does not differentiate between love and hate, does not rule.

This final appeal to a qualitative and in some attenuated sense rational difference between two passions, love and hate, is how Blake and Kierkegaard attempt to differentiate faith (love) and sin (hate) not only from each other but from error. "Sin is not a negation but a position," Anti-Climacus declares; in other words, sin is a *contrary* (*SUD*, 227). This contrary which Anti-Climacus calls a "position" Blake similarly calls a "positive;" in his words, "Con-

traries are Positives a negation is not a Contrary" (M, ıı, 30:fronti-
spiece; 129). As a position or positive, sin, like faith, is a *leap*: "When
sin is posited in the particular individual by the qualitative leap, the
distinction is then posited between good and evil," Haufniensis
declares (*CD*, 100). Once again, Blake and Kierkegaard attempt to
leap beyond the determinism which declares not only that one is
always already saved, but that one is always already in sin. The
system has annulled sin just as surely as it has annulled faith,
according to Kierkegaard. Again, logic claims to encompass or
understand sin; but "to want to explain logically the entrance of sin
into the world is a stupidity," Haufniensis exclaims (*CD*, 45); sin is a
spirited act of freedom, not a necessary and inevitable corruption
into which the individual gradually and imperceptibly declines, or
into which he is inevitably born. Hegelian Christendom "is so far
from being what it calls itself that the lives of most men are,
Christianly understood, too spiritless even to be called in a strictly
Christian sense sin" (*SUD*, 235). The spiritless are more properly in
the state of error or negation, the passive state which does not stand
in any relation to God (or to life), either in the relation of faith (love)
or in that of sin (hate).

Blake would seem to make a similar distinction in *The Four Zoas*
when he announces that "Error can never be redeemd in all Eternity / But Sin Even Rahab is redeemd in blood & fury & jealousy"
(*FZ*, ıx, 120:48–49; 390). He also makes this distinction in *A Vision of
the Last Judgment*:

Forgiveness of Sins is only at the Judgment Seat of Jesus the Saviour where
the Accuser is cast out. not because he Sins but because he torments the
Just & makes them do what he condemns as Sin & what he knows is
opposite to their own Identity. (93; 565)

The Accuser is cast out "not because he sins" but because he makes
people live a spiritual death instead of life; he hinders or negates them,
thus hindering action, the realization of one's "eternal validity" (in
Kierkegaard's phrase), identity, or living self. As Blake also says,

we do not find any where that Satan is Accused of Sin he is only accused of
Unbelief ... Satan thinks that sin is displeasing to God he ought to know
that Nothing is displeasing to God but Unbelief & Eating of the Tree of
Knowledge of Good & Evil (VLJ, 86; 564)

Only unbelief and eating of the tree of knowledge are displeasing to
God because they are errors of passivity and inaction. Unbelief is

passive because it is a negation of belief, a refusal to make the leap; eating of the tree of knowledge is passive because it is also a negation or abstraction which tyrannizes over life. Blake explicitly identifies unbelief with negation in *Jerusalem*, when he says "Negations Exist Not: Exceptions & Objections & Unbeliefs / Exist not" (J, I, 17: 34–35; 162). The distinction between sin and error is also implicit in Blake's remark that "when a Religious Man falls into Sin, he ought not to be calld a Hypocrite: this title is more properly to be given to a Player who falls into Sin; whose profession is Virtue & Morality & the making Men Self-Righteous" (J, III, 52; 201). The hypocrite once more is the plagiarist and pretender, the negation whose profession is good-and-evil. The context for this statement is also a diatribe against religions of vengeance, emphasizing that sin is what can be "forgiven," in contrast to the error which must be cast off: "Listen! Every Religion that Preaches Vengeance for Sin is the Religion of the Enemy & Avenger; and not of the Forgiver of Sin, and their God is Satan, Named by the Divine Name" (J, III, 52; 201). Forgiveness of sin is essential if one is to break out of the cycle, as we have seen; realizing this, Los declares

> If I should dare to lay my finger on a grain of sand
> In way of vengeance; I punish the already punished: O whom
> Should I pity if I pity not the sinner who is gone astray!
> O Albion, if thou takest vengeance; if thou revengest thy wrongs
> Thou art for ever lost!
>
> (J, II, 45:33–37; 194)

This rejection of vengeance is entirely in keeping with Blake–Los's "modulation of his fires" in the last three prophecies, and the corollary redemption or ransom of both contraries. And it is clear that this "forgiveness of sin" depends entirely upon making the distinction between sin and error.

We can see from all this what constitutes the brotherhood of human community for Blake and Kierkegaard, a brotherhood ideally of mastered passion or irony in which Abraham and Cain are true brothers. This brotherhood is potentially an all-inclusive but actually a rather exclusive one, for those who are "found to be neither cold nor hot will be spewed out," while the Devils and Inspired Men who "give themselves to their Energetic Genius" will constitute its membership. The criterion for membership, the ground of this community, is ideally not just private passion but a mastered passion – a passion that rationally knows what it is doing, in a sense – and in this is supposed to be its vitality. By insisting on a distinction not only between passionless outsiders and passionate insiders but between the passionate insiders themselves (those whose passion is love, the good, versus those whose passion is hate, the evil), this community tries to avoid celebrating a purely nihilistic unrestraint of the will, the condition of pure action or eros that would in fact destroy all community. And as always, only this distinction or choice between faith and sin, good and evil, love and hate, casts off the state of error and thus differentiates the sheep from the goats, the wise men from the fools, the brothers from the non-brothers. Yet the Devil and the Inspired Man are undeniably equal in their respective passions; the passionate choice for good or evil is more important than whether one chooses good rather than evil. Blake and Kierkegaard hope that through a kind of revelation or reason as "the bound or outward circumference of energy," we can never sin unknowingly. But when this knowledge does not seem to inhibit or restrain the choice for evil, it seems to abdicate its function. And when the revelation of Right and Wrong seems to *follow* the choice, producing either God or Lucifer, this attenuated form of revelation verges on collapse. When it makes no real difference whether one loves or hates, either choice bringing one equally into the community or brotherhood, the ground of the community seems precarious indeed.

Nonetheless, Blake and Kierkegaard do insist on this precarious ground; in both the sexual and ethical realms of human life, as we have seen, they attempt to found communities based not just on private eros or passion but on mastered passion. The aesthete who lives according to unmastered private passion never has to confront the choice, the incommensurability between his private autonomous self-creative project and the goals of public human community. Similarly, the ethical individual who lives wholly by public laws of marriage and of good and evil (the other form of unmastered irony) never has to confront the incommensurability between these laws and his private passions. But not to confront the incommensurability or choice or collision between the two is not to live, and indeed can only be sustained by removing oneself from life. Blake and Kierkegaard would argue that life always confronts us with the collision between the private and the public spheres (the real meaning of God's command to Abraham); to try to avoid those collisions or crises by living a wholly public or a wholly private life is to try to escape from life. Only by continually choosing between the private and the public does one keep alive the true difference between them, the incommensurability that is the source of life's true tension or eros. Only by keeping alive the difference between them through the choice can one preserve what "should always be concealed and hidden as the root of life always is" – the hiddenness at the heart of the truly erotic life.

Because they reconstitute the public for the sake of the private, reason for the sake of true passion, action, and life, Blake's and Kierkegaard's ground of life threatens to – and indeed must inevitably – founder. Yet their stubborn insistence on this ground does create an extraordinary tension between mastered and unmastered irony that decisively differentiates them from those whose communities, ungrounded on even this vestigial foundation, abdicate any attempt to keep alive the private and the public tension and deliberately dissolve all foundations in unmastered irony.

For such communities, the problem of language is paramount; to dissolve foundations may be to dissolve the possibility of public discourse. If language too is unmastered irony, communication threatens to dissolve altogether. But if language is entirely unironic, it will lose its vitality and hence perhaps equally its communicative function. We should now turn to see how our philosopher–poets deal with this third and perhaps most important realm of human community.

CHAPTER 5

Irony and authority

Los reads the Stars of Albion
The Spectre reads the Voids between the Stars
Blake, *Jerusalem*

What Tarquinius Superbus spoke in his garden with the
poppies was understood by his son, but not by the messenger.
Hamann; epigraph to *Fear and Trembling*

I never in all my conversations with him could feel the least
justice in calling him insane; he could always explain his paradoxes when he pleased, but to many he spoke so that 'hearing
they might not hear.'
John Linnell (artist friend of Blake)

Decisiveness is precisely the eternal protest against all fictions.
Johannes Climacus, *Concluding Unscientific Postscript*

Blake's spiritual friends and brothers converse together in
"Visionary forms dramatic," and "every Word and Every Character Is Human." But their experience of mutual interchange and
intellectual commingling is largely foreign to the majority of Blake's
readers, at least when they are reading Blake. His notorious obscurity, far from allowing such immediate (or unmediated) exchange,
has rather demanded, as the proliferating Blake industry bears
witness, the mediation of a host of critics and an ever-expanding
interpretive apparatus.

Hypotheses about the reasons for this obscurity are many. Blake
was mad, or close to it, increasingly entangled in the Urizenic
meshes of his own idiosyncratic and finally private symbolic net of
religion; he was a mystic, irrationally compiling esoterica from
disparate and often contradictory occult sources in the conviction
that all pointed to the same ultimately ineffable and wordless truth;
he feared censorship, in England's politically unstable and exces-

sively repressive climate following the French revolution, deciding that "deep dissimulation is the only defense an honest man has left;" he wished pedagogically to force his readers into an active grappling with his text, to "rouze [their] faculties to act," deliberately speaking in riddles and paradoxes so that "hearing they might not hear."

Like all useful simplifications, these may be caricatures of the usual hypotheses, but they are basically accurate ones. And far from being straw men, all are true in varying degrees. It seems clear first of all that much of Blake's obscurity was unintentional, and that it accordingly derived to some extent at least from a troubled and excessively introspective frame of mind, perhaps indeed from the spectre of melancholy so perennially dogging his footsteps. It is also true that Blake is in some sense – although a very qualified one – a mystic, if by mysticism we mean adherence to an "idea of the holy," as Rudolph Otto has called it, or to what I would call the qualitative otherness of transcendence. To the extent that this is so, Blake's obscurity may indeed partly originate in a mystical insistence that the nature of truth is such that it does indeed transcend or escape language. Yet the matter is rather more complex than this, for Blake is but perhaps more significantly not a mystic in any orthodox sense of the term. That Blake may have feared censorship is possible, and certainly David Erdman has made a convincing and provocative argument that this was so.[1] And while it may be true, as Erdman suggests, that Blake's fears were largely unfounded because he saw himself as more subversive than he actually was,[2] Blake's very real trial for sedition at Felpham suggests that indeed the English political climate of the time was an uncommonly suspicious one. The problem with hypotheses about either political or religious censorship, however, is that they ignore the extent to which Blake's obscurity may be fundamentally bound up with his redefinition or radicalization of religion. It is essential to the very character of his production or authorship, a way of reduplicating in language what Blake sees as the relation of error or obscurity to truth.

Blake's difficulty stems from a number of distinctive features: his catalogues of invented place and character names, identifiable to some extent through etymological roots or as mythological allusions, but for the most part demanding interpretation based on the internal coherence of Blake's symbolic system; the complex web of allusions from widely disparate sources constituting the basic texture of his myth; the sheer volume of bewilderingly "minute particulars," the descriptive detail which makes sifting through to the basic narrative lines of the last prophecies so difficult a task. He shares with Kierkegaard, however, several obscurities that are not only more arguably intentional strategies, but also more centrally implicated with the vision of life informing his entire myth. Like Kierkegaard, Blake radically destabilizes his own authority or authorial stance; like Kierkegaard, he further destabilizes his myth through an all-pervading perspectivism which in its linguistic form confronts his readers with apparently undecidable oppositions; and finally, as the direct consequence of these two forms of destabilization, Blake, like Kierkegaard, shifts the task of interpretation almost entirely upon the reader, who, with little in the way of guiding authorities in terms of either an author or a text, is radically thrown upon his or her energies of appropriation or interpretation. All of these strategies finally serve to ground the truth of interpretation in perspectivism or "error," appealing to a "point of view" to ground their authority, as we shall see. In this lie their profound affinities with and differences from the strategies of romantic and poststructuralist hermeneutics.

Blake and Kierkegaard destabilize their authority in markedly similar ways, fundamentally by displacing or concealing any univocal authorial voice through a series of dramatized voices or pseudonyms. The curious impersonality of Blake's poetry – the absence of a directly confessional lyric "I" – has always differentiated his poetry from that of such romantic lyricists as Wordsworth and Coleridge. Whatever autobiographical or confessional element Blake's poetry contains – and indeed I have been suggesting that his myth is largely about his personal struggles with melancholy and religious despair – is depersonalized or objectified in a number of ways, most notably in the later works by its dramatization in the characters of the Zoas and of Los and the spectre. This dramatization or projection of deeply felt psychic states onto "visionary forms dramatic" whose disembodied voices articulate those psychic conflicts is characteristic of all of Blake's poetry, early and late, although in the *Songs* these voices are somehow less disembodied and more lyrically realized.

But however lyrical and distinct the voices in the *Songs*, the personal voice of William Blake is, as many have remarked, curiously absent from most of his poetry, and he is in this sense an author who is, as Kierkegaard would put it, "without authority." Kierkegaard's careful construction of even more deliberate dramatic pseudonyms enacts a similar strategy of authorial concealment. He also repeatedly calls attention to his authorial absence, referring to himself as "an absent one" (*PV*), and when he does publicly acknowledge his authorship of the pseudonymous works, disclaiming any privileged authorial point of view on their interpretation: "*Without authority* to call attention to religion, to Christianity, is the category for my whole activity as an author, integrally regarded. That I was 'without authority' I have from the first moment asserted clearly and repeated as a stereotyped phrase. I regarded myself preferably as a *reader* of the books, not as the *author*" (*PV*, 151). If Blake's Los "reads the stars of Albion," Kierkegaard too is only a reader; both abdicate the author's point of view for the existing individual reader's, as we shall see.

This apparent abdication of authority to a multiplicity of readerly points of view or perspectives threatens to dissolve the authority of the text into radical perspectivism or unmastered irony. Other poetic strategies contribute to this dissolution: Blake's symbolism, for example, is fundamentally perspectival; as Frye points out, all of Blake's images can be read equally either as "symbols of the world of innocence when thought of in terms of eternal existence," or as "symbols of the world of experience when thought of in terms of death and annihilation."[3] This means that the same natural objects can be read from either of two perspectives: the imaginative, spiritual perspective of life, and the unimaginative, corporeal perspective of spiritual negation and death. Blake's tantalizingly brief little poem "The Clod and the Pebble" perhaps best exemplifies the interpretive stalemate in which his perspectivism may abandon us, a stalemate exacerbated by Blake's apparent refusal to step in as author to arbitrate. Whether love "builds a Heaven in Hells despair" as the clod of clay asserts or "builds a Hell in Heavens despite" as the pebble retorts is unresolved and seemingly unresolvable by any higher perspective outside of these other two – or more accurately, by any truth beyond all perspectivism. And while this poem might seem an unusually undecidable one, some would argue that it is no more nor less undecidable than all of Blake's poetry. After all, "I have represented it [vision] as I saw it," Blake calmly asserts, "to different People it appears differently" (VLJ, 68; 555).

A similar undecidability infects Kierkegaard's pseudonymous works, dissolved as they are into a multiplicity of pseudonyms. What the aesthete celebrates as the whole of life, the erotic, is from the ethical man's point of view a kind of stasis and spiritual death; yet the ethical man's celebration of marriage over the aesthetic life is from the religious man's point of view similarly limited. Nor is it clear that there is any ascending order or hierarchy to these spheres of existence: the aesthete's criticisms of the passionlessness and stasis of married life, its destruction of the erotic, have considerable force, as do the aesthete's and ethical man's criticisms of the religious man's unerotic and unethical otherworldly existence. It is unclear that there is any God's-eye or Hegelian point of view which will either transcend these points of view or subsume them within itself. Kierkegaard's *Fear and Trembling* further calls attention to this perspectival hermeneutic by presenting a number of readings of the Abraham – Isaac story, each interpreting that story differently; and nearly all the pseudonymous works rely heavily upon cryptic parables and analogies which obscure as much as – or more than – they clarify.

This authorial dissolution into perspectivism or interpretive undecidability evokes in Blake's and especially Kierkegaard's case two explanations: the "ethical-religious" and "the aesthetic." The religious reading interprets this perspectivism as a strategy designed to render the author a transparent medium through which speaks a higher religious Authority, and to demand from the reader an irrational choice, a "leap of faith" into a mystical embrace of this higher intention. The (related) ethical reading (henceforth identified with the religious) similarly sees this undecidability as issuing a moral imperative demanding an ethical choice, again for a higher, determinate intention. The aesthetic reading, finally, interprets this perspectivism as a deconstructive strategy that ironizes or dissolves the possibility of choice and any privileging of intention.[4]

We can see how Blake's and Kierkegaard's strategies not only invoke but indeed demand both (or either) of these kinds of readings. Understood as religious poets or prophets, Blake and Kierkegaard are ventriloquists who necessarily abdicate all authority to a higher truth which speaks through them. As merely vehicular forms by which the individual is led to vision or truth both author and text are in some sense empty or absent; they do not dogmatically impose themselves upon the reader, for to do so would be a kind of idolatrous substitution of themselves for the true Authority. "I see the Saviour over me / Spreading his beams of love & dictating the words of this mild song," says Blake in *Jerusalem*; and, as he told Mr. Butts (speaking of *Milton*), "I have written this Poem from immediate Dictation ... without Premeditation & even against my Will"

(April 25, 1803; 729). Kierkegaard similarly claimed that his entire authorship had been dictated by "Divine Governance:"

From the very beginning I have been as it were under arrest and every instant have sensed the fact that it was not I that played the part of master, but that another was Master ... The whole productivity has had in a certain sense an uninterruptedly even course, as if I had had nothing else to do but to copy daily a definite portion of a printed book. (*PV*, 69, 72)

Such a theory of "divine Governance" may indeed account in some measure for the curious combination of dogmatism yet anti-dogmatism, authority yet self-effacement, which characterizes Blake's and Kierkegaard's authorial presences. It means that their claim for a peculiarly individual prophetic authority yet disclaimer of authority need not be self-contradictory.[5]

The religious reading not only interprets authority as a kind of divine ventriloquism, but interprets writing as the poet-prophet's calling of his readers to a "Last Judgment," demanding from them a leap of faith that will differentiate the believers from the non-believers, the sheep from the goats. As a call to judgment, Blake's "prophetic art," as Jerome McGann observes, is a "revelation ... [that] exposes the inner condition of the listener. But beyond this, his art demands a choice. ... These are the prophet's functions. He does not teach, he declares that the time of choice has come."[6] Because he does not teach but instead presents his readers with a choice, Blake thus makes his art deliberately anti-dogmatic and to that extent perhaps "obscure." It does not present us with a completed vision – what Kierkegaard would call a Hegelian "result" – but rather leads us to the point at which we are ideally forced to actualize that vision or result ourselves, to fill in its conceptual content or meaning as Blake refuses to do for us. This makes his poetry "a call to judgment" in which we as readers are tried and revealed in our true or "eternal" selves, because how we choose (or refuse to choose) will ideally reveal us as we truly are. This emphasis on the reader's role or authority in interpretation is therefore not incompatible with the religious reading, for the claim is not that readers make or create their own texts but that they make a passionate leap of faith which actualizes an independently existing and "objective" text.

Kierkegaard's Johannes Climacus invokes a similar religious hermeneutic, one which also effaces the author and puts the burden of interpretation on the reader:

no anonymous author can more cunningly conceal himself, no practitioner of the maieutic art can more carefully withdraw himself from the direct relationship, than God. He is in the creation, and present everywhere in it, but directly He is not there; and only when the individual turns to his inner self, and hence only in the inwardness of self-activity, does he have his attention aroused, and is enabled to see God. . . . Is not this to behave, in relationship to the individual, like an elusive author who nowhere sets down his result in large type or gives it to the reader beforehand in a preface? And why is God elusive? Precisely because He is the truth, and by being elusive desires to keep men from error. (*CUP*, 218)

The implications for the Kierkegaardian reader seem clear. Like the Blakean reader, it is only when he "turns to his inner self . . . in the inwardness of self-activity" that he has his "attention aroused" in a Blakean rousing of the faculties which similarly does not present him with God (or with authorial meaning) as a finished result, but by which he is rather "*enabled* to see God" (my emphasis). Each reader must struggle to attain his own clarity of vision; each reader, like Blake's Los, must labor at the forge of his imaginative energies to shape a vision which actualizes his eternal self. "Let every Christian as much as in him lies engage openly & publicly before all the world in some Mental Pursuit for the Building up of Jerusalem," Blake exhorts, and that exhortation is indeed the call of all his poetry. Like Los's call to Albion, it calls to the reader to rouse himself from his slumbers of passivity to action and to life – to the activity of interpretation.

This call to action and to life – to the *activity* of interpretation – is however what leaves this religious hermeneutic wide open to the aesthetic reading. For the shift in emphasis from the object of interpretation (God, Being, Truth) to the activity of interpretation as the real interpretive goal marks what we might call an "aesthetic turn" from a truth to which language points or leads us to language as an end in itself. Perhaps the process of wrestling with perspectivism, undecidability, and error is more important than getting beyond that activity or process to a static Being or Truth. Blake's and Kierkegaard's art is after all the art of *life*, "an art that could not be turned into an abstraction, an art that no one would fall down and worship . . . an art that would urge no programs and offer no systems."[7] An art so described could indeed threaten to be radically perspectival and indeterminate, to "have no meaning" or to "mean anything."[8]

This aesthetic reading of Blake's and Kierkegaard's art as life argues that author, reader, and text are all in fact part of the flux of life that is language; they are reinscribed as merely differential effects or incompatible points of view within the activity of language and interpretation as life. Author and reader do not choose among (or "will") interpretations, for such freedom of choice presupposes a neutral stance outside of interpretation from which to choose, a neutral stance that would have to be (impossibly) outside of life and language. Kierkegaard and Blake may therefore try to confront their readers with a choice between or among different perspectives, demanding a leap of faith from their readers (runs the aesthetic argument), but they cannot either "impose" such a choice or "guarantee" that their readers will make the right choice.[9] Effacing the author and confronting their readers with perspectivisms and multiple points of view merely enacts the undecidability of life as art or poetry, its lack of any ground in a stable Being or Truth outside itself. Life, like art, is only indeterminacy and error.

What makes this aesthetic reading so compelling – especially in Kierkegaard's case – is that Blake and Kierkegaard do indeed want to create an art of life, and this aligns them more closely with the aesthetic reading (or misreading, as I shall argue) than with the religious one. Like the aesthetic ironist, they want to dissolve dogmatic foundational authorities, to destabilize text, author, and language because they have become empty, systematic abstractions from their vital, living forms. "Modern discourse about Christianity has lost the vigor that can come only from an energetically sustained terminology, and the whole is reduced to a toothless twaddle," complains Climacus (*CUP*, 325). This recalls Blake's parable in *The Marriage* of the poets who "animated all sensible objects with Gods or Geniuses, calling them by the names and adorning them with the properties of woods, rivers ... / Till a system was formd, which some took advantage of & enslav'd the vulgar by attempting to realize or abstract the mental deities from their objects; thus began Priesthood." This is a parable about language as well as religion, the emasculation of the true poetry – which for Blake in this context means the Gods or Geniuses residing in the human breast – by its ossification into doctrine and the systematic forms of language. As Climacus says, "Christianity is not a doctrine but an existential communication expressing an existential contradiction" (*CUP*, 339); it is, in Coleridge's words, "not a doctrine but a life."[10] Such doctrinizing of poetic truths substitutes false religion and false certainty for true: "at length they pronounced that the Gods had ordered such things. / Thus men forgot that all deities reside in the human breast." Men forgot, in other words, not that there are no gods, but that there are no gods abstracted from the human breast, no gods who are not *living* gods. This distinction, at once tenuous but critical, is the critical tenuousness permeating all of Blake's and Kierkegaard's thought.

Blake and Kierkegaard agree then with both the aesthete and the religious man that language has become error; by becoming systematized or abstracted from its originating genius, language has for them become entirely *fictionalized*. This however is where they begin their critical departure from the aesthete and the theologian. For the theologian, because language is error it must be cast off in a leap of faith beyond language into mystical silence, a wordless embrace of Being and Truth. For the aesthete, because language is error and there is nothing outside of language, error is all there is, the whole of life, life's *truth*; the distinction between truth and error effectively drops out of the picture. For Blake and Kierkegaard, however, this "either/or" is too extreme: the choice is not either to abandon language as error for mystical silence and truth, or to conclude that language and error is all there is.[11] For them, the choice is a more moderate one: between false language and true. What one casts off is not language (as the theologian does) but the false forms of language; conversely, what one embraces is not language (and life) as error (as the aesthete does) but language as a living truth. By insisting that language is inevitably error, the theologian and the aesthete equally empty it of its content and actuality; both forms of dogmatism, the overt dogmatism of the theologian and the covert dogmatism of the aesthete, evaporate or ironize language into a spectral abstraction from life.

Because language has degenerated into mere fiction, it must be destabilized through specifically rhetorical or fictional strategies of deception – through speaking in paradoxes, riddles, parables, and pseudonyms. One must fight illusion with illusion, fire with fire. The false Christian must first have his illusion exposed to him as such; he must be forced to defend his lie, as Blake puts it, "so that he may be snared & caught & taken." The truth is that he is not a living individual but an aesthete who has fictionalized and thus emasculated life; and his own aestheticism and web or system of fictions therefore becomes the very means of his entrapment, his snare.

This is why Blake–Los strives with fictions to deliver individuals from those fictions, fixing fictions into a permanent body or shape of falsehood that they may be cast off forever. He strives to master both kinds of fictions which negate or ironize the life of language: the extremism of the theologian who rejects language altogether and the extremism of the aesthete who embraces language as all there is. This ideal of mastered irony is an ideal of true, living language which speaks and yet remains silent, language which speaks in such a way that 'hearing they might not hear.' It is also the key to differentiating Blake's and Kierkegaard's poetics from romantic and postmodern poetics of undecidability or unmastered irony.[12]

All of the pseudonymous works embody or dramatize with great consistency Kierkegaard's theory of mastered irony. But perhaps the clearest example of what he means by the concept is in his final, posthumously published book, *The Point of View for My Work as an Author*. This work not only raises most explicitly the central problem of his authorship, its "ambiguity or duplicity" as both an aesthetic and a religious production, it is in some ways the most frequently misread of Kierkegaard's works. Misread as Kierkegaard's attempt to issue an unequivocally "magisterial fiat," a dogmatic (and unconvincing) defense of authorial intention appealing to a "providential ethics of interpretation," the work becomes a "direct communication" which effectively destroys the whole theory of indirect communication or mastered irony enacted in the pseudonymous works.[13] But *The Point of View* is much more subtle than this, as indirect a communication as any of the pseudonymous works, perhaps the culminating example of mastered irony. Despite its apparent disclosure of full authorial presence, for example, it makes this disclosure only because indeed its author is "an absent one," in the fullest sense of the phrase, because he is dead. It also gives the last word to a pseudonym, to "my poet," as Kierkegaard describes him. But more than this, as Kierkegaard makes clear, "the point of view for my work as an author" is in fact "the point of view for my work as a *reader*." As always, Kierkegaard abdicates his authority, any God's-eye point of view, to appeal to a point of view firmly situated inside, not outside, the life or activity of interpretation. As always too, this appeal to a point of view or perspective threatens to dissolve his authority altogether – the other reading (or misreading) of *The Point of View*, which makes it a particularly illuminating example of his theory of mastered irony in practice. Like all the pseudonymous works, it not only discusses but enacts – as indeed it must – mastered irony.

Kierkegaard begins *The Point of View* by explicitly inviting his readers to entertain two speculative hypotheses about his work, two antithetical perspectives or "points of view." "Let us try to explain the whole of this literary production on the assumption that it was written by an aesthetic author," he invites us; and, let us "experiment with the assumption that it is a religious author"(*PV*, 17). He invites us to such experimentation because, as he says:

I have little confidence in protestations with respect to literary productions and am inclined to take an objective view of my own work. If as a third person, in the role of a reader, I cannot substantiate the fact that what I affirm is so, and that it could not but be so, it would not occur to me to wish to win a cause which I regard as lost. . . . *qua* author it does not avail much that I protest *qua* man that I have intended this or that. But everybody will admit that when one is able to show with respect to a phenomenon that it cannot be explained in any other way, and that in this particular way it can be explained in every detail, or that the explanation fits at every point, then this explanation is substantiated as evidently as it is ever possible to establish the correctness of an explanation. (*PV*, 15–16)

We should note the modesty of Kierkegaard's claim here – that this explanation "is substantiated as evidently as it is ever possible to establish the correctness of an explanation." He quite reasonably makes no claims for demonstrably absolute or certain knowledge; yet it is this very reasonableness and even skepticism which is so often dismissed as a leap of faith.

This qualified, even skeptical appeal to two experimental hypotheses – to two hypothetical or "postulated" authors[14] – is interesting for several reasons. Firstly, it is an appeal to reason – to a process of rational testing. Yet this appeal to reason may be designed to confute reason; it may be that, try as it might, reason will be unable to resolve the antithetical points of view, and will only be able to reveal its own limits as error, unable to grasp any decisive truth. This is what an aesthetic or deconstructive reading might conclude: that reason can find no compelling reasons to decide for one interpretation or point of view rather than another and is thus halted and exposed in its impotence at a moment of aporia.

One can also regard this defeat of reason, again, as demanding a theological leap of faith, a choice for one interpretation over the other. One need not conclude that because reason cannot grasp or demonstrate the truth with absolute certainty the truth does not exist; the exposure of reason as error may only demonstrate reason's limitations. This again is why the deconstructionist and the theologian are sides of the same coin: both conclude that if reason cannot demonstrate the truth with absolute certainty then interpretation is radically undecidable – i.e., irrational – an irrationality the theologian calls "faith."

Yet Kierkegaard is the first to admit that he can give no guarantees of interpretive certainty, and to relinquish such demonstrable certainty as an interpretive goal. Nor, he readily admits, can he force the reader either to choose or to make the right choice. While by his strategies of indirection he hopes to lead his reader to the right interpretation, "this result is not in my power," he acknowledges:

it depends upon so many things, and above all it depends upon whether he will or no. In all eternity it is impossible for me to compel a person to accept an opinion, a conviction, a belief. But one thing I can do: I can compel him to take notice ... By obliging a man to take notice I achieve the aim of obliging him to judge. Now he is about to judge – but how he judges is not under my control. Perhaps he judges in the very opposite sense to that which I desire. (*PV*, 35)

As he further admits, "all doubly reflected communication makes contrary interpretation equally possible, and the judge will be made manifest by his judgment" (*PV*, 156). He cannot compel his readers to judge as he desires; he can however guide them not only to make a choice but the right choice, as we shall see. And if he cannot compel them to choose, existence does so compel them; for not to choose is not to live.

But how, on the basis of perspectivism, a point of view, can Kierkegaard even claim that choice is possible? He seems to take for granted the possibility of choice that deconstruction for example denies; as Derrida declares, "I do not believe that today there is any question of choosing" – presumably, because there can be no neutral ground independent of interpretation from which to choose.[15] Such a declaration, however, for Kierkegaard entails adopting a God's-eye point of view that is simply unavailable to the existing individual. Only the Hegelian, who sees life's oppositions as mediated within a higher unity, and the romantic ironist, who sees life's opposites as vacillating in a "higher madness" of undecidabilities, deny the possibility of choice from such God's-eye points of view. The existing individual reader firmly situated within concrete interpretive situations cannot "spectate" on life as such retrospective or prospective infinitude. To live means to act; to act means to choose; this is how, for Kierkegaard, life denies the impossibility of choice and "coerces us into freedom."[16]

Choosing one interpretation means casting off the error of undecidability to leap or commit oneself to a determinate interpretation, to a definite point of view true to the situatedness of life. In the Kierkegaardian interpretive act one chooses the author, the text, and oneself as reader out of the flux of textuality. One reconstitutes them as determinate entities out of a prior dissolution. This is neither a simple reactionary return to a naive interpretive voluntarism that grants an unproblematic freedom of choice, nor a naive interpretive faith in the unproblematic objectivity of author, text, and reader as entities independent of the interpretive act that constitutes them. For Kierkegaard, to insist on the necessity for choice is not to imply that we can adopt a neutral stance outside of interpretation – at least not in life, however possible this is in thought, as he readily acknowledges. Choice is dictated by the fact that to live one must situate oneself within an interpretive situation – or else one remains abstract.

Yet what prevents us from willfully "creating" rather than rationally "choosing" the right or wrong interpretation in any given interpretive situation, particularly when the choice seems to be such an irrational one, a leap of faith? For Kierkegaard, what prevents this is the fact that author, text, and reader are in some sense "given" prior to the interpretive act, as a locus of possibilities that must be actualized. Life is a given as well as a task, he claims: the task of realizing or choosing some of these possibilities. "That which is chosen does not exist and comes into existence with the choice," says Kierkegaard; yet "that which is chosen exists, otherwise there would not be a choice. For in case what I chose did not exist but absolutely came into existence with the choice, I would not be choosing, I would be creating; but I do not create myself, I choose myself"(*E/O*, II, 219–220). Whatever "being" author, text and reader have outside the interpretive act of choice is almost as irrelevant and philosophically uninteresting to Kierkegaard as it is to poststructuralists. Yet unlike Kierkegaard they reject this prior being on grounds he exposes as false: the assumption that to believe

in such a notion of potentiality involves adopting a neutral stance
outside interpretation which they declare is unavailable. On the
contrary, Kierkegaard replies: in any interpretive situation we
necessarily encounter texts and authors as givens that we must
actualize; it is those who deny this given or ground that are adopting
an abstract perspective removed from life. Only a perspective
outside of particular interpretive situations sees their grounds or
givennesses as groundless, themselves interpretive constructs.

Kierkegaard also insists on the critical role of reason in particular
interpretive acts – a reason that again prevents those acts from being
purely "creative" – as a return to our two hypotheses in *The Point of
View* should illustrate. For Kierkegaard's hypothetical aesthetic and
religious authors which he invites us to postulate are not in fact
equal and opposite as might first appear – at least, not to the
"energetic" reader to whom Kierkegaard ultimately directs his
writings. He speaks to two audiences, the wise men and the fools,
those who "hear" and those who "hearing do not hear." But the
energetic readers are not merely the theological believers who cast
off rational error to make a blind leap of interpretive faith to a
theological author; nor are the lazy readers the "non-believers" or
skeptics who remain passively in a state of error.[17] The energetic
readers are those who exercise their *reason* to its utmost limits – for
only by exercising it to those limits can the truth beyond those limits
stand revealed. For Kierkegaard's energetic readers, reason is not
sheer indeterminacy but a determinate guide to the truth, one that
reveals one hypothesis as less acceptable than the other.

Yet this rational, hypothetical, authorial guide is still for Kierkegaard "error," which cannot grasp the paradox of existence. To
appeal to a hypothetical or postulated author is still to appeal to a
purely rational and fictional construct, a relatively stable fiction to
stop the play of fictions.[18] This stopping-point is where Kierkegaard
makes his much criticized leap of interpretive faith, a leap which
demands two things apparently denied by Nietzschean interpretive
theories. The Kierkegaardian leap demands a radical separation of
author, text and reader, the separation that makes the leap both
possible and necessary; and it demands an interpretive voluntarism
– an act of will or passion – constituting the leap of interpretive faith
itself. But for Nietzschean interpretation, whether one speaks of
interpreting God, the world, or a text, all are indissociable from the
interpretive act which constitutes them; for such theories "the world

is alien to us only if we think of it as something that could finally be grasped only as the sum of 'every' possible point of view. Projecting a God's-eye point of view that is not a point of view is not merely useless but unintelligible."[19] It is the very existence of such a point of view which Nietzschean theorists would want to deny, for such an aperspectival perspective beyond all perspectives would clearly undermine the radical perspectivism of their view of life. Kierkegaard, by contrast, does insist on the *possibility* of a God's-eye (and non-constructed authorial) point of view. Yet paradoxically, he would emphatically agree that the existing individual should relinquish any attempt to aspire to or project a God's-eye point of view that is not a point of view, and would agree that such an attempt "is not merely useless but unintelligible." This is why he is at once so much like, yet so much unlike, Nietzschean theorists. Like them, Kierkegaard has virtually no interest in the author "behind" the text; in the being or Platonic truth "behind" the world and temporality; in the reader "in front of" the text; or in meaning "outside" of language. Existence and life are his gods: the author in the text, the being in time, the reader in the text, meaning in language. His interest, in other words, is in all of these presences as constituted by human perceivers and not as they might be in themselves. Kierkegaard's pervasive skepticism insists that the existing individual cannot know an abstract God-in-himself outside of life and temporality, or by analogy a similarly abstract author-in-himself outside the text. This is why aspiring after a totalizing perspective beyond all perspectives is for Kierkegaard precisely the opposite of the real route to truth. For him, only by choosing fully one's own limited perspective or interpretation – again, an act of *exclusion* (either/or) by which one commits oneself wholly to one's limited perspective or interpretation rather than an act of inclusion by which one attempts to grasp the whole (both-and) – can one paradoxically attain the fullness of the whole or the authorial intention. This is because only such an act of interpretive commitment reveals the *limitations* of that interpretation and hence the fullness of what escapes it. Each interpretive act, by sharply revealing the shape of its limitations, can paradoxically bring the individual into the full experience or "repetition" of the author's meaning.

This seems to imply, though, that the true interpretation will always be something radically other than – perhaps even the exact opposite of – one's limited and perspectival interpretation. And it further seems to imply that all interpretations, however limited and perspectival, can bring one into equal relation to the text's meaning: as long as one's interpretation is "passionately" made, the shape of its limitations emerges sharply enough to reveal the fullness of what it has failed to grasp. Yet these implications would be true only if Kierkegaard were a complete irrationalist in whose thought reason played no significant role. By contrast, reason – and in particular, the deployment of reason in the act of interpretation – is of great importance to Kierkegaard, for it is only when reason is brought to its *highest* point that the truth beyond reason can fully reveal itself. This means that interpretations, as rational hypotheses about the text's meaning, can for Kierkegaard be tested and ranked as better and worse. For Kierkegaard, the most comprehensive and rational of these interpretations would be the best – because it most closely approaches the hypothetical *rational* ideal. For in most closely approximating that ideal, Kierkegaard would claim, this interpretation reveals reason at its maximum capacity and hence in its truest, most "consolidated" shape. Only by thus forcing reason to its limits can the fullness of what escapes those limits – the true interpretation – be allowed to emerge. And clearly this "true interpretation" beyond those limits is not their exact opposite but simply always just a little "beyond" what reason can conclusively grasp or demonstrate. Kierkegaard's truth of life cannot be *fully* grasped by reason alone; but this does not mean that reason is "wrong." Reason just cannot go quite far enough – and it is only when it refuses to acknowledge this limitation and claims to grasp the whole of life that it is error.

But in what sense is this truth beyond reason *necessary* to interpretation? Unlike the postulated author, this "unknown something" seems to exert no constraints or authority over interpretation; it is merely an ineffable something that Kierkegaard insists is always "left over" when one has finished testing one's hypotheses about a text. Most resistance to this ineffable something is a resistance to its apparently theological implications; yet we need to remember that Kierkegaard is saying quite simply that we do not "think" the world or "existence" or "the other:" life *is not* (as Hegel for instance would claim) logic. He is insisting on the reality of an otherness that we do not create – the otherness of life or existence – despite the fact that (as he would be the first not only to acknowledge but to insist) it is nonetheless constituted for us only by our own acts of interpretation. While it is true that this otherness exerts no demonstrable constraints on interpretation and that its existence cannot be proven or demonstrated, its non-existence cannot be proven or demonstrated either. Most importantly, Kierkegaard would insist that without this sense of something beyond itself which it cannot grasp, reason would not be impelled to interpret; it is motivated, in a sense, by the desire to discover its own limits. Put in another way, man is fundamentally motivated by a desire for certainty or "the unconditional," Kierkegaard insists; give up the faith in and drive towards certainty and one gives up life.

Blake's perspectival dialectic of truth and error allows us to test the same two hypotheses which Kierkegaard invites us to apply to his work: that Blake is a "religious" or "truthful" author who uses aesthetics (meaning again irony, indirection, and error) only in the service of that religious end or truth; and conversely, that Blake is an aesthetic author for whom aesthetics and unstable irony are ends in themselves. Not surprisingly, there is far less debate about whether Blake is an intentionally aesthetic or skeptical author, although there are those who might argue that he unintentionally falls into unstable irony, the victim of his own – or perhaps language's – obscurities and fictions. But what seems more interesting is to consider how Blake conceived of the relation between art and life. Is it, as for Kierkegaard, the rather complex relation between error and truth?

Certainly if Blake's "prophetic art" above all presents us with a choice, demanding that one make a choice either for vision or against it, then it would seem that Blake does indeed insist that we go beyond the apparent contradictions or "errors" of his texts to a determinate truth of life or vision. Again, if we reconsider briefly the way in which "contraries" function in Blake's myth, we see a fairly consistent strategy that would seem to bear this out. For Blake consistently confronts us with contraries that seem to demand a choice: between innocence and experience, Orc and Urizen, reason and energy, Heaven and Hell, angels and devils. Yet the dynamics of this choice become increasingly complex, as we have seen – for one can easily argue that Blake's apparently equal and opposite contraries are designed to preclude the possibility of choice, to demonstrate rather the impossibility of choosing between them precisely because of their essential equality. If we consider this apparent equallizing of contraries as antithetical points of view the whole of Blake's strategy, this clearly makes him an "aesthetic" Blake, a master ironist who reduces life's contraries to indeterminacy. But I have argued that while Blake does indeed "deconstructively" abolish the principle of contradiction by levelling traditional distinctions or hierarchies in a play of undecidable (because equal) opposites, he then goes beyond this blurring of distinctions to reestablish a hierarchy out of their dissolution. The traditional hierarchy of (unfallen) innocence over (fallen) experience, for example, is equallized by Blake's argument that innocence can be fallen, and experience, a "*higher* innocence" (see chapter 2) – yet it may be that, as has been suggested, the two states were never in fact equal for Blake but rather at different stages of his career were alternately satirized and celebrated as "lower" and "higher."[20] And the observation that *The Marriage* is not truly a marriage of equal contraries but a celebration of one contrary, Hell, is surely correct. Blake does, it is true, present us with clearly opposed contraries – reason and energy, love and hate, devils and angels – that he wants us to transcend as neutralized or "dead". But at this point in his myth is there really any question whether we must instead choose between them – any question, that is, that one contrary is in Blake's eyes the true one? Only "The Clod and the Pebble," I would acknowledge, presents us with a genuine standoff of opposed contraries or perspectives. In "The Tyger," by contrast, while clearly calling into question the traditional hierarchy of good and evil, Blake nonetheless unambiguously celebrates the tyger himself – he does not stop with the levelling of good and evil, the exposure of error, but passes beyond that levelling to a positive vision of life. Whatever the speaker's ambivalence towards the tyger, do we really question Blake's celebratory attitude towards it? "The Tyger" is perhaps the most successful instance in Blake's early work of the deconstructive levelling of conventional contraries yet affirmative vision beyond that levelling – a reconstituted hierarchy of life over death – that comes to be his final ideal.[21] It is therefore much more successful than either *The Marriage*, in which Blake does not succeed in going beyond conventional contraries but instead only inverts them – and "The Clod and the Pebble," where the contraries are indeed equallized but thereby left in static opposition.

    What greatly complicates the issue of Blake's decidability, however, is the increasing turn to perspectivism I have traced in this study – his turn to a dialectic of exclusive perspectives rather than of inclusive contraries. (Again, while that perspectivism may have been implicit in the early myth, it becomes explicit only in the later myth with the introduction of the Spectre of Urthona.) In his early work, Blake might appear to have been more determinate or decidable because he had *separate* sets of images and ideas associated with each of the contraries: priests, laws, prisons, chapels, Heaven – all the restrictions associated with reason – were "good" (which is to say, "evil," or more properly, "dead"); while the lack of all such images of hindrance and the prevailing counter-images of Hell and fire, Blake's central symbol of imaginative energy and life, were "evil" (which is to say, "good" or "alive"). But in the later myth, the *same* images are associated with either death or life, so that "wheels" can be either "the Eternal Wheels of intellect" or "the wheels of Urizen & Luvah" that "perverse rolld ... back reversd" (FZ, 1,20:12–14; 313). This principle of reversal – of reversing one's perspective on the same image, the reversal I have called "the logic of error" – is all-pervasive in *Milton* and *Jerusalem*, where a tree can be either the Tree of Life or the Tree of Mystery, a city can be either Jerusalem or Babylon, looms and nets can be either death-dealing or life-affirming, and "generation" can be either death or the image of Regeneration (Eternity). *Jerusalem* "shows us two worlds," remarks Frye, "one infinite, the other indefinite, one our own home and the other that same home receding from us in a mirror" (384); the poem is built on a pattern of contrasts or reversals that are ultimately the single contrast of two perspectives: life versus death, Los versus the Spectre.[22]

By redefining life's conflict or dialectic as between opposite perspectives, then, Blake might seem to have rendered his myth even more indeterminate or obscure – for this turn to perspectivism dissolves the tangibility of the contraries and renders them seemingly more alike than different, mirror images whose true and false forms are as difficult to distinguish as is Los from his Spectre. And this perspectivism above all seems to equallize the poles in Blake's dialectic of life, for if they are both only perspectives, how can either claim to be higher than the other? How can Blake compel us to choose one rather than the other?

Indeed, he cannot compel us to choose, Blake might acknowledge; but neither does he wish to so compel us. And he can "compel us to take notice," as Kierkegaard asserts, even though how we choose is

not within his power. Besides, are these two perspectives with which
he confronts us really equal? They are indeed two opposite perspectives on life, two equally available options from which to choose. But
surely Blake has very definite ideas about which would be the right
choice; while he cannot compel us either to choose or to make the
right choice, he can *lead* us to see that one perspective is higher – that
there is or can be a determinate hierarchy of life over death. For
again, is there really any question that Los is life and the Spectre is
death, and that this contrast or difference is absolute? Can we read
Blake's Jerusalem as death and his Vala as life? His Tree of Life as
death and his Tree of Mystery as life? We can, of course – but only
by ignoring our authorial guide, whose assessment of their differences, despite his deliberately duplicitous structuring of their mirror
relationship, remains clear.

Blake's deliberate fostering of ambivalent perspectives may thus
indeed "obscure" his authorial intentions, his essentially dogmatic
purposes, rendering him as elusive as Kierkegaard's God. But that
obscurity need not obliterate those intentions – although it can, if
one refuses to try to penetrate those obscurities, to resolve the
ambivalence pervading the entirety of his work. Those apparently
equal and opposite perspectives do not in fact "make contrary
interpretation equally possible," as Kierkegaard states (or over-
states) his case; they do not cast Blake's poems "into antithetical sets
of terms whose significance can only be determined by a reader's
self-implicating decision."[23] For the Blakean and Kierkegaardian
reader has always an authorial guide for whom those perspectives of
life versus death are not equal and opposite but hierarchically
determined.

Further, this hypothetical authorial guide, 'Blake,' does not
demand an irrational leap of faith from his readers – a blind
conviction that their author is indeed "religious" (in its radical
Blakean sense) and not "aesthetic" – but like 'Kierkegaard,'
demands skepticism and the utmost exercise of reason in interpretation. Blake's obscurities, like Kierkegaard's, are deliberately
designed to challenge reason – to "rouze the faculties," especially
the faculty of reason, "to act." Since skeptical reason so loves to
master contradictions, Blake will puzzle it with ambivalent perspectives that demand reason's resolution. Only by issuing such a challenge can Blake lead reason to "defend a Lie," to consolidate itself as
error – by acknowledging that, try as it might, it cannot finally

resolve or master the "contradiction" that is life. Nor can it master the contradiction that is the author, for while it may weigh alternative hypotheses about whether he is "religious" or "aesthetic," rigorously evaluating the textual evidence for and against each hypothesis, it cannot prove with absolute rational certainty that the author is one and not the other. Reason may bring us very close indeed to grasping the "right" answer, the author's truth or life – but it cannot quite fully master or grasp it. For life, as something always just beyond purely rational demonstration, requires a final, critical, leap of faith.

This is why the Spectre, the consolidation of rational, skeptical error, is essential to Los's rebuilding of eternity. He need not be hostile to the truth but can be made its servant; while he threatens to dissolve the truth of life by his skeptical reasonings, through Los's mastery he is made the guide to that truth instead, a guide whose corrosive reasonings are not banished but centrally employed in the service of truth and life. He is "error" only when he claims to dissolve the final contradiction that is life; when he acknowledges that he is not the truth but the way, a partial perspective on life but not the whole, he is redeemed as its essential servant. This is why Blake's "indeterminate texts" are not indeterminate after all; for error is not sheer indeterminacy but has a consolidated shape, the shape of the Spectre, whose consolidation allows us to see him for what he is: a determinate guide for our interpretive way.

All of this suggests that Kierkegaard's invitation to his readers in *The Point of View* to weigh alternative hypotheses about his work as an author is neither a statement of extreme Nietzschean skepticism nor a theologically "magisterial fiat." Rather, it is simply another testing or calling of his readers to judgment – not an attempt to "demonstrate" conclusively his point of view, but to demonstrate merely the *method* by which his readers should try to "understand" it. And as always his call to judgment speaks to two different audiences: those who will seek "demonstration, blind to all the simple rules of life," as Blake puts it, and who, failing to find such rational certainty – such absolute proof that their author is not a radical perspectivist or ironist – will turn aside in skeptical disbelief; and those who will interpret reason's failure to provide certainty "differently." For Blake and Kierkegaard, reading should always demand the highest exercise of reason, the "burning fire of thought" and "thunders of intellect" in Blake's eternity. But it must also be the act of passion Kierkegaard calls faith, in which the reality of the author's otherness – an otherness we do not create, (however much it owes its existence to our constitution of it), the individual human voice of life – breaks through, in what finally resolves the question of irony. Such an appeal need not be a strictly theological or mystical one; Kierkegaard defines "a believer" as "one who is infinitely interested in another's reality" (*CUP*, 290), and surely there is a kind of hard-headed realism about this. After all, "If the Sun & Moon should doubt / Theyd immediately Go Out," as Blake caustically remarks ("Auguries of Innocence," 109–110; 492); if we are simply to go on reading, he and Kierkegaard might argue, we must at some point "believe" that this reading can enable us to encounter an other who is not ourselves. It is in this sense, finally, that the ultimate appeal is not simply to an orthodox God or a theological author but to life itself: the activity or life of interpretation. There may indeed be no demonstrable "grounding authenticity which can call a halt to the mazy indirections of language and motive;"[24] but what halts those mazy indirections is the "wirey bounding line" – or "limit" – of life.

The potentially radical ironizing powers of reason and aesthetics are for Blake and Kierkegaard finally not the truth but the way, and the negative way. But as error they are not so much wrong as *insufficient*, and this is the final critical point in understanding their relation to the truth of life and to the decidability of interpretation. As we should be able to see from the role of both reason and aesthetics as I have described it, it is a mistake to think that one must be either in a state of complete confusion or error, or in the opposite state of perfect clarity which is truth, with only a blind and irrational leap between the two. Even in the state of error one has a guide, that guide of course being reason or art themselves. And they do not mislead so much as *not lead one far enough*, a limitation which becomes an error only when we cannot see it for what it is – a part of life but not the whole, a means towards a further end. For Kierkegaard, as for Blake, error is neither mere formlessness nor the exact opposite of truth. It is the necessary guide – and guise – of their truth or being in time. As McGann reminds us, Golgonooza, Blake's city of art,

is not Jerusalem but the means towards it, and the function of his city of art is to reveal the whorish aspects of all creation. Golgonooza too must go to Eternal Death, for it stands not only as the promise of Jerusalem, but also as the last great temptation to retreat from vision. . . . We were never meant to live in it, or with it, but through it.[25]

Art and reason are our guides, but we should never be tempted to pursue them as ends in themselves, as the whole of life. In themselves they are spectral abstractions from life, not visionary forms dramatic.

This means, finally, that the limit of art and reason is not a logical contradiction or paradox but existence itself, which does not properly stand in any logical relation to reason. For Climacus, the paradox that reason cannot grasp has the character of existence: "it cannot be thought, and thus serves as a limit to thought."[26] This is the real otherness that reason is a part of but cannot grasp: not the otherness of logical paradox but the otherness of existence. Existence includes thought but cannot be thought, is Kierkegaard's basic assertion; existence cannot be made into a category of logic that can be assimilated into a logical system or an indeterminate dialectic. The real thrust of his polemic against idealist dialectics, and by extension perhaps poststructuralist thought, is that they abrogate the distinction between logic and life, thought and reality, in what can only be an abstract, God's-eye point of view. From the point of view of the existing individual logic is not life.

The parallels I have invoked here between romantic and poststructuralist thought are hotly disputed. Yet the basis of Kierkegaard's attack on the idealist hermeneutics of undecidability – that they abolish the principle of contradiction – is surely precisely what poststructuralism shares with those dialectics. (Indeed, poststructuralists might argue that the idealist dialectics did not go far enough towards abolishing that principle.)[27] If poststructuralism in some sense "reinscribes" contradiction as a purely "immanent" rather than ontological difference, this is surely what idealist dialectics did in "reinscribing" "Being" as an illusory appearance, a differential effect, within "Becoming." It is this reinscription of difference that for Kierkegaard negates life, in a spectral parody of true action and freedom. According to him, the dull and plodding Hegelian reader for whom "the inner is the outer" believes that all communication is direct – that words should simply be taken at face value. This is why he "understands" all communication so freely and readily as a conceptual object or "result," for he sees only a happy mediation of

language and meaning with no real struggle or contradiction
between the two. The romantic ironist seems rather more foxy and
alert, for he makes much of the irreconcilability of language and
meaning in the infinite play of an irony or contradiction that can
never be resolved in any stable presence or truth. For Kierkegaard,
what both kinds of readers share, however, is equal subjugation to
systematic theories of language, and as such they are equally victims
of necessity. The Hegelian reader assumes that truth or meaning is
always already mediated for him within language – that he need
make no leap beyond language to a truth towards which that
language merely points. Everything is always already interpreted
for him because language has already done his interpretation for
him. Yet he is therefore not free to misinterpret what he reads –
which leads us to realize (if we have not done so already) that he is
not free to interpret what he reads either. Curiously, he shares this
inability with the romantic ironist, who similarly can neither interpret nor misinterpret. Because the romantic ironist lives in the world
of infinite interpretive possibility (as opposed to the Hegelian's finite
world of interpretive "results"), he thinks that he therefore has
infinite freedom to interpret however he wants. Yet because he sees
language and meaning as "always not yet" interpreted in any
conclusive sense, he can neither interpret nor misinterpret. Despite
his illusory freedom and ceaseless activity, then, he is in fact just as
passive a reader as is the Hegelian. As we have seen before, both
kinds of readers are spectators, this time outside the game of interpretation.

The deconstructive reader would seem to be equally spectral and
outside the game, on Kierkegaard's terms, for like the romantic
ironist, he refuses to choose between apparently undecidable oppositions but instead stops short at this moment of *aporia*. This moment
is for him not a moment of choice but one that precludes choice or
illustrates the arbitrariness of choice; there is, he declares, no compulsion to go further. Like the Hegelian and Schlegelian reader, he
sees no compelling reason to convert both-and (equally for him a
neither/nor) into either/or – for any such "decisiveness," whether
exercised by author or reader, is arbitrary and can claim no privileged authority.

This deconstructive undecidability denies affinities with either
Hegelian or Schlegelian dialectic, but its affinities are what Kierkegaard perhaps indirectly exposes in his equation of the two. For

deconstruction's differences from Hegel are often argued on Sch-legelian grounds whose difference from Hegel Kierkegaard exposes as illusory. Derrida claims, for example, to suspend or "destroy" Hegelian both-and logic, defining *différance* as "precisely the limit, the interruption, the destruction of the Hegelian *relève* [*Aufhebung*] *wherever* it operates."[28] Yet does Derrida in fact simply by denying all real closure destroy both-and logic or merely like Schlegel re-enact it, not in the "positive unity" of Hegelian mediation, but in the "negative unity" of romantic irony? Romantic irony too claimed to be "unsystematic," unfinished process rather than finished "result," a process in which "the totalizing and teleological nega-tion of the negation is never realized."[29] But this supposed open-endedness is surely illusory, as Kierkegaard argues, merely an inver-sion of Hegel's positive unity into a negative one. In both dialectics (Hegel's and Schlegel's) contraries are equallized within some abso-lute that necessarily relativizes or negates them in a both-and pattern of logic; similarly, as "an absolutist without absolutes," Derrida can only relativize contraries within some kind of absolute, no matter how negative and in effect non-existent he tries to make it. Both deconstructive strategies of insisting on the irreducibility of contraries and of collapsing apparent opposites into each other – of asserting both the irreconcilability and identity of opposites – in themselves seem to enact an implicit recognition that they are governed by both-and logic.

If deconstruction denies affinities with Hegelian dialectic on the grounds that unlike mediation it denies any closure, it equally denies affinities with romantic irony on the grounds that the romantic ironist has a "nostalgia" for closure or for a lost presence. As Candace Lang puts it, romantic irony is a "despondent idealism," whereas "the truly postmodern work (of literature or of criticism) is anything but an impotent wordplay symptomatic of the 'sickly longing' of romanticism."[30] The romantic ironist longs for a lost *actuality*, whose loss deconstruction does not mourn but joyfully affirms. Yet this seems to overlook the extent to which Schlegel too defined romantic irony not as a negation but as an affirmation of life, a losing of oneself in its abundance or *Fülle*. More significantly, Lang does not analyze the underlying logic of romantic irony in relation to that of deconstruction. As M.H. Abrams has remarked, Derrida is "a logical prestidigitator who acknowledges and uses, as a logocentric 'effect,' the logic of noncontradiction, yet converts its either/or into a simultaneous neither/nor and both-and."[31] Again, this equallizing of oppositions which is both a creative "both-and" or plenitude of meanings and a destructive "neither/nor" or emptying out of meanings seems very like the romantic ironist's creative and destructive *Fülle*. And in the end, "You say 'I can either do this or do that, but whichever of the two I do is equally mad, *ergo* I do nothing at all,'" as Judge William tells the romantic ironist; life comes to a stop at the interpretive *aporia*.

Whatever the differences in attitude towards the abolition of the principle of contradiction, all three of these forms of dialectic do abolish it. And Kierkegaard's point is simply that to abolish it is to abolish the truth of life; for life, he insists, is contradiction and choice. Only by exercising the power of choice – in interpretation as in all things for Kierkegaard – does one act and therefore live. Not to choose is to succumb passively to a kind of spectral death-wish of interpretation; and as Kierkegaard says, whether his reader is able to master this death-wish "above all ... depends upon whether he *will* or no" (my emphasis). Granted, one can refuse to live, and refuse to interpret, but this is not so much a choice as a negation of choice. And Kierkegaard's point is that one should not be under any illusion that one is thereby either living or interpreting texts.

Choosing is of course in a sense what the romantic ironist and deconstructionist are always already doing, for revelling in the relative arbitrariness of all choices frees them to create and destroy readings at will. But Kierkegaard would insist that this is "creating" not "choosing," and on a critical, however precarious, distinction between the two. Deconstruction claims to evoke what Sylviane Agacinski calls a "nondialectizable negativity," an "alterity" that "ironically" escapes the abstract logical system of idealist dialectics;[32] it claims not only to expose the limits of reason as error, but to evoke something that escapes those limits. Kierkegaard's reply is that only an act of choice beyond the exposure of those limits can evoke and even grasp – without sublating, dialectizing, or ironizing – the otherness of existence. For him, the only way to preserve the integrity of otherness is through an act of exclusion or choice; attempts to be all-inclusive (as in Hegelian mediation and all dialectics of negation) dissolve the very otherness they claim to preserve. The true "other" is that which is excluded; but paradoxically, it is grasped in its otherness by this exclusion. Only an act of choice puts one in relation to that which is excluded as well as to that which is included; only an act of choice puts one in relation to life. To view life as undecidable is to remain trapped in the error of all the idealist systems – in their unmastered irony that abstracts from and negates life. It is to claim a God's-eye point of view that by virtue of its absolutism sees not an alterity but "nothing outside itself." From the point of view of the existing individual, the individual who acts and lives, "decisiveness is precisely the eternal protest against all fictions" (*CUP*, 203).

Blake and Kierkegaard want to insist that life is not art; life is not entirely willed or constructed but chosen, in some greatly attenuated sense a given. It has a Being or ground that is negatively realized through the interpretive act of choice or Becoming. This Being is attenuated to the point of disappearance, reconstituted on perspectival grounds; it is reduced to "the bound or outward circumference of energy." As such, it is precarious indeed, almost dissolved by the perspectival act of Becoming through which it is constituted. But their insistence on this precarious limit, this undemonstrable, unprovable, resistant qualitative otherness,[33] is what differentiates Blake and Kierkegaard not only from romanticism as that has come to be identified with idealist dialectics, but from the poststructuralist theories which romanticism has spawned.

Conclusion. *Los and the Spectre: master and slave in the labor of the negative*

Los compelld the invisible Spectre
To labours mighty, with vast strength, with his mighty chains,
In pulsations of time, & contentions of space, like Urns of
  Beulah
With great labour upon his anvils [;] & in his ladles the ore
He lifted, pouring it into the clay ground prepar'd with art;
Striving with Systems to deliver Individuals from those Systems
                                            Blake, *Jerusalem*

Doubts are always pernicious Especially when we Doubt our
Friends Christ is very decided on this Point. "He who is Not
with Me is Against Me" There is no Medium or Middle State
& if a Man is the Enemy of my Spiritual Life while he pretends
to be the friend of my Corporeal he is a real Enemy
                              Blake, Letter to Mr. Butts, April 15, 1803

While Socrates politely and indirectly took away an error from
the learner and gave him the truth, speculative philosophy
takes the truth away politely and indirectly, and presents the
learner with an error.
            Johannes Climacus, *Concluding Unscientific Postscript*

In his battle to master the Spectre, Blake's Los labors "negatively"
to cast off all spectral abstractions from life: to consolidate these
spectral abstractions as inaction, negation, irony, and error. But
beyond this corrosively negative exposure of error, Los labors to
actualize a living truth of action and life, a full and positive presence
of sorts which stands revealed beyond that negative exposure. This
presence is by definition virtually impossible to figure or symbolize
concretely, for to do so would be to impose a new consolidation of
error dogmatically tyrannizing over life. The closest Blake comes to
imaging this presence is the figure of Christ which appears in
Jerusalem; but this presence is also simply Los himself. Los is after all

174

the living individual "truth" which stands revealed once he masters or casts off his own spectral negation. It is remarkable the extent to which Blake succeeds in presenting Los as sheer activity, defined mostly by his incessant labor at the forge of life. Yet Los is also the embodiment of imagination or "Intellect," the living expression of an idea which attempts to combine true reason and true passion as the two living principles or true contraries of life. These true contraries of reason and will attain full symbolic presence in the characters of Socrates and Christ.

A. CHRIST AND SOCRATES: MASTERED IRONY AS THE PASSION OF REASON

Blake and Kierkegaard willfully and energetically refashion traditional Socratic and Christian principles (much as Blake refashions Milton) to figure forth their truth of life as a form of "passionate intellect." Kierkegaard's Christ and Socrates are "masters of irony" who master the potentially dissolving ironies of both reason and will, "converting" Schlegel's debased form of will and Hegel's debased form of reason into their true and living forms. Christ and Socrates lived exemplary lives of passionate intensity, according to Kierkegaard, because both lived according to the "paradox" or "difference" in which life consists, sustaining the extraordinary tension that is life. Understanding just how this is so consolidates our understanding of this difficult dialectic of life, for in Christ and Socrates it finds its culmination. They dramatize the essential perspectivism of the dialectic – its attempt to cast off or master the false forms of reason and will (the abstract perspective which negates their energy) for the true (the concrete, living perspective which revitalizes them). Beyond this, they lived the kind of life the dialectic advocates: through the paradox of "knowledge" and "ignorance" (Socrates) and the paradox of "God" and "man" (the incarnation of Christ), both lived the paradox or difference of life. The philosophic and religious rhetoric here should not obscure the fact that both lived according to the *same* paradox: the difference between either knowing one's life (through pure philosophy and reason) and creating one's life (through pure poetry, passion, or will), in the ideal tension between knowing and creating that constitutes the Blakean and Kierkegaardian choice.

As a philosopher, Socrates knew life through the exercise of reason. But according to Kierkegaard, he knew life in a way that corrects or redeems the way the Hegelian knows life, and hence corrects or redeems the claims of Hegelian reason. Further, Kierkegaard's Christianized Socrates knows life in a way that corrects and redeems not only Hegelian reason but reason itself, by bringing reason out of the realm of abstraction into the realm of life through the exercise of Christian will involved in the act of choice. Through these subtle permutations of a Christianized Socrates Kierkegaard tries to limit but not dispense with the claims of philosophy and reason to grasp life.

"Socrates was great for the fact that he 'distinguished between what he understood and what he did not understand,'" Vigilius Haufniensis quotes Hamann (epigraph to *CD*). Socrates lived according to the distinction between knowledge and ignorance, between what he could know and what he could not know. In other words, unlike Hegelian reason, which claims to know everything, to penetrate reality completely, Socratic reason knew its *limits*. Kierkegaard's Socrates knew better than to try to adopt the illusory, all-inclusive, omniscient perspective of Hegelian mediation; by acknowledging the limits of his reason he lived as an existing individual should and can only live: within his own partial, "exclusive" perspective.

Unlike Hegel, Socrates did not claim to know "the System" or the whole of life; but also unlike Hegel, Socrates thereby knew *himself* – again, a part of life but not the whole.[1] By relinquishing any attempt to know the whole of life, by living instead by the dictum "know thyself," Socrates "consolidated" his finite perspective, the only perspective available to the existing individual, and thereby paradoxically grasped the whole of life. For by living with full awareness of the distinction between "what he could understand and what he could not understand," Socrates lived according to the distinction or difference that for Kierkegaard constitutes life itself.

As commentators have noted, Kierkegaard's idea of Socrates undergoes substantial revision between the early *Concept of Irony* and the later pseudonymous works.[2] And this revision essentially takes the direction of "Christianizing" Socrates by investing him with the Christian element of will. In *The Concept of Irony*, Kierkegaard interprets the Socratic dictum "know thyself" as having no positive content; it simply means "separate yourself from 'the other,'" he claims (*CI*, 202). Knowing oneself is therefore only negatively defined as against a kind of limit or otherness. This early Socrates is "pure negativity" without content; despite Plato's attempt "poetically" to invest Socrates with such content, he claims, the "actual" Socrates "seizes the columns bearing the edifice of knowledge and plunges everything down into the nothingness of ignorance" (*CI*, 77). "Plato has attempted to fill in the mysterious nothingness which constituted the essential point in Socrates' life by giving him the Idea," Kierkegaard complains (*CI*, 181); but insofar as Socrates has the Idea he has it "not [as] a manifestation but [as] a limit" (*CI*, 158, 231). Hence there is "an absolute dissimilarity between Socrates and Christ," says Kierkegaard, for "the ironical personality [Socrates] is therefore merely the outline of a personality," whereas "in Christ dwelt the immediate fullness of the godhead" (*CI*, 242n.). Any similarity between Christ and Socrates "consists in dissimilarity, and ... there is only an analogy because there is an opposition" (*CI*, 52n.). The Socratic intellect or irony therefore serves only to empty actuality of its content by exposing it as error, yet not in the interests of a higher truth. This means that in *The Concept of Irony* at least, Socrates cannot himself embody the mastered irony which Kierkegaard elaborates at the very end of the work:

When irony has first been mastered it undertakes a movement directly opposed to that wherein it proclaimed its life as unmastered. Irony now limits, renders finite, defines, and thereby yields truth, actuality, and content. (*CI*, 338)

Socrates' knowledge, since at this point only a knowledge of ignorance, is therefore not yet mastered irony but is purely rational and corrosive; it exposes only its own limits, not any positive content beyond those limits.

Kierkegaard thus at this point invokes Socratic reason simply to diminish the claims of Hegelian reason (and hence of philosophy) to grasp the whole of life through reason – to "know" life. Socratic reason exposes this Hegelian claim as illusory; it criticizes in particular Hegelian reason's inability to explain or know the individual (in whom it has no interest). But Kierkegaard does not rest content with diminishing the claims of Hegelian reason; he must diminish the claims of Socratic reason as well, by destabilizing it with the element of Christian will. Socratic reason is too sure of itself, too grandiose in its claims that to know oneself is to grasp life; for despite

its attention to the individual, Socratic reason is still for Kierkegaard
too abstract and contemplative to grasp life itself, lacking the essential movement (and content) that is life. Although the Socratic
individual knows himself, Judge William declares,

> this knowledge is not mere contemplation (for with that the individual is
> determined by his necessity), it is a reflection upon himself which itself is an
> action; and therefore I have deliberately preferred to use the expression
> "choose oneself" instead of know oneself. So when the individual knows
> himself he is not through; on the contrary, this knowledge is in the highest
> degree fruitful, and from it proceeds the true individual. (*E/O*, II, 263)

True knowledge for the existing individual is action, involving the
exercise of the will. One does not know oneself until one exercises
one's freedom, the freedom of choice to "decide" who one is. It is
here that Kierkegaard Christianizes Socrates by adding the critical
element of the will. Only by choosing oneself does one actually grasp
life, and this is how Kierkegaard dispenses with reason's claims to
master life. Introducing the will means that despite knowing the
distinction between truth and error one can still refuse to embrace
that truth and thus reject the dictates of reason. It introduces a
critical uncertainty into reason's claims, because the will is free to
reject them.

   All of this serves to undermine the dogmatic authority of reason
and philosophy; but it also serves ideally to redeem or reconstitute
their authority as a more moderate and a more concrete, living one.
For the conversion of knowing to choosing converts knowledge out
of the static realm of thought into the dynamic realm of action and
life; and it combines will and reason in the act of choice: reason
presents the will with the distinction between the contraries, and the
will actualizes the distinction through the choice. Nonetheless, Kierkegaard's destabilization of reason and philosophy in the service of
life may succeed too well; for in his "conversion" (destabilization
and redemption) of Socrates the only true knowledge becomes
action, the act of will or faith by which one embraces life. As we have
seen throughout this study, it is after all only by choosing between
the contraries of life that one brings their distinction – and hence the
distinction between truth and error – into being, that one "knows"
the difference between them. However much Kierkegaard clings to
his claim that these distinctions exist somehow prior to the choice
and are merely actualized or realized by the choice, this prior
knowledge of the distinction is at best a dim apprehension of a

potential distinction, a precarious limit. This is why, again, skeptical readings can so easily collapse choosing into creating, and this moderated reason into pure will; for in his attempt to destabilize, moderate, and redeem the excessive claims of reason and philosophy, Kierkegaard elevates the agent of that moderation and redemption, the will, to a position dangerously close to being higher than that of philosophy and reason.

We can see, however, how he hoped that his converted Socrates might embody his ideal of an undogmatic but nonetheless still authoritative reason that would check or limit but not tyrannize over the will. Socrates exemplifies, in other words, the ideal of moderate reason and moderate will, the single ideal of "intellect," we have repeatedly seen throughout this study. And in so far as Blake is "Socratic," it appears to be in similar ways. Although Blake makes few references to Socrates, he clearly shares this paradoxically anti-philosophical and anti-theological Socratic Christianity. This is most evident in the fact that, like Kierkegaard, he sustains the two categories of (Socratic) error and (Christian) sin, as we have seen (chapter 4). But Blake also insists that poetic inspiration, passion, or faith is a kind of higher knowledge in his well-known objection to Plato's comment that the poet is a kind of inspired madman who does not know what he is saying: "Plato has made Socrates say that Poets & Prophets do not Know or Understand what they write or Utter this is a most Pernicious Falshood. If they do not pray is an inferior Kind to be calld Knowing Plato confutes himself" (VLJ, 70; 554). What Blake objects to here is not the idea that poets are inspired, but the idea that this passion is not true knowledge, is not objective in some sense, rather than being a merely subjective frenzy. He objects to the idea that poets in their passion do not *know* what they are doing but do it blindly without real vision. True poets are always passionate, Blake would agree; *and*, true poets always know what they are doing. True poets are clear-sighted visionaries who see the truth which inspires them.[3]

Blake also however makes some statements so entirely Socratic that they seem to exclude the element of will: "Truth can never be told so as to be understood, and not be believ'd," he declares (MHH, 10:69; 38); and in his Last Judgment, error is "Burnt up the Moment Men cease to behold it" (VLJ, 95; 565). The implications here seem most Socratic – that the moment one clearly sees or understands the truth, error simply vanishes. There seems to be no choice or leap involved, no option to disregard this truth that has been revealed. This seems to be a Last Judgment entirely of the reason, with little or no place for faith, will, or choice. Yet here again a closer look at Blake's contraries suggests otherwise. Although error is burned up, the distinction between the contraries continues even on the day of judgment. This day (remembering that this is not necessarily a strictly historical day of judgment, but the judgment that occurs each time one differentiates truth from error) ranges the true contraries of life against each other: in William Blake's Day of Judgment, "Bacon & Newton & Locke" stand over against "Milton & Shakespear & Chaucer" (J, IV, 98:9; 257). And it is crucial to remember that one casts off error *by* choosing between the contraries: the intellectual distinction between truth and error, while logically prior to the leap of faith, is virtually simultaneous with it. One has not *chosen* between truth and error, despite the fact that one has *seen* their distinction intellectually, *until* one has chosen between the contraries, ideally making intellect and will, knowledge and faith, virtually one.

Blake also Socratizes his Christianity – insisting on the role of intellect in matters of faith or passion – by Socratizing his vision of Christ. Blake's Christ, throughout all the changes in his myth, engages in the intellectual activity of exposing error. Again, he is not a "yea nay Creeping Jesus," the "Divinity of Yes & No too," but a Christ who comes to separate the sheep from the goats. "Jesus Christ did not wish to unite but to seperate them [the Two Classes of Men]," declares Blake, "as in the Parable of sheep & goats! & he says I came not to send Peace but a Sword" (MHH, 17; 40). And while this is indeed the early, satirical Blake, this same definition of Christ's activity as fundamentally divisive persists in Blake's later thought as well, when he declares "Jesus does not treat [all alike] because he makes a Wide Distinction between the Sheep & the Goats consequently he is Not Charitable" (Miscellaneous Prose, 73; 695). Blake marks the opening plates of *Jerusalem* "sheep" and "goats" in opposite margins (J, 1, 3; 145); and in *A Vision of the Last Judgment* he similarly declares "Christ comes as he came at first to deliver those who were bound under the Knave not to deliver the Knave He Comes to Deliver Man the Accused ... & not Satan the Accuser" (VLJ, 86; 564). Blake's ideal is a kind of "passionate intellect" combining will and intellect, Christ and Socrates; as he stoutly declares in *A Vision of the Last Judgment*,

Men are admitted into Heaven not because they have curbed & governd their Passions or have No Passions but because they have Cultivated their Understandings. The Treasures of Heaven are not Negations of Passion but Realities of Intellect from which All the Passions Emanate Uncurbed in their Eternal Glory ... Those who are cast out Are All Those who having no Passions of their own because No Intellect. Have spent their lives in Curbing & Governing other Peoples by the Various arts of Poverty & Cruelty of all kinds (VLJ, 97; 564)

Beyond these rather scattered instances of a Socratized Christianity in Blake's work, however, is the more profound idea of the incarnation that for both Blake and Kierkegaard dramatizes the central paradox and "difficulty" of life. If our Socratically philosophical (yet anti-philosophical) Kierkegaard has more to say about how Socrates masters the potentially dissolving irony of reason, our Christianly theological (yet anti-theological) Blake can tell us more about how Christ masters the dissolving irony of will or passion. Kierkegaard does however also centrally invoke the paradox of the incarnation, if not the figure of Christ himself, and it is in this paradox that his affinities with Blake's Christianity may come to the fore.

Again, the religious language of the incarnation-as-paradox should not blind us to the fact that it is the living paradox of will and reason and the paradox of two perspectives on life: "God's" (the all-inclusive, abstract, omniscient perspective of both-and) and "man's" (the exclusive, concrete, partial perspective of either/or). That Blake and Kierkegaard should have parallel ideas about the incarnation-as-paradox may seem unlikely; and indeed, we can hardly expect Blake to have worked through the complexities of the Kierkegaardian paradox. But for both the incarnation is a *radical* paradox, taken to its absolute extreme, and in this basic radicalism may lie their affinity. The potent paradoxicality of the Blakean incarnation has often been noted, for Blake radicalizes the Christian paradox to its extreme by conflating incarnation, crucifixion, and Last Judgment in a moment of choice that seems rather Kierkegaardian, as we shall see.

For Blake, the incarnation *is* the "consolidation of error," a conflation of the incarnation with the crucifixion and in turn with the Last Judgment, the moment of Blakean choice or differentiation. This extraordinarily potent paradox seems very like what Kierkegaard means by the incarnation, for Johannes Climacus remarks that it is "faith's crucifixion of the understanding" (*CUP*, 501). That is, the incarnation symbolically crucifies reason on the cross of faith – or, we might say here, on the cross of the will. What he means on its most obvious level is that the paradox that God becomes man, or that the eternal enters time, or that Being enters Becoming – is an "affront" that reason cannot possibly grasp. It cannot understand how the eternal could at one and the same time be the temporal, how God could be man – it baulks at the incomprehensibility of this claim, and thus is thrown back upon or forced to confront its own limits. Paradoxically, reason thus contributes to its own demise or crucifixion, and in doing so it redeems itself. Its error is to think that it can grasp the whole of life; when it is forced to acknowledge its limits – that it inevitably falls short of the whole of life – it is crucified but also redeemed. Further, it is redeemed by making itself the servant of this higher truth of life that escapes it. Reason serves this truth because it is itself the agent of its own revelation as error. It is reason's passion to master paradoxes or apparent contradictions, says Kierkegaard – to seek to resolve or dissolve them. It is "the passion of reason" to discover its own limits and in a sense to crucify itself – to strive at mastering contradictions until it confronts the one paradox or difference that it cannot master: the difference that for Kierkegaard is life itself. But without reason's passion – its striving to "know" itself through discovering its own limits – one could not grasp the truth of life that stands revealed beyond their sharp differentiation.

This paradox seems very like Blake's dramatization of the incarnation-as-crucifixion in the figure of Orc–Luvah, for this act is also the consolidation of reason as error on the Tree of Mystery. In Blake's incarnation–crucifixion, reason declares itself in its true shape, the shape of error and the body (hence the conflation with incarnation). That is, skeptical reason tries to claim that life can be reduced to or grasped by reason, that life is only the body or purely material existence. This skeptical reason which tries to grasp life by reducing it to these things must be forced to consolidate itself and thus be crucified in what is at once incarnation (consolidation of error), crucifixion, and last judgment (rejection of that error). Only through this complex act can the true "spiritual body" or Truth (symbolically, Jesus) stand revealed, as what error and reason are *not*. As Los relates to Enitharmon in *The Four Zoas*,

the Lamb of God Descended thro Jerusalems gates
To put off Mystery time after time & as a Man
Is born on Earth so was he born of Fair Jerusalem
In mysterys woven mantle & in the Robes of Luvah

He stood in fair Jerusalem to awake up into Eden
The fallen Man but first to Give his vegetated body
To be cut off & separated that the Spiritual body may be Reveald.

(FZ, VIII, 104:32–8; 378)

For both Blake and Kierkegaard the paradox of the incarnation is that it reveals the antithesis of error (reason, the body) and truth: it is simultaneously the consolidation or revelation of error and of the truth that is beyond it, the simultaneous revelation of the Anti-Christ and Christ in their moment of sharpest opposition. As the apotheosis of reason – the revelation of its limits – it is for Blake and Kierkegaard clearly the same paradox as that between Socratic knowledge and ignorance. Both the Socratic and Christian paradoxes reveal the limits of reason or knowledge, and define true knowledge as ignorance – that is, as a leap of faith beyond the limits of finite reason. Socratic reason is in other words an analogy for Christian faith: both ignorance and faith transcend the limits of reason, and this is why the two paradoxes are one and the same.

All of this suggests that Blake and Kierkegaard are simply irrationalists whose absolute is a mystery transcending reason. If so, then the difference between their incarnation as radical paradox and Hegel's incarnation as the mediation of God and man is easily explained. If finite reason cannot "know" the nature of God or the nature of man, as Blake and Kierkegaard seem to claim, then it cannot mediate them: for to reconcile A (God) and Not-A (man) as Hegel does presupposes that reason can know the nature of A, that it can know the nature of Not-A, and that it can therefore resolve the paradox or contradiction as a merely apparent one.[4] Yet it is precisely Kierkegaard's claim that such knowledge is simply unavailable to the existing individual, who cannot adopt this God's-eye Hegelian perspective on the paradox. This means that it is not even strictly correct to call the Kierkegaardian paradox a paradox; Kierkegaard's paradox is simply "that which cannot be thought," that which reason cannot grasp: existence or life, which baulks or "affronts" reason and therefore serves as its limit.[5]

At the same time, the fact that reason cannot wholly grasp the "paradox" of life does not mean that reason plays no role, as we have repeatedly seen. "Calling the paradox the boundary of reason by no means implies that it is illegitimate for reason to *attempt* to understand it," as C. Stephen Evans remarks; "It is precisely by attempting to understand the paradox that reason can discover that it is truly the paradox, not a merely relative paradox" (222). Or as G. Schufreider puts it, "the positing of the paradox does not occur through the dismissal of reason, but instead presupposes its rigorous application. . . . Only the relentless employment of reason can guarantee that its breakdown is genuine, that it occurs in the face of the incomprehensible, of that which cannot be understood, not in the face of that which we have simply not bothered to understand."[6] In this interpretation, faith is not outside but always subject to rigorous rational scrutiny. Further, faith is in a sense the passion of reason, the result of reason's passionate consolidation of its own limits in an attempt to discover and transcend them, to discover that which cannot be thought – existence, itself the "paradox" of life. This insistence on the critical – if subservient – role of reason is why Blake vehemently denounces all religions of "mystery," which he regards as religions of Reason. Reason *creates* religions of mystery and superstition, according to Blake, precisely by its claim that faith is irrational, is not a kind of "knowledge" but something totally irrational (again, his objection to Plato's characterization of the poets). It is why in Blake's myth Reason is crucified on the Tree of Mystery (whose "combats" are those of "good and evil"), which Blake opposes to the Tree of Life (whose combats are those of truth and error).

In their idea of the incarnation we see the culmination or apotheosis of Blake's and Kierkegaard's dialectic of truth and error, in what seems an extraordinarily potent paradox. For this incarnation–crucifixion is not only reason's passion as it crucifies itself on the cross of faith, it is faith's – or passion's passion too. And this dynamic strife of a higher reason and a higher passion – of Socratic intellect and Christian will – as the true Contraries is for Blake and Kierkegaard what constitutes life.

This apotheosis of the dialectic reveals most clearly however its deeply problematic nature and utter precariousness. On the one hand, the paradox suggests that Blake's and Kierkegaard's "God" is simply a mystery transcending reason, and that their "theology" is therefore a traditionally Augustinian one. Yet this is not only complicated by Blake's vigorous denunciation of such religions of mystery, it is complicated and radicalized by Blake's and Kierkegaard's insistence that the idea of *choice* is the key to their antitheological theology of the paradox. It is the choice, after all, which decidedly separates (as opposed to mediating) the poles of the paradox that is life, and which radicalizes the apparent Augustinianism of their paradox. Reason cannot grasp their truth of life not because life is a mystery transcending reason, but because life is a choice transcending reason. For Blake and Kierkegaard, the moment of choice is what brings the paradox into existence, and this is why reason can never capture or resolve it. Reason reasons but it cannot choose; choosing requires the will. Reason is thus forever impotent in the face of life – "knowing / And seeing life, yet living not," as the Spectre wails to Los (J, 1, 10:56–7; 154) – for without choice there is no life.

What this seems to mean, however, is that the dialectic must inevitably founder into one of pure passion or will. For there is apparently no "absolute paradox" for reason to attempt to master *until* the choice brings that paradox into being. The exercise of reason that supposedly labors to distinguish truth from error seems to follow rather than guide the choice. Kierkegaard and Blake seem to be caught in a logical impasse. They want to claim that the contraries of life are chosen not created – that reason presents the will with the contraries which the will subsequently actualizes or realizes through the choice. But at the same time, as we have repeatedly seen, they claim that the distinction between the contraries does not really exist until the act of choice brings it into being, which seems to mean that the contraries are "created" by the will after all.

But this is where Kierkegaard makes the appeal upon which his definition of the paradox finally rests, for he simply insists that the otherness constituting the paradox is not a creation of the will but that it is a *given*. If "life is a given, but also a task" – the task of becoming oneself, as Kierkegaard says – we should remember conversely that if "life is a task it is also a given" – the Being that realizes itself in the task of Becoming. Life in some sense presents itself to the reason and to the will as something other that they cannot grasp even before the will actualizes that otherness. Life has an irreducible otherness or Being that cannot be mediated by or dissolved into either the reason or the will, despite the fact that both are the necessary agents of its appropriation. Will, like finite reason, bumps up against this inevitable limit, "the bound or outward circumference of energy." This assertion of the givenness of Being as an empty limit that at once motivates and curbs or "masters" the passions of reason and of will is all that stands between Kierkegaard's – and Blake's – dialectic of Being and the idealist dialectics of Becoming, their precarious yet intractable "difference" of life.

B. LOS AND THE SPECTRE

The dialectic of either/or rests finally on the qualitative disjunction between two perspectives – those of God and man, or the eternal and the temporal. But as we have seen, this claim is a precarious one, compromised by the fact that this difference is apparently not an absolute one, but one merely of perspectives. As the spectral inversion of the dialectic of either/or, the mediated contraries of both-and logic bear the same close resemblance to it that the Spectre bears to Los, a resemblance that makes their differentiation very difficult. Like Hegel, Blake and Kierkegaard see the human condition as one of alienation or estrangement from eternity or true spiritual values; like Hegel, they share an ideal of unity which brings these values into human life. Like Hegel, Blake and Kierkegaard want to emphasize life or this world, not some otherworldly realm, as the locus of meaning or value. Yet, according to their dialectic of choice, Hegel's characterization of this ideal is deeply erroneous, primarily because it sees alienation as a merely relative difference: man is only quantitatively removed from truth or the eternal. From their perspective, this is on the one hand not true alienation but false alienation; it is in fact *mediation*, the exact opposite of alienation. The eternal has supposedly already been mediated, in both-and logic, so that the alienation it speaks of is merely illusory. On the other hand, according to Blake and Kierkegaard this mediation is itself merely illusory, and in fact signals the profoundest possible alienation from eternity. For to assume that the eternal has always already been mediated within existence is to be at the furthest possible remove from actually grasping the eternal. In sum, the dialectic of choice or existence represents man's condition in a way at once identical yet opposite to "mediation's" characterization of it: Blake and Kierkegaard agree that man's condition is one of alienation from eternity; but they *reverse* mediation's definition of alienation by saying that man is alienated from, *because he thinks he is mediated with*, eternity. Far from unifying the individual with eternity or with life, mediation is actually what alienates him from it, precisely by giving him a false sense of security, an illusory confidence that he has already grasped it. Lulled into this false security by mediation, he absentmindedly dreams his life away, in the sleep of Blake's Albion: why struggle for what is already in his grasp? What mediation calls "existence," then, is according to Blake and Kierkegaard only a ghostly mockery of it, a dream of reason disturbed, deep down, by the nightmare of warring zoas struggling for life. "Is this to be A God far rather would I be a Man," exclaims Tharmas to the Spectre; "Death choose or life thou strugglest in my waters, now choose life" (FZ, IV, 51: 29, 52:2; 334–5).

This oddly identical yet inverse relationship of the two dialectics is what makes them appear to move in opposite directions: both-and logic seems to move from a state of alienation or warring contraries to one of mediation or unity of the contraries; the dialectic of either/or apparently moves from a state of mediation to one of increasing differentiation of the contraries and finally to the casting-off of one of them. Yet this latter move is in fact from a state of illusory mediation which is in truth profoundest alienation to a state of radical differentiation which is in truth profoundest unity.

Because both dialectics are simply perspectives on life, however, this perspectivism may finally collapse the logic of either/or into that of both-and. Each perspective claims to grasp the whole of life: both-and logic claims that its perspective encompasses the whole of life, and that the differentiations or crises of either/or are subsumed within this higher both-and unity. But either/or logic claims that *its* perspective is the true whole of life, and that both-and logic is merely a partial view of life, the limited view of finite reason subsumed within its higher view of life. Yet does the either/or dialectic in fact make this claim? The greatest irony – or paradox, perhaps – is that it claims to grasp the whole of life only by insisting on the partial nature of its perspective. For the either/or dialectic is finally partial because it is the perspective of the existing individual, who cannot attain the perspective beyond all perspectives of both-and logic. There may be just two perspectives on life, which as perspectives are in some sense then merely equal. But Blake and Kierkegaard would argue I think that one perspective is higher than the other, and that this perspective is in the end not a perspective at all, because it is absolute. Ironically, this may be the perspective of both-and logic, which means that both-and logic may well be the whole vision of life and not merely a partial one. "Reality itself is a system – for God," Climacus readily concedes; "but it cannot be a system for any existing spirit" (*CUP*, 107). The subtlety of this dialectic of warring perspectives is that the "exclusive" perspective may be in an absolute sense the lower one because it is man's as an existing individual, while the "inclusive" perspective may be in an absolute sense the higher one. But the crucial point is that the exclusive perspective is the highest one for the existing individual, who cannot and should not try to adopt a God's-eye perspective (which Blake refers to as "Four-fold Vision"); and the inclusive perspective is the lowest one for the existing individual because it is a delusion of finite reason. This is the real difference, the real dualism, that Blake and Kierkegaard might argue stabilizes their irony or fluctuation of apparently equal perspectives into the hierarchy of mastered irony.

The logic of this claim seems to me to be inescapable: if indeed Kierkegaard in particular believes that there is a higher perspective that is not a perspective – however unavailable he declares it to be to the existing individual – then this dialectic of apparently equal perspectives resolves itself into a reconstituted hierarchy that does not negate the principle of contradiction but rather rescues it from its dissolution and reaffirms it. Yet we must acknowledge, I think, that the uncertainty here is very great indeed, for Kierkegaard cannot assert that he believes there is such a perspective or God without contradicting his entire philosophy. Nor can we "prove" with absolute rational certainty that Kierkegaard (and Blake) do or do not "believe" in the reality of such a God's-eye point of view that is not a point of view. Furthermore, the thrust of the either/or dialectic is such that, with the emphasis so entirely on the individual's perspective in existence, on the status not of Being (God) but of Being-in-time (Christ), it becomes very easy indeed to dispense with the reconstituted Being, the higher reason or Intellect that supposedly stabilizes the dialectic. Blake and Kierkegaard may insist, as I have argued, on the presence of a qualitative otherness "behind" existence: on a Being that does not dissolve into Becoming; on an otherness that finite reason cannot grasp; on a reality that simply cannot be "thought;" on a higher reason that cannot be dissolved by the will but rather serves as its limit. But again, we must remember that Blake and Kierkegaard reintroduce Being for the sake of Becoming; they reintroduce reason for the sake of the will. Without faith in "the unconditional" we will not strive, is their claim, and we will not act or live. Yet one might ask whether this sense of the unconditional may not degenerate into an ethical fiction: in order to act and to live we must proceed "as if" there is a God, a Being, an Author – for only such a desire for the unconditional, for something beyond what finite reason can grasp, will propel us out of our aesthetical–metaphysical narcissism into the struggle that is life.[7] Blake and Kierkegaard would I think deny that their Being so essential to realizing and stabilizing the Being-in-time is merely a necessary fiction; yet the God or qualitative otherness in their thought is undeniably attenuated almost to the point of disappearance. He is, as Kierkegaard said of Socrates, "not a manifestation but a limit" – a curiously empty God almost entirely displaced by the Being-in-time that is Christ. After all, says Climacus, "only so much of eternity is present as to be a restraining influence in the passionate decision" (*CUP*, 272). Their insistence on a qualitative otherness that cannot be relativized or mediated, their emphasis on the Being in Being-in-time, nonetheless reverses itself into an undeniable displacement: by being placed at the very heart of their reconstitutive enterprise, Blake's and Kierkegaard's Being or God is paradoxically displaced to the bound or outward circumference of the energy which is life; he is "eccentric," placed at its very limits, himself a kind of spectre or ghostly shadow of his former self. It is in this respect that Blake and Kierkegaard are "in between Kant and Hegel yet closer to Kant," as I have stated; for the closest analogy to their vestigial Being outside or beyond their Being-in-time may well be the noumenon or *Ding-an-sich* of Kantian philosophy. It too is simply "that which cannot be *thought*," an empty limit; and it too is placed so radically beyond the limit of certain kinds of human experience that it becomes all too easily dispensable to those who follow.

Kant may indeed have opened up the highway to idealism by insisting upon the otherness of his noumenon, an otherness making it dispensable to the idealists following in his wake. But he was not himself an idealist, that is, one who would say we create rather than merely constitute reality – that thought *is* reality, the qualitative difference between them abrogated – and his refusal to abolish this noumenon, however problematic, testifies to this. Similarly, Blake and Kierkegaard may have opened up the highway to existentialism (understood that is as a philosophy of existence without transcendence in which we entirely *create* our values) and to nihilism, but they were themselves neither existentialists nor nihilists. And their insistence on the intractability of "the other" was not merely a naively essentialist, theological, utopian, or quixotic attempt to prevent the collapse of value distinctions attending the increasing secularization of the romantic age, but a hard-headed insistence that logic *is not* reality or life.

In the ambiguous yet decisive relationship between the dialectics of either/or and both-and lies the key to Blake's and Kierkegaard's "eccentricity" in most respects: their confusing logic (or illogic) which does more than simply invert or reverse ideas in straightforward ironic fashion; their simultaneous indeterminacy, ambiguity, or relativizing of distinctions, and determinacy, decisiveness, or absolutizing of distinctions; their systematic yet puzzlingly antisystematic (and even asystematic) quality of thought; their radical perspectivism yet claim for a precarious limit to that perspectivism; their philosophical conservatism which conserves identity at the same time that it revolutionizes it into complete otherness. It may also be the key to understanding their rather eccentric relationship to romanticism as a literary movement and to the literary theories that romanticism has spawned.

The issue of romantic doubt has come increasingly to the fore in recent years, in a general attempt to differentiate it from the radical skepticism of postmodernism. (This began as an attempt not perhaps to repudiate so much as to complement M. H. Abrams's definition of romanticism in *Natural Supernaturalism*, a definition usually held to be too "optimistic" in its vision of an achieved romantic wholeness or unity of life.)[8] That Blake and Coleridge suffered severe religious doubts is plain to see in their poetry; that Wordsworth experienced a crisis of doubt in part at least religious he tells us in *The Prelude*; and that the second generation of major English romantics (Byron, Shelley, and Keats) were profoundly skeptical (a different kind of doubt, it would seem) has been widely recognized and brought to our attention. All of this supposedly calls into question the achieved romantic unity of life for a vision that may instead be profoundly fragmented and incomplete, the pervasive melancholy and disintegration of the self dissolved by philosophical and religious doubt. Coleridge and Wordsworth "retreat" from this fragmentation into orthodox religion; Byron overcomes the melancholy his skepticism brings him by celebrating it in the playfulness of romantic irony; Shelley alternates between a visionary idealism and a thoroughly Kantian skepticism; Keats gluts his sorrow in the morning rose, succumbing perhaps, like Wordsworth in Blake's opinion at least, to the "natural man" whose heart's desire is death.

What makes Blake "eccentric" is his fierce resistance to all of these alternatives. In the face of romantic doubt – a doubt not merely about the truths of orthodox religion, but about its supposed alternative, the potentially self-destructive nature of the romantic ideal of life – he will not retreat into orthodox religion; nor will he become the Idiot Questioner, always questioning and never answering. Nor will he indulge in the playful (albeit often melancholy) enthusiasm yet skepticism of the romantic ironist and aesthete; nor will he settle for a "happy synthesis" which is not true to his turbulent – and often corrosively skeptical – experience of life. T. S. Eliot once remarked upon Blake's "peculiar honesty, which, in a world too frightened to be honest, is peculiarly terrifying,"[9] and it is this grim and determined honesty which keeps Blake along a particularly rocky path, the "perilous paths" instead of "the paths of ease" (MHH).

It is also Blake's will which differentiates him from his fellow romantics, for only Byron among the English romantics has anything approaching the strength and intensity of Blake's will to life. Yet Blake's will is not a Byronic (or Shelleyan) Prometheanism – nor is it a Nietzschean will-to-power – simply because the annihilation of just such forms of "selfhood" is for him so critical a preliminary to the embrace of life. As Los exclaims to the Spectre, "I act not for myself: for Albions sake / I now am what I am." Again, the spectre to be mastered is the selfhood of pure will or of pure reason – a totalizing will-to-power threatening to negate all that Blake calls life. Blake's insistence on a bound or outward circumference of energy as a limit on the will is clearly meant to combat precisely this kind of fully emancipated and potentially annihilating Will.[10] Similarly, his emphasis on the "partiality" or perspectivism of the existing individual's stance in life – on his task in life as one of exclusion rather than inclusion, a consolidation of one's partial vision in an acknowledgement of its finite nature – also resists the totalizing impulse to leap to a God's-eye perspective without the limits that existence itself places on such a leap.

In these ways, then, Blake refuses to endorse an absolutist Will in either its rationalist or its irrationalist extremes. Yet Blake wills fiercely and consistently to overcome all passivity, the death-wish of the spirit, the feeling of necessity that so powerfully negates life. We cannot help but think of the difference from Coleridge here – for although we should perhaps avoid taking Coleridge's low self-evaluations at face value, clearly by his own admission a weak will was his greatest problem, threatening to doom him to a life of utter passivity and indolence. Like Rousseau, Coleridge confesses that as soon as anything becomes a duty he cannot bring himself to do it; and this offers a profound insight into the truth of Blake's realization that the feeling of necessity is the centrally romantic manifestation of a kind of death-wish of the spirit.[11] As Blake seems to see so clearly, it is precisely this feeling that life is ruled by necessity or duty which must be mastered if one is to act and to live – and it is just this mastery that Coleridge thought himself unable to achieve or will.

Coleridge was by no means an aesthete, yet his indolence and melancholy were also defining characteristics of the romantic ironist and aesthete, as we have briefly seen in chapter 3. Coleridge was in other words not the only romantic to succumb to the chains of necessity Blake so abhorred; but at least, Blake might claim, Coleridge knew he was not free, and in this knowledge therefore may have had some chance of redemption. From the Kierkegaardian and Blakean perspective, the problem with the romantic ironist is that he lives in a dream of his own freedom, ceaselessly striving, to be sure, but never bringing that striving to any completion or birth, the birth of life and actuality. His potentially redemptive melancholy, the symptom of his soul's disease, becomes not just his pain but his pleasure in an autoerotic cycle. His labors are fruitless ones, doomed to a cycle of infinite becoming.

Blake's Los absolutely rebels against this tyranny of becoming, this Coleridgean spectre of unfulfilled life-in-death. He will not be ruled by the Will, either in its masterful yet ultimately tyrannical Promethean form, or in its weaker, aestheticized, romantic ironic form. He will not, conversely, be ruled by an abstract Reason, equally annihilating as "fictions" the minute discriminations of life in its path. Instead, as we have seen, he labors to master those extremes by forcing them to acknowledge the "error" of their essentially totalitarian impulse, their claim to encompass the whole of life.

This labor of the negative, Los's consolidation of error by hammering it into shape upon his anvil, is thus very different from the labor of the negative in the idealist dialectics of becoming. For both-and logic, master becomes slave and slave becomes master in an eternally equallizing dialectic of necessity which relentlessly forces that illusory change or becoming upon them. In either/or, by contrast, master and slave attempt to escape the abstract tyranny of necessity that dooms them to their static cycle of equal slavery and negation. They try to escape through Los's exercise of the power of exclusion – in other words, through his exercise of the power of choice and hence of action, a power which decisively emphasizes the temporality, finitude, partiality, and "exclusiveness" of our perspective as existing individuals. Yet this power of choice and exclusion is ideally thereby inclusive after all, bringing into existence the qualitative difference between the temporal and eternal which is life.[12]

The spectre is therefore not enslaved but liberated by Los, for by being forced to declare himself in his true shape he thus redeems himself and his place in the final vision of life. Yet this voluntarism or willful power of choice in Blake's Los, the exercise of the action and the freedom that is life, is precisely what is denied by skeptics as an impossibility. To those who assert absolutely that there is no such freedom of choice, that choice is the great illusion or error, Blake and Kierkegaard would have a very caustic reply. Some abstract perspective beyond all perspectives may try to claim that we have no power of choice, that all is necessity, that all is the system. But they would ask whether life always and inevitably tells us this or whether our everyday experience of life tells us that we can and do experience some considerable power of choice. For them, life forces us to choose and to act, and thus "coerces us into freedom," (as Mackey said of Kierkegaard's rhetoric). To speculate on some higher abstract perspective from which we are not free "is not merely useless but unintelligible." Again, they might acknowledge that we can adopt such a perspective – however illusory – but they would insist that the question becomes which choice is better if we are to act and to live. Their faith in or appeal to life as a reliable guide is admittedly a precarious one; their faith is that life will not only compel the existing individual to choose, but will guide him to the right choice (for no man can sin "unknowingly," as we have seen).

Like the Daughters of Albion, Los "labour[s] for life & love, regardless of any one." Yet if indeed he so masters necessity as Blake claims, we might ask whether he does not thereby abrogate the so-called "reality principle" altogether. This is a charge frequently levelled at Blake as at Kierkegaard – that their perspectivism, their claim that a change of perspective changes reality in some sense absolutely – thus effectively banishes a recalcitrant reality, a true otherness, altogether.[13] But I have argued here throughout that precisely the opposite is the case: that their emphasis on the consolidation of a temporal, finite reality in opposition to thought, their insistence that life or existence as the irreducible paradox of matter and spirit cannot be entirely thought or mentally created, is an attempt to be true to the difficulty of life, our experience of reality as somehow intractable and as very difficult to change. This leads in turn, however, to the opposite charge that if Blake and Kierkegaard assert that we can only change perspectives and not reality (including the reality of political tyrannies) itself, then they are passive defenders of the *status quo*, for whom no actual change is possible. This charge may indeed carry some force: for if the solution to the "tyranny" of marriage bonds, for example, is not to break those bonds but to find a way of experiencing them as free – of living "in yet not of" them, altering the spirit but not the letter of the law – then the potential for real political change seems small. Yet again Blake and Kierkegaard might reply that only by first mastering those chains of necessity in some mental way can one hope to begin to step outside those laws as the necessary preliminary to actual change. We also need to remember that their change of perspective can and does have some real effects on reality itself; again, their ideal is very much one in this world, not some purely private or mystical one. To say that either they must change reality absolutely or they do not change it at all is to misunderstand the paradoxical moderation of their either/or, which rejects just this extremism of alternatives.

To argue for Blake's "realism" – or rather, for his peculiar version of skeptical idealism – may well be heretical in Blake studies, for we are all accustomed to the visionary Blake for whom the only reality is a purely mental or imaginative one. But I am suggesting here, again, that such a point of view is not incorrect but rather only partially right; and further, that such a point of view results from misreading – or not reading carefully enough – Blake's doctrine of the consolidation of error and hence misunderstanding the dynamic of his truth-error dialectic. There is a strong strain of almost Humean skepticism in Blake – as some commentators indeed have noted – a strain that has been remarked in Kierkegaard as well.[14] And it is significant that such Humean skepticism leads almost invariably to the profound melancholy over one's abstraction or alienation from life which Blake and Kierkegaard attack as the central sickness of the romantic self.

M. H. Abrams has recounted the consequences of that melancholy for Hume, consequences that would seem to bear out not only Blake's and Kierkegaard's diagnosis of the sickness, but to some extent the medicine that they propose for its cure. "Having reached his skeptical conclusions," Abrams tells us, "Hume finds himself ... in a condition of 'melancholy' and 'despair,' 'affrighted and confounded with that forlorn solitude in which I am plac'd in my philosophy:'"

From this dire condition he finds himself rescued not by further reasoning, but by the peremptory intrusion of a life-force – 'an absolute and uncontrollable necessity' that he calls 'nature.' 'Nature herself ... cures me of this philosophical melancholy and delirium. ... I dine, I play a game of back-gammon, I converse, and am merry with friends; and when after three or four hours' amusement, I wou'd return to these speculations, they appear so cold, and strain'd, and ridiculous, that I cannot find in my heart to enter into them any farther.' Hume finds that he cannot *live* in accordance with his skeptical philosophy ...[15]

"As a consequence," Abrams concludes, "Hume finds himself living (and recommends that others should also live) a double life: the life of human society, and the life of reason that disintegrates all the beliefs on which social life is founded into fictions and illusions." Blake and Kierkegaard similarly lead such a double life, yet theirs is a double life with a difference, again, the difference of mastered irony. For while Hume, by Abrams's account at least, lives a life in which both strains – the skeptical and the affirmative – are sustained in the equal and opposite tension of unmastered irony, Blake and Kierkegaard live a life in which one continually struggles to master the skeptical, to place and keep it hierarchically below the life-force Hume calls nature but which they would call simply existence or life. Life and action indeed rescue them from skepticism and despair – and it is in this sense that their final appeal is to the God of life.

If Blake has proved recalcitrant to most recent definitions of romanticism, he has proved equally resistant to recent theories of language and meaning. Given the roots of these theories in romantic thought – and particularly within the logical pattern of idealist dialectics – this would seem entirely consistent. For if Blake resists Hegelian mediation and Schlegelian romantic irony it should not be surprising that he resists the theories of meaning implicit in these dialectics – theories made explicit, I have argued, in Kierkegaard's thoroughly articulated critique of those theories and proposed antidote or solution (chapter 5). Blake's and Kierkegaard's theories of authorial and readerly roles in interpretation (again, both implicit and explicit) resist easy assimilation into the current literary theories derived from romantic thought. For while, as I have argued, in keeping with poststructuralism they insist on the radically perspectival nature of interpretation, on all interpretation as error, they also resist and attempt to master that perspectivism or hermeneutics of undecidability, imposing decisiveness as "the eternal protest against all fictions." While they acknowledge and indeed insist on the "always already constructed" nature of both author and reader, on their constituted "being-in-the-text" as in some sense their only existence, they also insist on a vestigial author behind-the-text who is chosen, not created, and chosen by a reader who similarly chooses rather than creates him or herself in the act of interpretation. They insist in other words on lived interpretation as involving individual acts of choice and will, the choice of the individual author who "wills one thing" rather than another, and the choice of the individual reader who wills to reconstruct it. In this insistence on interpretation as an exercise of choice and freedom they deny the necessity of the structuralist and poststructuralist system, the necessity which declares that author and reader are always already constituted in and by the linguistic system of the text, mere effects of its differential play of meanings. Yet I have argued that one cannot thereby place them in the traditionalist camp of literary theorists – for their theory accommodates, as authentically as poststructuralism claims to do, the potentially radical skepticism and perspectivism of interpretation. Their work offers rather "an ethical riposte to the current claims of deconstruction," as Norris describes Kierkegaard's enterprise; or, as Mitchell describes it, it attempts to master or dominate the discourse from which they are excluded.

Their final appeal or authority for interpretation is not merely to a theological author but to the life of interpretation itself; and this is why they differ so markedly from those whose appeal is to the play of differences within the linguistic system. Such an appeal is for them an appeal to death, to a spectral parody of the life of interpretation. The life of interpretation, like all forms of life, for them necessarily demands action and hence choice. Not to act – that is, not to choose one interpretation rather than another but rather leave contradictory interpretations in undecidable oscillation – is for them simply not to live the life of interpretation. And not to choose the author's meaning is to succumb passively to one's own annihilating (and ultimately self-annihilating) interpretive Selfhood, which willfully refashions the other into a mere projection of itself. They insist always on adopting what we might call an existential stance in relation to the activity of interpretation, a concrete, living "point of view:" for them, we are never in the perspective beyond all perspectives within which we, the author, and the text itself are mere moments or effects in a vast all-comprehending system. Our lived experience of interpretation is as a series of acts of choice, in which we encounter an other who is not ourselves; and any theory which refuses to acknowledge this experiential truth would for Blake and Kierkegaard be an abstraction from and denial of life as we live it. For them, there must always be something "left over" – not least that "little minikin," "the existing Herr Professor who writes the system."

Again, one must admire the vitality of this attempt to reconstitute author and reader out of their dissolution; yet again, we can see its undeniable precariousness. For if the energy of one's choice of the author (and concomitantly, of oneself as reader) is more important than whether one chooses the "right" interpretation, willful misreadings are almost as valid as willful readings; what matters is the energy of the choice. This is why their appeal to a "transfiguring act of choice" is indeed aligned with deconstruction, perhaps inadvertently contributing to the very destruction of what it hoped to salvage: a truth-content for poetry, poetry as a kind of knowledge, philosophy for the sake of poetry.[16] Their heroic attempt to resist this dissolution of philosophy into poetry through a radical "poetics of incommensurability" does result however in an extraordinary tension differentiating them both from their postmodern successors and from what we have come to call "romanticism."

W.J.T. Mitchell's suggestion – with which I began this study – that Blake is "the marginal figure who infiltrates the center" of poststructuralist romantic criticism, the figure "who thus cannot be looked at directly but must be mediated through other poets, especially Wordsworth," correctly implies, I think, that although Blake has always had to be mediated through other figures, he is also simply much more difficult to mediate than are any of the other romantic poets. He is very different from "romanticism" as it has come to be defined, as virtually synonymous with the idealist dialectics of Hegelian mediation and Schlegelian romantic irony. Yet Blake is deeply romantic; he saw with great clarity the true form of the romantic ideal, and he saw it because his temperament was so much more vigorously polemical than those of the other romantics so much more easily mediated within systematic patterns of thought. Blake remained more stubbornly "transcendent," more physically and intellectually isolated from his time, and the either/or dialectic which in part results from this is truer not only to his personal circumstances and temperament, but also to the nature of the romantic ideal he so clearly saw. It *was* to be an ideal in which the qualitatively distinct values of transcendence were not to be lost; and who could better preserve them than this poet whose own independence of thought had been so steadily and obstinately preserved in the face of neglect and public ridicule? Blake stands outside of, sharply differentiated from, "romanticism" as it became embodied in systematic patterns of thought; he stands on its margin, as Mitchell says, and in some sense casts it off as error.[17] Yet he also embraces romanticism, or more accurately the romantic ideal, in its truest form, with equally great intensity. His romanticism is "the same and yet not the same" as the romanticism we have come to accept.

Like Blake, Kierkegaard stands beyond or outside of romanticism as it came to be defined; as Blake stands at its beginning, Kierkegaard stands at its end. His peculiarly intense vision of the romantic ideal may have gained its clarity from this perspective, this vantage point from which he could look back and trace the decay of that ideal. And again as in Blake's case, his intensity of vision was also due to a polemical temperament exacerbated by an exceptionally isolated existence, an atmosphere of alternate neglect and ridicule in which he held his own not only against these "outer demons" but also against the inner demons of melancholy and despair which this isolation fostered. If Blake is one of the most curious eccentrics in the canon of English literature, how much the more so is Kierkegaard – a Dane writing in and against the German idealist tradition in the middle of Copenhagen – in the history of philosophy. His intense individualism puts him beyond the usual systematic categories, including that of romanticism – yet like Blake, while he casts off or leaps beyond this romanticism as error, Kierkegaard embraces it in perhaps its truest, most intense form. He also is "the same and yet not the same" – romantic, yet in a way which is in many respects the opposite of what has come to be called romanticism.

Blake's and Kierkegaard's eccentric perspective on romanticism, a "point of view" deliberately ambiguous, duplicitous, yet finally I would argue "decisive," may well provide us with a truer perspective on the romantic ideal. Kierkegaard's dialectic is particularly suited not only to Blake's fierce individualism, but also to the essential individualism or qualitative transcendence of the romantic ideal of *unmediated* vision. It does not necessarily provide a systematic paradigm for interpreting other individual romantic poets, a totalizing impulse which should in any case perhaps be resisted. Only Blake in his polemical individualism so closely matches Kierkegaard; what they both do, however, is define with greater clarity the ideal for which all the romantics, in their different ways, may have struggled. Curiously, this ideal may have been best defined by A. O. Lovejoy, who insisted on "ethical dualism," appropriated from Christianity, as a centrally defining feature.[18] Romanticism is not a *monistic* ideal, he argued, complaining "It is one of the many paradoxes of the word, and of the controversies centering about it, that several eminent literary critics and historians of our time have conceived the moral essence of Romanticism as consisting in a kind of 'this-worldliness' and a negation of what one of them has termed 'the Christian and classical dualism'" (247). Romanticism, Lovejoy claimed (quoting Schleiermacher's definition of Christianity) "is *durch und durch polemische*; it knows no truce in the warfare of the spiritual with the natural man" (248). Certainly for Blake and Kierkegaard at least, there is indeed no permanent truce in the warfare between Los and the Spectre.

Not "the generalizing law" but "the exception" *is* the rule for the romantic ideal. Perhaps this dialectic of the exception, a dialectic which is itself an eccentric exception to the generalizing laws of idealist dialectics, is closer to providing the rule for the romantic ideal of life. Not an abstract, indefinite unity or system but the concrete individual man is for romanticism the true measure of all things, the God of life. And neither nihilism nor religion but a tension between nihilism and religion stretched to its very breaking point constitutes the fiercely self-consuming energy that burns, like Blake's tyger, at the heart of the romantic ideal. In their eccentricity, the marginal figures of Blake and Kierkegaard may indeed "infiltrate the center," as Mitchell suggests; by providing the bound or outward circumference of the field of energy we call romanticism, they may give that circle its defining center.

Notes

INTRODUCTION

1 See for example (on Blake and Jung) Christine Gallant, *Blake and the Assimilation of Chaos* (Princeton: Princeton University Press, 1978); on Blake and Freud, Diana Hume George, *Blake and Freud* (Ithaca and London: Cornell University Press, 1980); Brenda Webster, *Blake's Prophetic Psychology* (Athens, Georgia: University of Georgia Press, 1983); and Morris Dickstein, "The Price of Experience: Blake's Reading of Freud," in *The Literary Freud: Mechanisms of Defense and the Poetic Will*, ed. Joseph H. Smith (New Haven: Yale University Press, 1980), pp. 67–111. On Blake and Marx, see Minna Doskow, "The Humanized Universe of Blake and Marx," in *William Blake and the Moderns*, ed. R.J. Bertholf and A.S. Levitt (Albany: SUNY Press, 1982), pp. 225–240; Fred Whitehead, "William Blake and Radical Tradition," in *The Weapons of Criticism: Marxism in America and the Literary Tradition* (Ramparts Press, 1976), pp. 191–214; Jackie Disalvo, *War of Titans: Blake's Critique of Milton and the Politics of Religion* (Pittsburgh: University of Pittsburgh Press, 1983); and David Punter, "Blake: Creative and Uncreative Labor," in *Studies in Romanticism* 16 (Fall 1977), 535–561 and "Blake, Marxism, and Dialectic," in *Literature and History* 6 (1977). Curiously, Punter seems to have seen no contradiction between these claims for Blake's dialectical materialism and those of his later study *Blake, Hegel, and Dialectic* (Amsterdam: Rodopi, 1982), which grounds Blake's notion of dialectic in Hegelian idealism. While Punter's is the only extended comparison of Blake with Hegel, their likeness is assumed or implied by many if not most Blake critics. See, finally, Joachim J. Scholz, *Blake and Novalis: A Comparison of Romanticism's High Arguments* (Frankfurt am Main, Bern, Los Vegas: Peter Lang, 1978); Martin Bidney, *Blake and Goethe. Psychology, Ontology, Imagination* (Columbia: University of Missouri Press, 1988); and (on Blake and Schlegel) Steven E. Alford, *Irony and the Logic of the Romantic Imagination*, American University Studies, series III: Comparative Literature, vol. 13 (New York, Bern, Frankfurt-am-Main, Nancy: Peter Lang, 1984).

2 W.J.T. Mitchell remarks that "Blake's technique of contrary or diaboli-
cal reading, . . . , which proceeds by inverting the privileged oppositions
in a text (. . .) and then by calling into question the whole system that
keeps them opposed, seems very close to the method of deconstruction,"
in "Visible Language: Blake's Wond'rous Art of Writing," from *Romanticism and Contemporary Criticism* (Ithaca: Cornell, 1986), p. 90. Mitchell
has also prophesied however that Blake will "outlive" deconstruction
precisely because he anticipates it "and offers such profound antidotes
to its skeptical and nihilistic tendencies . . . his work is one long struggle
with the forces of negation" (*Studies in Romanticism*, 21, Fall 1982, 416).
David Simpson points out that Blake "both perpetrates and subverts
the mythology of the primacy of speech over writing," in "Reading
Blake and Derrida – Our Caesars Neither Praised nor Buried," from
Unnam'd Forms: Blake and Textuality, ed. Nelson Hilton and Thomas
Vogler (California, 1986), p. 13. In "A Wall of Words: the Sublime as
Text" (also in Hilton and Vogler), V.A. DeLuca concludes that despite
the presence of a deconstructive *aporia* or moment of undecidability in
Blake's texts this is for Blake merely a moment to be transcended in a
full metaphysics of presence. Quoting Blake's dislike of the levelling of
contraries effected by the French Revolution (which has made
"Englishmen all Intermeasurable One by Another"), David Wagenknecht asks the very interesting question "Is Derrida, from Blake's
point of view, the very embodiment of the effect of the French Revolution, or are the two of them, caught on the verge of anathematizing
their enemies, not surprisingly unantithetical?," in *Critical Paths: Blake
and the Argument of Method*, ed. Dan Miller, Mark Bracher, and Donald
Ault (Duke, 1987), p. 311. Critics who consider the tension between
deconstructive and anti-deconstructive tendencies in Kierkegaard's
work (as opposed to declaring Kierkegaard unequivocally a
deconstructionist) include Christopher Norris, "Fictions of Authority:
Narrative and Viewpoint in Kierkegaard's Writing," from *The Deconstructive Turn:Essays in the Rhetoric of Philosophy* (Methuen, 1983); and
Candace Lang, in *Irony/Humor* (Johns Hopkins, 1988).

3 Among the first to suggest a thoroughly skeptical (although not
deconstructionist) Kierkegaard are Josiah Thompson, in *Kierkegaard: A
Biographical Essay* (Knopf, 1973), and especially Henning Fenger, *Kier-
kegaard: the Myths and their Origins*, transl. George C. Schoolfield (Yale,
1980). Deconstructionist readings include, centrally, those by Sylviane
Agacinski, *Aparté:Conceptions and Deaths of Søren Kierkegaard*, transl.
Kevin Newmark (Florida State, 1988); Patrick Bigelow, *Kierkegaard and
the Problem of Writing* (Florida State, 1988); Louis Mackey, *Points of
View: Readings of Kierkegaard* (Florida State, 1986); and Mark C.
Taylor, "Transgression," in *Altarity* (Chicago,1987), pp. 305–353.

4 Mitchell, "Visible Language," p. 91.

5 Among the many studies of Kierkegaard and Hegel see especially

Stephen Crites, *In the Twilight of Christendom: Hegel vs. Kierkegaard on Faith and History* (AAR Studies in Religion, no.2, 1972). While it is generally agreed that *The Concept of Irony* is Kierkegaard's most Hegelian work, S.N.Dunning argues that the structure of Kierkegaard's thought remains fundamentally Hegelian throughout all the pseudonymous works, in *Kierkegaard's Dialectic of Inwardness: A Structural Analysis of the Theory of Stages* (Princeton, 1985). The debates over Blake's Hegelianism or anti-Hegelianism are too numerous to catalogue here, often proceeding under the rubric of whether Blake is "systematic" or "anti-systematic," with respect both to his idea of "contraries" and to the overall shape of his myth. Most critics who argue for one or the other position generally run up against contradictions, of which Leopold Damrosch probably shows himself most aware, acknowledging both Hegelian and anti-Hegelian features in Blake's thought. See *Symbol and Truth in Blake's Myth* (Princeton, 1980). Northrop Frye is generally credited with initiating the "systematic" (Hegelian) reading of Blake; yet curiously, it is Frye who comments on the anti-Hegelian "crisis" structure of Blake's dialectic. See especially p. 260 of *Fearful Symmetry* (Princeton, 1947).

6 Essentially, deconstruction claims to be genuinely anti-foundational as romantic irony is not. There is some truth to this: as Richard Rorty points out, the German idealists "went only halfway" towards the anti-foundationalism of deconstruction and poststructuralist thought because they only halfway repudiated "the idea that truth is 'out there.' They were willing ... to see matter as constructed by mind ... but they persisted in seeing mind, spirit, the depths of the human self, as having an intrinsic nature – one which could be known by a kind of nonempirical super science called philosophy." (*Contingency, Irony, and Solidarity* [Cambridge: Cambridge University Press, 1989]), p. 4. Candace Lang makes a similar point when she argues that Schlegel's romantic irony still depends on a disjunction between essence and phenomenon (or Being and Becoming), whereas "postmodern" irony is purely "phenomenal," that is, an irony of pure Becoming that dispenses with the category of Being altogether. (*Irony/Humor* [Baltimore and London: The Johns Hopkins University Press, 1988], p. 33). Lang's formulation echoes Gilles Deleuze's distinction between "Platonic" and "Nietzschean" irony in *Logique de sens* (discussed in J. Hillis Miller's *Fiction and Repetition* [Cambridge: Harvard University Press, 1982], pp. 1–21).

Despite the "quasi-foundationalism" of idealist dialectics, however, Kierkegaard certainly saw Hegel and Schlegel as in some sense the first "anti-foundationalists," who dissolved all stabilities of Being and individual selfhood within the contingencies of the Hegelian and Schlegelian systems of pure Becoming. Rorty in fact seems to acknowledge Hegel's critical role as a kind of historicist father of anti-foundationalism when he remarks on the "historicist turn" since Hegel to the idea that "socialization, and thus historical circumstance, goes all the way down – that there is nothing 'beneath' socialization or prior to history which is definatory of the human" (p. xiii). This is precisely Kierkegaard's complaint (however unfair) against Hegel: that Hegel dissolves the individual "beneath" or "prior to" socialization and history. Kierkegaard sees Hegel and Schlegel as Rorty's "two kinds" of historicist: the former emphasizing a socialization that "goes all the way down," the latter emphasizing, like Nietzsche, the "desire for self-creation and autonomy" (pp. xiii and xiv). Both kinds of historicists for Kierkegaard equally dissolve all Being within Becoming, reason within passion or will, philosophy within poetry. Fundamentally, he would argue, anti-foundationalism shares with idealist dialectics the repudiation of the principle of contradiction (or non-contradiction) which is central to his attack on Hegel and Schlegel; see chapter 5.

7 Frye, chapters 7 and 8, pp. 187–262. For the inseparability of Orc from Urizen see especially pp. 210, 214, 215, and 219.

8 Harold Bloom, Commentary to David Erdman's 1982 edition of *The Poetry and Prose of William Blake* (New York: Doubleday and Co., Inc.), p. 897. Bloom does however elsewhere deny that Blake's notion of dialectic is Hegelian, claiming "Blake does not build truth by dialectic, being neither a rational mystic like Plato nor a mystic rationalist like Hegel" ("Dialectic in *The Marriage of Heaven and Hell*," PMLA 73, 1958, 502) – the first part of which claim I would also dispute. Like Kierkegaard, Blake is indeed "a rational mystic like Plato," as we shall see, with a dialectic that is in essence (or attempts to be) a radically Christianized version of Socratic dialectic.

9 Damrosch, *Symbol and Truth in Blake's Myth*, pp. 179–181.

10 Steven Shaviro, "Striving with Systems: Blake and the Politics of Difference," *boundary* 2, 10.3 (1982), 231–232.

11 Martin K. Nurmi, *Blake's "Marriage of Heaven and Hell": A Critical Study* (Kent, Ohio: Kent State University Bulletin, April 1957), p. 20.

12 Tilottama Rajan, *The Supplement of Reading* (Cornell, 1990).

13 For good accounts of the political and social background to Kierkegaard's thought, see John Elrod, *Kierkegaard and Christendom* (Princeton, 1981), and Bruce H. Kirmmse, *Kierkegaard in Golden Age Denmark* (Indiana, 1990).

14 W.J.T. Mitchell observes that, after all, Blake's Urizen satirizes both reactionary and revolutionary elements: not only repressive "English reaction in the late 1790s," but also the "revolutionary utopian reformer who brings new laws, new philosophies, and a new religion of reason." While it may be "heresy to suggest Blake could have held any reactionary opinions or agreed with Edmund Burke about anything," Mitchell remarks, "the general prototype for Urizen's 'dividing and measuring' is, of course, Edmund Burke's characterization of the 'geo-

metrical and arithmetical constitution' of the new French Republic."
See "Visible Language," p. 58.

15 JP, III, 3724; quoted in Elrod, p. 302.

16 For an interesting discussion of this problem for Blake studies, see
Michael Ferber, *The Social Vision of William Blake* (Princeton, 1985), pp.
21–25.

17 For more specific discussions of Blake's relation to eighteenth and
nineteenth century German thought, see L. M. Trawick, "William
Blake's German Connection," in *Colby Library Quarterly* 13 (No. 4,
December 1979), 229–245, and Michael Ferber, *The Social Vision of
William Blake*, pp. 33–34. While both Trawick and Ferber suggest the
usual shared source in Jacob Boehme, Trawick argues for a more
immediate influence in Henry Fuseli and Johann Lavater, two
German–Swiss contemporaries of Blake. Most interesting is Jerome
McGann's recent argument that Blake knew German Biblical criticism
through his knowledge of Dr. Alexander Geddes' scholarly reviews; see
"The Idea of an Indeterminate Text: Blake's Bible of Hell and Dr.
Alexander Geddes," in *Social Values and Poetic Acts* (Cambridge:
Harvard University Press, 1988), pp. 152–172.

18 For the most extended and carefully documented version of this argument, see Henning Fenger's *Kierkegaard: The Myths and Their Origins*.

19 "Letter on Blake," from Samuel Palmer to Alexander Gilchrist, quoted
in Gilchrist's *Life of William Blake* (London and Cambridge: Macmillan
and Co., 1863), p. 301.

20 See especially Patrick Bigelow, "Kierkegaard and the Hermeneutical
Circle," *Man and World* 15 (1982), 67–82; B. Pedersen, "Fictionality
and Authority: a Point of View for Kierkegaard's Work as an Author,"
Modern Language Notes 89 (December 1974), 938–56; and Christopher
Norris's "Fictions of Authority" (see note 2).

21 Shaviro, p. 230.

22 Kevin Newmark, for example, says in his introduction to Agacinski's
Aparté that for Agacinski's Kierkegaard "what we do when we read ... a
story as a temporal unfolding, is to *impose* in turn a meaningful narrative
on an ironic structure that in and by itself is devoid of any sequence or
meaning whatsoever. The technical term Paul de Man has given to
such narratives is, of course, allegory ... "; p. 30. I shall be arguing
instead that for Kierkegaard one "chooses" a meaningful narrative
rather than "imposes" such a narrative, in an act of reading that is
between knowing and creating (or imposing) that meaning.

23 See for example Leslie Brisman's *Milton's Poetry of Choice and its Romantic
Heirs* (Yale, 1978). Stephen Behrendt's *The Moment of Explosion: Blake
and the Illustration of Milton* (Nebraska, 1983) does however more fully
discuss the thematics of choice central to Blake's "corrections" of
Milton both philosophically and pictorially. David Wagenknecht's
focus on "choice" in his afterword to *Critical Paths* nonetheless concludes

that this moment of choice is entirely consistent with the deconstructive *aporia*.

24 "Afterword," in *Critical Paths*, ed. Miller et.al.

25 "The Aim of Blake's Prophecies and the Uses of Blake Criticism," in *Blake's Sublime Allegory*, ed. Stuart Curran and J.A.Wittreich (Wisconsin, 1973),pp. 3–21.

26 See for example Donald Ault's claim that "apart from perspective relationships there are no events in *The Four Zoas* ... no substructure of specifiable events which is distorted or partially interpreted by the perspectives," argued in "Incommensurability and Interconnection in Blake's Anti-Newtonian Text," *Studies in Romanticism* 16 (summer 1977), 277–303; and more recently, in "Re-Visioning *The Four Zoas*," from *Unnam'd Forms: Blake and Textuality*, pp. 105–139.

27 "One must adopt either the way of imagination or the way of memory; no compromise or neutrality is possible. He who is not for imagination is against it. Religion insists that however mixed good and bad may be in this world, there are eternally only heaven and hell, with a great gulf between. For the apocalypse or vision of eternity is at the same time a Last Judgment, an absolute separation of sheep from goats, of the men who have used their varying amounts of talents from the men who have hidden theirs. In eternity all the confused and eclectic and weakly tolerant are obviously on the wrong side. Hence the duty of the imaginative man is to force the issue and compel decisions;" p. 55.

28 *Literature Against Itself. Literary Ideas in Modern Society* (Chicago, 1979), p. 39.

29 See for example Agacinski's claim that "for Kierkegaard irony will always be what eludes Hegelian sublation (*Aufhebung*)," in *Aparté* (p. 74), and "irony represents a means of criticizing or resisting the 'System' in a noncontradictory, thus in principle, in a nondialectizable way – perhaps one of the only means of 'contesting' speculative dialectics without immediately becoming part of it. By not stepping onto the field of its oppositions, irony exasperates dialectical thought: it displaces without opposing, it contests without contradicting. As a result, dialectics cannot figure out what to do with irony: neither how to get hold of it nor how to get rid of it" (pp. 60–61). This is exactly how for Kierkegaard "life" or "existence" eludes the system. But he does not call "existence" "irony"; rather, existence for him is what resists or escapes irony *and* the System, the latter synonymous terms. Candace Lang similarly describes irony as what is "undialectizable," in *Irony/Humor*, pp. 24 and 35.

30 Again, both Agacinski and Lang privilege *The Concept of Irony* in this way.

31 See for instance Lee Patterson's complaint that the "argumentative structure" of New Historicism "tends to be incorporative rather than differentiating, both/and rather than either/or: ... history is finally as

undecidable as poetry, as of course it must be when read as a poem. Absorbing the historical into the textual, New Historicism endows it with the irresolution that, for deconstruction, characterizes textuality per se." These "irresolutions and undecidabilities valued by contemporary techniques of interpretation" "subvert the category of the historically real" and lead to "a world strangely drained of dynamism" (*Negotiating the Past. The Historical Understanding of Medieval Literature* [Madison: University of Wisconsin Press, 1987], pp. 62–63). Arguments about the possibility of "determinate meaning" have been waged exhaustively in critical books and journals for at least the last twenty years, many in reaction to E.D. Hirsch's defense of authorial intention in *Validity in Interpretation* (New Haven: Yale University Press, 1967) – a book, it should be noted, now nearly twenty-five years old yet still under continual attack. Cogent recent discussions of the issues involved in specifically deconstructive indeterminacy include M.H. Abrams, "Construing and Deconstructing," in *Romanticism and Contemporary Criticism*, ed. Morris Eaves and Michael Fischer (Ithaca and London: Cornell University Press, 1986), pp. 127–182; Michael Fischer, *Does Deconstruction Make Any Difference?* (Bloomington: Indiana University Press, 1985); John M. Ellis, *Against Deconstruction* (Princeton: Princeton University Press, 1989); and Gerald Graff, "Determinacy/Indeterminacy," in *Critical Terms for Literary Study*, ed. Frank Lentricchia and Thomas McLaughlin (Chicago: University of Chicago Press, 1990), pp. 163–176.

32 Michael Fischer emphasizes the extent to which Derrida, for instance, acknowledges the necessity of interpretive constraints such as context and authorial intent for "minimum readability," a "doubling commentary" that is logically prior to its own deconstruction. See *Does Deconstruction Make Any Difference?; p. 39.*

33 See especially Fenger's argument that possibly "one girl, or perhaps even two, had entered his life before the queen of his heart appeared," thus falsifying Kierkegaard's claim for the uniqueness of his experience with Regina, in *Kierkegaard: the Myths and their Origins*, pp. 150–157. Somewhat surprisingly, perhaps, Sylviane Agacinski's deconstructionist reading does not question the authenticity of Kierkegaard's crisis with Regina and in fact makes much of Kierkegaard's claim that he owed the pseudonymous authorship to her – that she had made him a "poet." Agacinski also discusses at length the influence of Kierkegaard's father on his "religious" works, a discussion again taking seriously the influence of these biographical relationships on Kierkegaard's writing. See pp. 238–258.

34 FZ, VIII, 115:41–51; p. 381. See also Frye's explication of the Seven Eyes, especially pp. 128–134; 311; 320–347; 360–371; 410.

35 Jerome McGann's recent work on Blake does not single out the Spectre per se, but it does focus on Blake's poetics of "error" much as I am doing

here, observing that because "Blake's new anatomy of truth is actually a set of directions for how to deal with falsehood and error," "Blake's truth is much closer to a Socratic (which is not to say a Platonic) form of truth than to anything else." The result, McGann argues, is a poetics of "action," a "literature of knowledge" which lays claim to a kind of truth-content neither wholly philosophical nor wholly poetic but somewhere between the two. See *Towards a Literature of Knowledge* (Chicago: University of Chicago Press, 1989), pp. vii–37. For excellent discussions of the spectre see Nelson Hilton's chapter on spectres in *Literal Imagination. Blake's Vision of Words* (Berkeley, Los Angeles, London: University of California Press, 1983), pp. 147–172; Edward J. Rose, "Blake and the Double: the Spectre as Doppelganger," *Colby Library Quarterly* 13, No. 2 (June 1977), 127–139; and Wayne Glausser's "The Gates of Memory in Night VIIa of *The Four Zoas*," *Blake Illustrated Quarterly* 18 (Spring 1985), 196–203. Mary Lynn Johnson and Brian Wilkie also usefully discuss the spectre's role in *The Four Zoas* in "The Spectrous Embrace in *The Four Zoas*, VIIa," in *Blake Illustrated Quarterly* 12 (1978), 100–106. Janet Warner catalogues the spectre's symbolic representation of melancholy, despair, pride, passivity, *accidie*, and materialism in "Blake's Figures of Despair: Man in his Spectre's Power," in *William Blake: Essays in Honor of Sir Geoffrey Keynes*, ed. Morton Paley and Michael Phillips (Oxford: Clarendon Press, 1973), pp. 208–224. Morton Paley discusses "Spectre and Emanation" in chapter five of *The Continuing City: William Blake's 'Jerusalem'* (Oxford: Clarendon Press, 1983), a section that usefully recapitulates his earlier article on the spectre as Blake's fear of meeting William Cowper's fate of madness and religious despair: "Cowper as Blake's Spectre," *Eighteenth Century Studies*, 1 (1968), 236–252. Blake's illustrations of the spectre are examined by Geoffrey Keynes and Alice Mills in (respectively) "Blake's Spectre," *Book Collector* 28 (1979), 60–66 and "The Spectral Bat in Blake's Illustrations to *Jerusalem*," *Blake Studies* 9 (1980), 87–99; Nelson Hilton's very fruitful discussion also includes the drawings as well. Finally, J.R. Scrimgeour has suggested the Spectre's affinities with Kierkegaardian despair in a short article, "'The Great Example of Horror & Agony': a Comparison of Søren Kierkegaard's Demonically Despairing Individual with William Blake's Spectre of Urthona," in *Scandinavian Studies* 47 (Winter 1975), 36–41.

36 In this respect they seek to increase the tension between poetry and philosophy – "the tension between an effort to achieve self-creation by the recognition of contingency and an effort to achieve universality by the transcendence of contingency," as Rorty defines that tension or "quarrel" – instead of trying in true romantic fashion to collapse philosophy into poetry. Yet finally, it may be that their attempt to strengthen philosophy ends up instead establishing "honorable terms

on which philosophy might surrender to poetry," in Rorty's wonderfully apt formulation. See *Contingency*, pp. 25–26.

37 Quoted in Dan Miller's introduction to *Critical Paths*, p. 3.

CHAPTER 1. THE SPECTRE AND THE LOGIC OF ERROR

1 See Lillian Swenson's preface to *Either/Or*, Vol. 1 (Princeton: Princeton University Press, 1944). Walter Lowrie also discusses at length this relationship and its consequences for Kierkegaard's life and work in his biography *Kierkegaard* (London, New York, Toronto: Oxford University Press, 1938); see especially "Regina," pp. 191–231. Sylviane Agacinski's provocative discussion of Regina's – and "woman's" – role in Kierkegaard's thought runs throughout *Aparté*, but is concentrated mostly in pages 131–158 and 238–241. For disagreement that this crisis was in any sense real or decisive for Kierkegaard see especially Fenger, pp. 150–157.

2 He does say in his *Journal*, "My intellectual life and my significance as a husband are two incommensurable qualities" (quoted in Lowrie, p. 229). And he wrote a book entitled *Prefaces* (not translated into English) of which Lowrie says "In the preface to *Prefaces* the pseudonymous author, Nicholas Notabene, confides to the reader that he is not permitted to write a *book* because his wife is jealous of his preoccupation with such work, and hence he resorts to the expedient of writing a volume of *prefaces*" (*Either/Or*, II, pp. x-xi, translator's preface).

3 Quoted from Kierkegaard's *Journal* by Lowrie in his introduction to *Fear and Trembling* (Princeton: Princeton University Press, 1941), p. 19.

4 Quoted in Lowrie, *Kierkegaard*, p. 209.

5 Lowrie, p. 267; Agacinski, p. 137.

6 Lowrie, p. 194; Agacinski, pp. 146–150.

7 From 1844 to 1859, Kierkegaard published an average of two books per year.

8 Quoted in Lowrie, p. 220.

9 Stephen Crites, *In the Twilight of Christendom: Hegel versus Kierkegaard on Faith and History* (American Academy of Religion Studies in Religion, No. Two, 1972), 4–5.

10 As Agacinski puts it, "if the family accomplishes only the law of woman, if reappropriation [the *Aufhebung* of the "singularity of the husband" within the family] is always feminine, then it would be necessary to say that, for Kierkegaard, the Hegelian dialectic is feminine;" *Aparté*, p. 177.

11 David Erdman, ed., and Harold Bloom, commentary, *The Poetry and Prose of William Blake* (Garden City, New York: Doubleday & Company, Inc., 1982), p. 915.

12 For a detailed account of the Felpham incident (or incidents), includ-

ing Blake's correspondence, see G. E. Bentley, Jr.'s *Blake Records* (Oxford: Clarendon Press, 1969), "Patronage and Dependence," pp. 62–174. Despite several chapters on Blake's time at Felpham, Alexander Gilchrist greatly downplays Blake's falling-out with Hayley in his *Life of William Blake*; this and Mona Wilson's standard account in her *The Life of William Blake* (London: P. Davies, Ltd., 1932) contrast with Frye's highly interpretive account (and almost entirely biographical reading of *Milton*) in *Fearful Symmetry* ("Comus Agonistes," pp. 313–355). Margaret Storch gives the incident a persuasively Freudian reading as Blake's symbolic confrontation with his father, in "The Spectrous Fiend Cast Out: Blake's Crisis at Felpham," in *Modern Language Quarterly* 44 (June 1983), 115–135.

13 Such a theory of Milton's influence on Blake need not involve a Bloomian anxiety of influence; indeed, as J. A. Wittreich and others have pointed out, Milton's "fatherly" influence on Blake is in this poem (and one might argue, ultimately) not repressive but liberating. See J. A. Wittreich, Jr., *Angel of Apocalypse: Blake's Idea of Milton* (Madison: University of Wisconsin Press, 1975), and the introduction to *William Blake and the Moderns*, ed. Robert J. Bertholf and Annette S. Levitt (Albany: SUNY Press, 1982). Bertholf and Levitt propose, instead of "a metaphysical scheme of influence dominated by the anxiety of that influence and the obligation to remove that antecedent force," a "tradition of enacted forms" in which "one artist comes into the possibilities of his own imagination in the works of another" – certainly a more accurate description of how Blake dramatizes his relation to Milton here.

14 Review of Anne K. Mellor's *Blake's Human Form Divine* (Berkeley, Los Angeles, London: University of California Press, 1974) in *Blake Newsletter* 8 (Spring 1975), 117–119.

15 E.D. Hirsch, Jr., *Innocence and Experience: An Introduction to Blake*, second edition (Chicago: University of Chicago Press, 1975), p. 103.

16 *Blake Records*, pp. 62–174. Margaret Storch confirms this pattern of "exaggerated trust" in male mentors followed by bitter fallings-out in "The Spectrous Fiend Cast Out" – see note 12.

17 In Shaviro's words, "The statement that 'they should be enemies' is at once the expression of a particular perspective (one of the Contraries) and a meta-statement which thereby surpasses that, or any other particular perspective. ... No dialectical reconciliation of the Contraries is permitted, and yet it is in an authoritative statement, one which would have to transcend the contradiction, that the Contraries are maintained as Contraries, as states defined in opposition to and by means of a struggle with one another" (p. 233).

18 See for example several attempts to explain the mechanism or dynamic of what Mary Lynn Johnson has called Blake's "conversion of sets of twos (apparent opposites) into threes (genuine contraries separated

from an unreal negation)," in "'Separating What Has Been Mixed': A Suggestion for a Perspective on *Milton*" (*Blake Studies* 6, Fall 1978, 11–17). This includes Jeffrey Mitchell's similar attempt in the same issue of *Blake Studies*, "Progression from the *Marriage* into the Bard's Song in *Milton*" (35–45). Dan Miller's remark that "religion separates what cannot be separated in order to reconcile what cannot be reconciled: dualism and monism are identical errors" succinctly argues for *The Marriage of Heaven and Hell* what my entire chapter here argues for *Milton* ("Contrary Revelation: 'The Marriage of Heaven and Hell," in *Studies in Romanticism*, vol. 24, no. 4, Winter 1985, 491–509; 500).

19 Frye, chapters seven and eight (pp. 187–268).

20 In Night I Los repents of striking Enitharmon (p. 303); in Night IV Tharmas expresses regret over Enion, whom he has cast out, and pities those he is about to destroy (p. 325); in Night V Los repents chaining down Orc (p. 335). Most notable, however, are Urizen's expressions of repentance in Nights V (pp. 336–337), VI (p. 341), and especially in Nights VIII and IX (p. 367, pp. 375–376). His repentance in Night IX results in his complete transformation into a "radiant Youth" (p. 376). Blake–Los has discovered that he must "modulate his fires" for redemption (p. 357). He has discovered to his astonishment that he loves Urizen (p. 357) – a redemption made possible by the spectre, the negation whose destruction redeems the contraries.

21 Storch, "The Spectrous Fiend Cast Out;" see note 12.

22 *Blake Records*; quoted in Damrosch, p. 272.

23 Gregor Malantschuk, *The Controversial Kierkegaard*, transl. Howard V. Hong and Edna H. Hong (Waterloo, Canada: Wilfred Laurier University Press, 1980), pp. 62–65.

24 Quoted in Lowrie, p. 20.

25 *Ibid.*, p. 48.

26 Quoted in Malantschuk, p. 63.

27 Quoted in Malantschuk, p. 65.

28 For an alternative and controversial reading of Blake's Oedipal struggles as ending in defeat, see Brenda Webster's *Blake's Prophetic Psychology*. Webster argues that Blake's lifelong Oedipal jealousies culminate at last, in *Jerusalem*, in a consummation of Jerusalem and Albion which is ultimately incestuous "because Los, Blake and Christ are imagined as participating, through merger with the father, in the embrace of the mother." Unable to renounce the mother for a healthy wife-substitute, "Blake as poet [thus] insists on participating with the father in the primal scene," and, unable either to fully accept or to circumvent this embrace of the mother celebrated by his poetry, simply stops writing poetry altogether (p. 293). Webster's reading hence interprets negatively the increasing embrace of male figures, or fathers and sons, that most commentators (myself included) interpret positively as a successful resolution of Oedipal strife. Agacinski similarly

argues that Kierkegaard's relationship to his father remained deeply
conflicted and unresolved, characterized by Oedipal jealousies finally
repressed as "the secret of a secret": "This ... mimetic identification of
the son with the father, then, would not have had as its goal and effect
the resolution of a conflict ... but would rather be the avoidance of
even the slightest contact with the question of the father, so as to modify
in no way the paternal figure;" *Aparté*, pp. 251–252.

29 Abrams, chapter three, "The Circuitous Journey: Pilgrims and Prodi-
gals," pp. 141–195, especially pp. 164–169, "The Prodigal's Return."

CHAPTER 2. THE SPECTRE AS KIERKEGAARD'S CONCEPT OF DREAD

1 Annotations to Lavater, Erdman and Bloom, p. 601.
2 Lowrie, p. 233.
3 See, for example, *CUP*, p. 484, where Kierkegaard speaks of the
"voluptuous, soft exaltation of despair" characteristic of his age.
4 Quoted in Lowrie, pp. 220–221.
5 *Blake Records*, p. 221.
6 "'The Great Example of Horror and Agony': A Comparison of Søren
Kierkegaard's Demonically Despairing Individual with William Blake's
Spectre of Urthona," in *Scandinavian Studies* 47 (Winter 1975), 36–41.
7 "The Gates of Memory in Night VIIA) of *The Four Zoas*," *Blake Illustrated
Quarterly* 18 (Spring 1985), 196–203.
8 For an excellent discussion of the spectre as memory, see Glausser's
article (noted above). As Glausser remarks, the spectre is a potentially
redemptive kind of memory, one that "will become a dynamic revision-
ary force rather than a disabling belief that the past cannot be
changed" (p. 201). Los's embrace of the spectre is thus "a striking act of
memory," for "in its most important Blakean meaning, to remember
means to make in the present an act of judgment about your identity –
to recognize what belongs to you, to find or find again what has been
forgotten or repressed" (p. 201). In this respect Los's embrace of
memory constitutes a Kierkegaardian "repetition" rather than a
Freudian entrapment in repetition as neurosis – see further discussion of
this in the following chapter.
9 Edward J. Rose calls this potential for either salvation or damnation
the "mythic pattern" of "the double," quoting Otto Rank's description
of the pattern thus: "'Originally conceived as a guardian angel, assur-
ing immortal survival of the self, the double eventually appears as
precisely the opposite, a reminder of the individual's mortality, indeed,
the announcer of death itself'" (from "The Double as Immortal Self,"
in *The Double: A Psychoanalytic Study*, tr. and ed. Harry Tucker, Jr.),
quoted in Rose's article "Blake and the Double" – see introduction,
note 35. Hence, concludes Rose, "the fate of the universal man depends

upon Los's abilities to maintain the Divine Vision, to make the double a reflection of man's immortality and not a twin who seeks to displace man's true self" (p. 136).

10 "The Echoing Green," lines 23–30; E8.

11 Agacinski's reading characteristically denies any such realm of Being or potential, any such "ground;" see her discussion of "the fall" in *Aparté*, pp. 97–105.

12 For Kierkegaard's very full discussion of "childish Christianity" – that is, the mistaken identification of true "spirit" with the state of innocence – see especially *CUP*, pp. 523–537.

13 James Scrimgeour identifies the spectre with this particular form of despair of the various kinds which Kierkegaard describes; see note 6.

14 Frye, pp. 292–299.

15 Part of this confusion undoubtedly results as well from the confused order of the plates (and Nights) in the poem. In his most recent (1982) edition of Blake's poetry, David Erdman has changed the order of Night viia from that of the 1965 edition; see also his article "Night the Seventh: the Editorial Problem," in *Blake Illustrated Quarterly* 12 (Fall 1978), 135–139, an issue devoted almost entirely to the question of which of the two existing versions of Night vii is the authoritative one, and on what grounds. Another of the contributors, John Kilgore, argues convincingly that the "traditional explanation" making Night viia – containing the confrontations of Los, the spectre, and Enitharmon – the authoritative version is not necessarily affected by disputes about which version came first. Whatever the order of the nights, he argues, it seems clear why Blake's discovery of the spectre was indeed an "imaginative crisis" that "burst the whole Zoa scheme altogether" as Frye originally proposed (Frye, p. 298). Kilgore suggests that Blake's increasing rejection of "clock-time" resulted naturally in "a crisis of disenchantment with narrative itself," in which he "found himself less and less inspired to resolve the narrative tangles of the Nights Seven" ("The Order of Nights viia and viib in Blake's *The Four Zoas*," p. 112). The simplest and most compelling argument for the centrality of Night viia, however, is surely the fact that confrontation with the spectre does become the narrative center in *Milton* and *Jerusalem*.

16 Frye, p. 278.

17 Donald Ault suggests that the spectre represents the Newtonian doctrine of *"prisca sapientia"* – that is, the doctrine of "the one true system," "a false integration of modes of explanation," thus reinforcing his role as both false reason and false unity. See "Incommensurability and Interconnection in Blake's Anti-Newtonian Text," in *Studies in Romanticism* 16 (Summer 1977), 277–303, especially 290–292.

18 See for instance Damrosch, pp. 220–243.

CHAPTER 3. THE SPECTRE AND THE LINE OF LIFE

1 Hilton suggests that perhaps Blake's idea of the spectre as "spectator" derived from Adam Smith's *The Theory of Moral Sentiments*: "Perhaps reading Smith or Godwin, Blake realized that the 'spectator within' was the 'spectre,' the philosophical *spectator ab extra* that demands intellectual detachment from areas of emotion. This verbal relation leads to the other psychological root of the spectre. It is not merely a thing seen, but something seeing us, the vision of division" (pp. 154–155). The phrase "the vision of division" wonderfully encapsulates the ambiguity of the spectre's role as a kind of vestigial awareness or memory of the prelapsarian state and subsequent fall into division – an awareness, again, potentially damning or redemptive.

2 "*Jerusalem* is harsh: the Lord's Prayer is not very euphonious when said backwards, and *Jerusalem* is continually muttering or howling sinister spells to compel the devil to appear in his true shape;" *Fearful Symmetry*, p. 358.

3 For fuller descriptions of this fundamentally post-Kantian pattern of logic in romantic poetry, see E. D. Hirsch, Jr., *Wordsworth and Schelling: A Typological Study of Romanticism* (New Haven: Yale University Press, 1960), chapter 2, "The Structure of Experience," pp. 15–25; Anne K. Mellor, *English Romantic Irony* (Cambridge: Harvard University Press, 1980), chapter 1, "The Paradigm of Romantic Irony," in particular pp. 25–30; and especially, Leonard P. Wessell, Jr., "The Antinomic Structure of Friedrich Schlegel's 'Romanticism,'" in *Studies in Romanticism* 12, Summer 1973, no. 3, 648–669.

4 In *William Blake's Theory of Art* (Princeton: Princeton University Press, 1982), Morris Eaves has remarked upon the "obstinately metaphorical nature of Blake's linearism," which forces us to wonder "what a distinct, sharp, and wirey bounding line will look like when discovered in the language of a poem," asking "Does Blake's poetry before or after 1805 reveal the verbal counterpart of pictorial distinct line and formal clarity?" (p. 43). (Eaves also remarks that Blake "joins the linearists by employing the conventional association between line and intellect" – p. 19). Clearly, in the either/or dialectic, I am proposing, we find just such a verbal counterpart, if not in a formal sense then in a thematic one.

5 Frye, pp. 246–247.

6 *Friedrich Schlegel's 'Lucinde' and the Fragments*, transl. Peter Firchow (Minneapolis: University of Minnesota Press, 1971), No. 51, p. 167.

7 In his introduction to Agacinski's *Aparté*, Kevin Newmark deconstructs "the arbitrary play between *Gave* (gift) and *Opgave* (task)" to argue that one cannot "mediate the aporia between *Opgave* as meaningful thesis (task) and *Opgave* as arbitrary positing;" pp. 28–30. In this way he qualifies and indeed dissolves the passionate Kierkgaardian "leap" from potential to actual, necessity to freedom, death to life.

8 Frye, p. 248.
9 Glausser, p. 202.
10 *Gesammelte Werke*, 13, p.38; quoted by George J. Stack in "Repetition in Kierkegaard and Freud," *Personalist* 58 (July 1977), 249–260; 257.
11 Stack, p. 251. Blake's insistence on the individual's ability to escape all deterministic cycles of necessity is why Harold Bloom's essentially Freudian theory of anxieties of influence does not apply to Blake – or at least, to Blake's intentions and to his own theory of Milton's influence (see chapter 1, note 12). Diana Hume George admirably charts the ways in which Blake would reject as limited and deterministic the Freudian world-view in *Blake and Freud*.

CHAPTER 4. MASTERED IRONY AS THE GROUND OF HUMAN COMMUNITY

1 This distinction is Richard Rorty's, in *Contingency, Irony, and Solidarity* (Cambridge: Cambridge University Press, 1989), pp. xiii-xiv. Gary Handwerk argues that radical irony can be entirely commensurable with human community, claiming that Schlegel's irony has "an ethical and consensual force;" see *Irony and Ethics in Narrative from Schlegel to Lacan* (New Haven and London: Yale University Press, 1985). Agacinski's discussion of the politics of radical irony is especially interesting; she argues for instance that "Christianity for Kierkegaard can never have anything but an ironic relationship with the political order. The *extremely* ironic religious attitude, carried far enough, would consist in *defending* the powers that be, *no matter which ones*, out of indifference" (*Aparté*, p. 56). She does not discuss how "the extremely ironic *aesthetic* attitude" would escape this "political blameworthiness."
2 See *Fear and Trembling*: "The Hegelian philosophy holds that there is no justified concealment, no justified incommensurability;" p. 92.
3 Agacinski offers a sustained gender critique of Kierkegaard's "Christian indifference" as covertly appropriating the feminine virtues of 'castration' for an exclusively virile potency of impotence; see *Aparté*, pp. 167–184.
4 Leonard W. Deen, *Conversing in Paradise: Poetic Genius and Identity-as-Community in Blake's Los* (Columbia and London: University of Missouri Press, 1983), pp. 121–122.
5 See for example Susan Fox's claim that Blake's females are "either passive or pernicious," in *Poetic Form in Blake's 'Milton'* (Princeton: Princeton University Press, 1976), p. 214, and Anne K. Mellor's fundamental agreement with Fox that Blake's women are always "either passively dependent on men, or ... aggressive and evil," in "Blake's Portrayal of Women," in *Blake Illustrated Quarterly* 16 (Winter 1982–83), 148–155; 148.
6 Mellor, p. 153.

7 This assumes of course that for Blake only heterosexuality can be erotic, which may not necessarily be the case. Brenda Webster for example sees a strong homoerotic impulse in Blake's vision, in *Blake's Prophetic Psychology*.

8 "Because Eden is neither Generation nor Beulah, in Blake's poetry Eros plots are often converted into or dominated by redemption plots, as in *The Four Zoas* and *Jerusalem*;" Deen, p. 15.

9 See for example Michael Ferber's "Nature and the Female," in *The Social Vision of William Blake*, pp. 89–115.

10 *Blake and Freud*, p. 197.

11 As Jean Hagstrum remarks, "love" in Blake's eternity is "not *agape* alone but a combination of *eros* and *agape*," in *The Romantic Body: Love and Sexuality in Keats, Wordsworth, and Blake* (Knoxville: University of Tennessee Press, 1985), p. 110. This concurs with Thomas Frosch's insistence on the Blakean "renovation" of the body as being "not a transcendence but a reorganization of the given," in *The Awakening of Albion: the Renovation of the Body in the Poetry of William Blake* (Ithaca, New York: Cornell University Press, 1974), p. 10, and with Diana Hume George's remark that "Regeneration is an inclusive concept that includes Generation," p. 180.

12 Alicia Ostriker, "Desire Gratified and Ungratified: William Blake and Sexuality," in *Blake Illustrated Quarterly* 16 (Winter 1982–83), 156–165.

13 Kevin Newmark argues that these spheres do not constitute "a hierarchy in which the single individual [is] subjectively free to choose between the relatively independent spheres that move upward in linear fashion from an aesthetic (or prephilosophical) to an ethical (or philosophical) stage, and finally on to the religious (or postphilosophical) stage," endorsing Maurice Blanchot's aesthetic focus on language which he claims radically "unsettles" this traditional understanding. Such an aesthetic focus "serves to place the three categories" in "a differential structure of signification that is not necessarily either temporal or subjective" – effectively destroying Kierkegaard's emphasis on freedom and choice; *Aparté*, pp. 8–9.

14 Gregor Malantschuk, *The Controversial Kierkegaard*, pp. 60–61.

15 The Abraham–Isaac metaphor may not be without Oedipal significance, the same curiously *reverse* Oedipal implications involved in the relationship between Orc and Los in *The Book of Urizen*, *The Four Zoas* and in *Milton*. The binding of Blake's Orc by his parents on the top of a mountain (BU, VII; FZ, V, pages 60–63) is in some respects very like Abraham's parental binding of Isaac. Los binds his son out of "jealousy" in an oddly reverse Oedipal situation: "Los beheld the ruddy boy / Embracing his bright mother & beheld malignant fires / In his young eyes discerning plain that Orc plotted his death" (FZ, V, 60:7–9; 340). We are told of course that Abraham's motives are very different – that his ritualistic binding of Isaac is entirely at God's command. Yet this may not be the whole story, as Kierkegaard seems to force us to

consider. It is not farfetched to speculate, I think, that there may be a sense in which Abraham too binds his son out of a sense of jealousy – because his son, like Los's Orc, is a sign of his own mortality, or because his son represents a powerful force which somehow prevents him from attaining what he wants. Just as Orc's desire for Enitharmon blocks or threatens Los's desire for her as the vision of all that he pursues, so Isaac, insofar as he symbolizes Abraham's great love for the finite or this world, may thereby block Abraham from his true love, love for the infinite or for God. In other words, both sons are "jealously" regarded as in some sense obstacles to what their fathers most desire, the visionary state of unity with the infinite or with life.

Blake's and Kierkegaard's apparent sympathy with the father as opposed to the son in these circumstances – their reverse Oedipal identification with the father's rather than the son's jealousy – clearly contains the seeds of the redemptive or conversion experience in which they will themselves return to or identify with "the father" not as the origin of jealousy, the tyranny of the absolute, but as the agent of liberation from a new kind of tyranny, that of the relative (the son) holding itself up as the absolute (the father). Significantly, this is why, in *Milton*, Blake has Milton, once considered the tyrant of the absolute, function as the agent who frees Orc from his Chain of Jealousy:

> At last when desperation almost tore his heart in twain
> He recollected an old Prophecy in Eden recorded
> And often sung to the loud harp at the immortal feasts
> That Milton of the Land of Albion should up ascend
> Forwards from Ulro from the Vale of Felpham; and set free
> Orc from his Chain of Jealousy, he started at the thought
> (M, 1, 20:56–61; 115).

16 As Michael Ferber has noted, Blake is in fact ambivalent about equality despite his endorsement of liberty and fraternity; see *The Social Vision of William Blake*, pp. 67–88.

17 For an excellent detailed reading of *Cain*, see Paul Cantor's *Creature and Creator* (Cambridge: Cambridge University Press, 1984), pp. 135–155.

18 As Martin Bidney so accurately observes, "*Cain*, when viewed from a Blakean standpoint, constitutes a searching and penetrative examination of the psychology of the state of 'Generation,' a condition of mental constraint resulting from one's inability to transcend, or rather transvalue, the Natural cycle," in "*Cain* and *The Ghost of Abel*: Contexts for Understanding Blake's Response to Byron," *Blake Studies* 8 (1979), 145–168; 148–49.

19 Bidney argues convincingly however that Cain's rejection of love as it is offered to him by his wife Adah is, like Blake's rejection or demotion of Beulah, the rejection of a "tranquil pastoral Arcadia of reverie and mild repose" (p. 158); her love is therefore not a real option for the visionary Cain.

CHAPTER 5. IRONY AND AUTHORITY

1 In a very interesting reading of Tharmas's role in *The Four Zoas*, Erdman suggests that the epic is largely about "the Tongue's [Tharmas's] plight in exile and under censorship, an aspect of Blake's own predicament after 1795." See *Blake: Prophet Against Empire*, third edition (Princeton, 1977), pp. 298–308.

2 Erdman, p. 153.

3 Frye, *Fearful Symmetry*, p. 382.

4 Christopher Norris gives *The Point of View for my Work as an Author* a religious reading only to deconstruct it into an aesthetic one, thus providing a good example of both; see "Fictions of Authority: Narrative and Viewpoint in Kierkegaard's Writing," in *The Deconstructive Turn* (London and New York: Methuen, 1983), pp. 85–106.

5 As W.J.T. Mitchell remarks, "We may say, of course, that this guise of impersonality is a transparent fiction ... yet we also have to acknowledge that, for Blake, the claim of individual expressive authority and the disclaimer of authority (...) involves no contradiction, for the universal poetic genius that is God acts only through individuals. That is why Blake can seem to be the author of original writings and merely a conduit through which innumerable writings (...) transmit themselves." ("Visible Language," in *Romanticism and Contemporary Criticism*, p. 75).

6 Jerome McGann, "The Aim of Blake's Prophecies and the Uses of Blake Criticism," in *Blake's Sublime Allegory: Essays on 'The Four Zoas,' 'Milton,' and 'Jerusalem,'* ed. Stuart Curran and J. A. Wittreich (Madison: University of Wisconsin Press, 1973), pp. 3–21; p. 11.

7 Ibid., p. 10.

8 Ibid., p. 11, 14.

9 See Norris: "Kierkegaard undoubtedly labours to interpellate a reader who will find herself obliged to choose once and for all between alternative positions. But his text is unable to *impose* that choice – or even to state its necessity;" ("Fictions of Authority," p. 103). See also Agacinski's remark that "there is no precautionary measure – ever – that is capable of guaranteeing in an absolute sense the earnestness of a given discourse" (*Aparté*, p. 78). This is of course true; what is not true is that radical undecidability therefore inevitably follows.

10 Quoted in Lowrie's introduction to *Postscript*, p. xviii.

11 Agacinski imposes this false "either/or" on Kierkegaard when she claims that Kierkegaard's knight of faith, Abraham, does not speak (*Aparté*, pp. 138–9, 141, 237). Critically, the knight of faith does in fact speak; although language is indeed a form of (Hegelian) mediation, he finds a way of speaking so that "hearing they might not hear" – that is, of mastering irony. As Johannes de Silentio reports,

Only one word of his has been preserved, the only reply to Isaac, which is also sufficient proof that he had not spoken previously. Isaac asks Abraham where the lamb is for the burnt offering. And Abraham said, 'God will provide Himself the lamb for the burnt offering, my son.' ... In so far as I can understand the paradox I can also apprehend the total presence of Abraham in this word. First and foremost, he does not say anything, and it is in this form he says what he has to say. His reply to Isaac has the form of irony, for it is always irony when I say something and do not say anything. (FT, 124–5, 127–8)

Several Blake critics also correctly see that Blake does not impose a mystical (theological) or a deconstructive "either/or" on language: as Hazard Adams has pointed out, the Blakean "fall" is not from a pre-existent reality outside of language into language, but from an originally mythic language into a "spectral hardening" or negation of itself; see p. 145 of "Blake, *Jerusalem*, and Symbolic Form," in *Blake Studies* 7, no.2 (Spring 1975), 143–166. Robert Gleckner has similarly observed that "concomitant with the Blakean Fall into disintegration, fragmentation, and dislocation, is the fall of the Word into words;" in "Most Holy Forms of Thought: Some Observations on Blake and Language," in *English Literary History* 41 (Winter 1974), 555–577; 556. Mitchell perhaps makes this point best, when he remarks that Blake "treat[s] writing and printing as media capable of full presence, not as mere supplements to speech," reminding us that Blake is very different from the other romantics in this respect: "Blake continued ... to think of writing as a 'wond'rous art' when many of his contemporaries were blaming it for all the evils attendant on modernity" ("Visible Language," p. 51, 55). For Blake, unlike Shelley for example, the "deep truth" is neither imageless nor wordless. See also Michael Fischer's lucid explication of the extreme "either/or" of deconstruction in *Does Deconstruction Make Any Difference?*, p. 40.

12 Again, as I remarked in my introduction, the arguments over indeterminacy and the possibility of interpretive validity have pretty much run their course, and should not need extensive rehearsing here. It is worthwhile, nonetheless, to trace the extent to which Kierkegaard anticipates not only the strategies of deconstructive indeterminacy, but the most powerful arguments against them. Most telling perhaps are not his arguments for the *possibility* of "decidability" (now accepted in fact by most sophisticated deconstructionists) but his arguments about the implications of a hermeneutics of undecidability: that it leads to stasis and inaction, a spectral negation of action and life.

13 See Norris; the phrase "magisterial fiat" is his (p. 102).

14 See Alexander Nehamas, "The Postulated Author: Critical Monism as a Regulative Ideal," *Critical Inquiry*, vol.8 no.1 (Autumn 1981), 133–149. As Nehamas points out, even deconstructive criticism accepts it as "self-evident" that "literary texts are produced by agents and must be understood as such;" p. 145. David Hoy lucidly extends the implications of Nehamas's idea of the postulated author for poststructuralist theory (i.e., as entirely consistent with its radical perspectivism) in

"Different Stories," *London Review of Books*, January 8, 1987, 15–17. I am indebted to my colleague Eugene Hill for bringing this review article to my attention.

15 There can be no question of choosing, Derrida completes this remark, "because here we are in a region (let's say, provisionally, a region of historicity) where the category of choice seems particularly trivial;" see "Structure, Sign and Play," in *The Structuralist Controversy*, ed. Richard Macksey and Eugene Donato (Baltimore and London: The Johns Hopkins University Press, 1972), p. 265.

16 Louis Mackey, *Kierkegaard: A Kind of Poet* (Philadelphia: University of Pennsylvania Press, 1971), pp. 293–294.

17 Norris, p. 90.

18 See Hoy, 15–17.

19 Hoy, 15.

20 This is E.D. Hirsch's argument in *Innocence and Experience*; see chapter 1.

21 For a complex deconstructive reading of "The Tyger" see Steven Shaviro's "'Striving with Systems': Blake and the Politics of Difference," in *boundary* 2, 10.3 (1982), 229–249.

22 For accounts other than Frye's of this pattern of reversals in *Jerusalem*, see in particular "Perspectives on *Jerusalem*," in *Blake Studies* 7, 1 (1974), ed. Edward J. Rose.

23 McGann, p. 13.

24 Norris, p. 88.

25 McGann, p. 20.

26 C. Stephen Evans, *Kierkegaard's 'Fragments' and 'Postscript': the Religious Philosophy of Johannes Climacus* (Atlantic Highlands, N.J.: Humanities Press, 1982), p. 226.

27 See introduction, note 6.

28 Jacques Derrida, *Positions*, transl. Alan Bass (Chicago: University of Chicago Press, 1984); quoted in Shaviro, p. 235.

29 Shaviro, p. 235.

30 Candace Lang, *Irony/Humor. Critical Paradigms* (Baltimore and London: The Johns Hopkins University Press, 1988), p. 61.

31 M.H. Abrams, "Construing and Deconstructing," in *Romanticism and Contemporary Criticism*, p. 155.

32 *Aparté*, p. 58.

33 As McGann so aptly describes this otherness, "what is missing rises up before us as what has been rejected by the imagination, rises up as the absent reality – rises up, finally, as objectivity and otherness, without which imagination must become a hollow idea rather than what it is, a form of human action." (*Towards a Literature of Knowledge*, p. 36).

CONCLUSION. LOS AND THE SPECTRE IN THE LABOR OF THE NEGATIVE

1 See *The Concept of Dread*, p. 70, and *Concluding Unscientific Postscript*, p. 276.

2 Candace Lang claims that this revision happens within *The Concept of Irony*, but this seems to me mistaken. Although Kierkegaard does indeed end the work with a description of "mastered irony," he does not say in this work that Socrates embodies such irony. The point would be unimportant did it not suggest further possible misunderstandings of Kierkegaard's concept of irony. Deconstructionist readings of Kierkegaard, for example, rely almost exclusively upon the "infinitely negative" Socrates of *The Concept of Irony*, ignoring his later revision; see for example Agacinski's *Aparté*. More accurate is W. E. Nagley's article, "Kierkegaard's Early and Late Views of Socratic Irony," in *Thought* 55 (1980), 271–282.

3 Jerome McGann makes a very similar and more extended argument for the truth-claims of Blake's poetry in *Towards a Literature of Knowledge*; see Chapter One, "William Blake Illuminates the Truth," pp. 9–37.

4 For an excellent account of the Kierkegaardian paradox, see C. Stephen Evans, *Kierkegaard's 'Fragments' and 'Postscript': the Religious Philosophy of Johannes Climacus* (Atlantic Highlands, New Jersey: Humanities Press, 1983), pp. 207–245.

5 As Agacinski puts it, this otherness of existence "resists" rather than "opposes" speculative thought (the latter term suggesting a logical rather than "existential" opposition); "it displaces without opposing, it contests without contradicting." See *Aparté*, pp. 60–61.

6 G. Schufreider, "The Logic of the Absurd," in *Philosophy and Phenomenological Research* 44 (S 1983), 61–84; 70.

7 C. Stephen Evans argues persuasively against this criticism that Kierkegaard's God is merely an ethical fiction in "Kierkegaard on Subjective Truth: Is God an Ethical Fiction?", *International Journal for Philosophy of Religion* 7 (1976), 288–299.

8 Yet the romantic poets, Abrams remarks, "felt intensely the strength of the temptation to hopelessness and apathy which is chief (...) among 'all that is at enmity with joy,' hence with life and creativity. ... Romantic affirmations do not eliminate, nor, taken in their full context, do they minimize the agony and strife of human hearts. To justify evil by placing it in a larger conceptual overview is not to annul it, or to lessen the pain of suffering; an excess of suffering does not foster character but destroys it; and the tragic paradox is that the values of life are valuable precisely because they are limited and defined by death" (*Natural Supernaturalism*, p. 442, 444). Seminal works initiating the "other, skeptical romanticism" of a more fragmentary or sometimes failed vision include Paul De Man's "The Rhetoric of Temporality," in

which De Man argued that a more skeptical notion of language as
"allegory" (in which "the allegorical sign refer[s] to another sign that
precedes it") should replace the elevation of "symbol" (seen as a
"happy synthesis" of mind and nature, language and reality) as para-
digmatic of romantic thought; see *Interpretation: Theory and Practice*,
ed. Charles Singleton (Baltimore: The Johns Hopkins University Press,
1969), pp. 173–209. De Man's numerous "allegorical" readings of
romantic poets have been collected within a single volume, *The Rhetoric
of Romanticism* (New York: Cornell University Press, 1984), a volume
which De Man described as representing, with the "possible addition"
of "The Rhetoric of Temporality," "the main bulk of what I have
written on romanticism" (p. vii). Deconstructionist readings of the
romantic poets by Harold Bloom, Geoffrey Hartman, and J. Hillis
Miller appear in *Deconstruction and Criticism*, ed. Harold Bloom et. al.
(New York: The Seabury Press, 1979); other skeptical readings (by
now legion) include such works as Anne K. Mellor's *English Romantic
Irony* (Cambridge, Mass., and London: Harvard University Press,
1980) and Thomas McFarland's *Romanticism and the Forms of Ruin*
(Princeton: Princeton University Press, 1981).

9 T.S. Eliot, "William Blake," in *Selected Essays* 1917–1950 (New York:
Harcourt Brace Jovanovich, Inc., 1964).

10 J. Kellenberger makes a similar argument for the Kierkegaardian will
in "Religious Faith and Prometheus," *Philosophy* 55 (1980), 497–507.
The denial of self in the act of faith is exactly the opposite of the
"prideful" assertion of self in romantic Prometheanism, he argues; his
argument however may overlook the extent to which a vigorous,
spirited assertion of the will remains vital to Kierkegaard's conception
of faith.

11 "By the long Habit of the accursed Poison i.e. Opium my Volition (...)
was completely deranged ... so that I was perpetually in the state, in
which you see paralytic Persons, who attempting to push a step forward
in one direction are violently forced round to the opposite ... the worst
was, that in *exact proportion* to the *importance* and *urgency* of any Duty was
it, as of a fatal necessity, sure to be neglected;" *Collected Letters of Samuel
Taylor Coleridge*, ed. E.L.Griggs, vol. II, pp. 489–490. See Rousseau's
"Sixth Walk," in *Reveries of the Solitary Walker*, in which he complains of
how even the most natural and generous of human impulses – charity –
becomes irksome once it becomes (as society inevitably makes it
become) a duty.

12 Los's labor of exclusion and choice is fundamentally a kind of *praxis*, for
its emphasis is on actively realizing or actualizing the individual self.
David Punter gives this element of *praxis* a Marxist reading, remarking
"Los's work shares the basic characteristics of Marx's description – the
notions of man's continuing self-creation, of his self-realisation through
the creation of objects, of work as a guarantee of freedom," in "Blake:

Creative and Uncreative Labor," *Studies in Romanticism* 16 (Fall 1977), 535–61, 546). Michael Ferber similarly emphasizes the material (as well as spiritual) dimension of Los's labors and the many images of machines (looms, furnaces, wheels) throughout Blake's myth, briefly discussing as well Los's labor to consolidate error (p. 146), in *The Social Vision of William Blake*, pp. 131–151.

13 Damrosch, for example, argues that Blake "openly defies the reality principle:" "In *The Ego and the Id* Freud discusses the ego's subservience to three masters, 'the external world, the libido of the id, and the severity of the super-ego' ... All three 'masters' are visible in Blake's myth, but he asserts that they are false and can be dispensed with. The external world is a Lockean–Newtonian fiction; the libido is a caged Orc who can be healed ... by the sacrifice of Jesus in Luvah's robes of blood; and the superego is the brooding Urizen whose Satanic state can be abolished ... Freud would diagnose this as wish-fulfillment of a peculiarly comprehensive kind" (*Symbol and Truth in Blake's Myth*, p. 163).

14 Damrosch points out that in "The Tyger" Blake "starts out from the same questions that a skeptic would put, in this case the argument from Cicero that Hume quotes in *Dialogues Concerning Natural Religion*" (p. 377). The Humean skeptic of course appears always in Blake's poetry as the enemy he attacks; yet this enemy may well be a voice within Blake himself. Blake shares the skeptic's distrust of empirical phenomena, sense impressions, or "objective knowledge" as the basis for certainty, in a peculiar combination of empiricism and idealism. Damrosch suggests Blake's insistence that abstract universals can be known only through "minute particulars" "derives from that part of empiricism (as in Berkeley) which he was unwilling to reject" (pp. 20–21n.). Andrew M. Cooper has recently explored in interesting and useful ways the relation of eighteenth-century skepticism to romantic doubt, in *Doubt and Identity in Romantic Poetry* (New Haven and London: Yale University Press, 1988), remarking of Blake that "by recognizing difference or otherness to be an irreducibly mysterious fact of immediate sense experience, Blake in effect beats the sensationalists at their own game" (p. 42) – essentially, I think, what I am arguing here. Stephen Crites reports (and accepts) being corrected by Robert L. Perkins on the issue of Kierkegaard's supposedly Kantian "critical idealism" with the retort that "'the only authors he [Kierkegaard] refers to with approval on epistemological matters are Hume and the Greek skeptics ... All objective knowledge for Kierkegaard is empirical, and it is in every sense an approximation. ... Objective knowledge is an approximation, but more like Hume's skepticism than Kant's synthetic a priori'" (*Twilight*, p. 22n.).

15 M.H.Abrams, "Construing and Deconstructing," in *Romanticism and Contemporary Criticism*, p. 132.

16 Michael Fischer points out the affinities of Northrop Frye's belief in "a revolutionary and transforming act of choice" (which Frye acknowledges as Blake's influence on his thought) with deconstruction in *Does Deconstruction Make Any Difference?* See Chapter 2, "The Imagination as a Sanction of Value," pp. 14–31.

17 As Jerome McGann remarks, Blake's "stubborn insularity of mind" produced "a philosophy of imagination, or an imagination of mind, which stood in the sharpest critical relation to the philosophical (and imaginative) spirit of the age;" in *Towards a Literature of Knowledge*, p. 16.

18 A.O. Lovejoy, "On the Discrimination of Romanticisms," *Essays in the History of Ideas* (Baltimore: The Johns Hopkins University Press, 1948), pp. 228–253.

Bibliography

I. BLAKE

PRIMARY WORKS

Blake, William. *The Poetry and Prose of William Blake*. ed. David Erdman, with commentary by Harold Bloom. Garden City, New York: Doubleday & Co., 1982.

SECONDARY WORKS

Abrams, M.H. *Natural Supernaturalism*. New York: W.W. Norton & Co., Inc., 1971.

Adams, Hazard. "Blake, *Jerusalem*, and Symbolic Form," *Blake Studies* 7, no.2 (Spring 1975), 143–166.

Alford, Steven E. *Irony and the Logic of the Romantic Imagination*. American University Studies, Series III: Comparative Literature, vol. 13. New York, Berne, Frankfurt am Main, Nancy: Peter Lang, 1984.

Altizer, Thomas J.J. *The New Apocalypse: the Radical Christian Vision of William Blake*. East Lansing, Michigan: Michigan State University Press, 1967.

Aubrey, Bryan. *Watchmen of Eternity. Blake's Debt to Jacob Boehme*. Lanham, New York, London: University Press of America, 1986.

Ault, Donald. "Incommensurability and Interconnection in Blake's Anti-Newtonian Text," *Studies in Romanticism* 16 (Summer 1977), 277–303.

"Re-Visioning *The Four Zoas*," in *Unnam'd Forms: Blake and Textuality*. ed. Nelson Hilton and Thomas A. Fogler. Berkeley, Los Angeles, London: University of California Press, 1986, pp. 105–139.

Behrendt, Stephen. *The Moment of Explosion: Blake and the Illustration of 'Milton.'* Lincoln: University of Nebraska Press, 1983.

Bentley, G.E. *Blake Records*. Oxford: Clarendon Press, 1969.

Bertholf, R.J. and Annette S. Levitt, eds. *William Blake and the Moderns*. Albany: SUNY Press, 1982.

Bidney, Martin. *Blake and Goethe. Psychology, Ontology, Imagination*. Columbia: University of Missouri Press, 1988.

225

"*Cain* and *The Ghost of Abel*: Contexts for Understanding Blake's Response to Byron," *Blake Studies* 8 (1979), 145–165.

Bloom, Harold. *Blake's Apocalypse*. Ithaca and London: Cornell University Press, 1963.

    The Visionary Company. Ithaca and London: Cornell University Press, 1961.

    "Dialectic in *The Marriage of Heaven and Hell*," PMLA 73 (1958), 501–504.

Bracher, Mark and Donald Ault, eds. *Critical Paths: Blake and the Argument of Method*. Durham and London: Duke University Press, 1987.

Curran, Stewart, and Joseph Wittreich, eds. *Blake's Sublime Allegory: Essays on 'The Four Zoas,' 'Milton,' and 'Jerusalem.'* Madison: University of Wisconsin Press, 1973.

Damrosch, Leopold, Jr. *Symbol and Truth in Blake's Myth*. Princeton: Princeton University Press, 1980.

Davies, J.G. *The Theology of William Blake*. Oxford: Clarendon Press, 1948.

Deen, Leonard W. *Conversing in Paradise: Poetic Genius and Identity-as-Community in Blake's Los*. Columbia and London: University of Missouri Press, 1983.

De Luca, V.A. "A Wall of Words: the Sublime as Text," in Hilton and Vogler, pp. 218–241.

Dickstein, Morris. "The Price of Experience: Blake's Reading of Freud," *The Literary Freud: Mechanisms of Defense and the Poetic Will*, ed. Joseph H. Smith (Psychiatry and the Humanities, vol.4). New Haven and London: Yale University Press, 1980, pp. 67–111.

DiSalvo, Jackie. *War of Titans: Blake's Critique of Milton and the Politics of Religion*. Pittsburgh: University of Pittsburgh Press, 1983.

Doskow, Minna. "The Humanized Universe of Blake and Marx," *William Blake and the Moderns*, ed. Bertholf and Levitt, pp. 25–240.

Eaves, Morris. *William Blake's Theory of Art*. Princeton: Princeton University Press, 1982.

    and Michael Fischer, eds. *Romanticism and Contemporary Criticism*. Ithaca and London: Cornell University Press, 1986.

Erdman, David V. *Blake: Prophet Against Empire*. Third Edition. Princeton: Princeton University Press, 1977.

    and John Grant, eds. *Blake's Visionary Forms Dramatic*. Princeton: Princeton University Press, 1970.

Essick, R.N., and D. Pearce, eds. *Blake in His Time*. Bloomington: Indiana University Press, 1978.

Ferber, Michael. *The Social Vision of William Blake*. Princeton: Princeton University Press, 1985.

Fisher, Peter. *The Valley of Vision. Blake as Prophet and Revolutionary.* ed. Northrop Frye. Toronto: University of Toronto Press, 1961.

Fox, Susan. *Poetic Form in Blake's 'Milton.'* Princeton: Princeton University Press, 1976.

"The Female as Metaphor in William Blake's Poetry," *Critical Inquiry* 3 (1977), 507–551.

Frosch, Thomas R. *The Awakening of Albion; The Renovation of the Body in the Poetry of William Blake.* Ithaca: Cornell University Press, 1974.

Frye, Northrop, ed. *Blake: A Collection of Critical Essays.* Englewood Cliffs, New Jersey: Prentice-Hall, Inc., 1966.

Fearful Symmetry: A Study of William Blake. Princeton: Princeton University Press, 1947.

"The Keys to the Gates," *Some British Romantics: A Collection of Essays,* ed. James V. Logan, John E. Jordan, and Northrop Frye. Columbus: Ohio State University Press, 1966, pp. 3–40.

Gallant, Christine. *Blake and the Assimilation of Chaos.* Princeton: Princeton University Press, 1979.

George, Diana Hume. *Blake and Freud.* Ithaca: Cornell University Press, 1980.

Gilchrist, Alexander. *Life of William Blake.* London and Cambridge: Macmillan and Co., 1863.

Gillham, D.G. *Blake's Contrary States: the 'Songs of Innocence and Experience' as Dramatic Poems.* Cambridge: Cambridge University Press, 1966.

Glausser, Wayne. "The Gates of Memory in Night vııa of *The Four Zoas,*" *Blake Illustrated Quarterly* 18 (Spring 1985), 196–203.

Gleckner, Robert F. "Antithetical Structure in Blake's 'Poetical Sketches,'" *Studies in Romanticism* 20 (Summer 1981), 143–162.

Blake and Spenser. Baltimore and London: The Johns Hopkins University Press, 1985.

"Most Holy Forms of Thought: Some Observations on Blake and Language," *English Literary History* 41 (Winter 1974), 555–577.

Hagstrum, Jean. *The Romantic Body. Love and Sexuality in Keats, Wordsworth, and Blake.* Knoxville: The University of Tennessee Press, 1985.

Hilton, Nelson. "Blakean Zen," *Studies in Romanticism* 24 (Summer 1985), 183–200.

Literal Imagination: Blake's Vision of Words. Berkeley, Los Angeles, London: University of California Press, 1983.

and Thomas A. Vogler, eds. *Unnam'd Forms. Blake and Textuality.* Berkeley, Los Angeles, London: University of California Press, 1986.

Hirsch, E.D., Jr. *Innocence and Experience. An Introduction to Blake.* Chicago: University of Chicago Press, 1964, 1975.

Johnson, Mary Lynn. "'Separating What has Been Mixed:' A Suggestion for a Perspective on *Milton,*" *Blake Studies* 6 (Fall 1973), 11–17.

and Brian Wilkie. "The Spectrous Embrace in *The Four Zoas*, VIIa," *Blake Illustrated Quarterly* 12 (1978), 100–106.

Keynes, Geoffrey. "Blake's Spectre," *Book Collector* 28 (1979), 60–66.

Kilgore, John. "The Order of Nights VIIa and VIIb in Blake's *The Four Zoas*," *Blake Illustrated Quarterly* 12 (Fall 1978), 107–113.

Klonsky, Milton. *William Blake: The Seer and His Visions*. New York: Harmony Books, 1977.

Lindsay, Jack. *William Blake: His Life and Work*. New York: Braziller, 1979.

McGann, Jerome J. "The Aim of Blake's Prophecies and the Uses of Blake Criticism," *Blake's Sublime Allegory*, ed. Curran and Wittreich, pp. 3–21.

Social Values and Poetic Acts. The Historical Judgment of Literary Work. Cambridge, Massachusetts and London, England: Harvard University Press, 1988.

Towards a Literature of Knowledge. Chicago: University of Chicago Press, 1989.

Mellor, Anne K. "Blake's Portrayal of Women," *Blake Illustrated Quarterly* 16 (Winter 1982–83), 148–155.

Miller, Dan. "Contrary Revelation:'The Marriage of Heaven and Hell,'" *Studies in Romanticism* vol.24 no. 4 (Winter 1985), 491–509.

Mills, Alice. "The Spectral Bat in Blake's Illustrations to *Jerusalem*," *Blake Studies* 9 (1980), 87–99.

Mitchell, Jeffrey. "Progression from the *Marriage* into the Bard's Song of *Milton*," *Blake Studies* 6 (Fall 1973), 35–45.

Mitchell, W.J.T. "Visible Language: Blake's Wond'rous Art of Writing," *Romanticism and Contemporary Criticism*, ed. Morris Eaves and Michael Fischer; pp. 46–95.

Murray. E.B. "*Jerusalem* Reversed," *Blake Studies* vol. 7 no.1 (Fall 1974), 11–25.

Murry, J. Middleton. *William Blake*. London: Jonathan Cape, 1933.

Nurmi, Martin K. *Blake's "Marriage of Heaven and Hell:" A Critical Study*. Kent, Ohio: Kent State University Bulletin, April, 1957.

Ostriker, Alicia. "Desire Gratified and Ungratified: William Blake and Sexuality," *Blake Illustrated Quarterly* 16 (Winter 1982–83), 156–165.

Paley, Morton. "Cowper as Blake's Spectre," *Eighteenth Century Studies* (1968), 236–252.

Energy and the Imagination: A Study of the Development of Blake's Thought. Oxford: Oxford University Press, 1970.

The Continuing City: William Blake's Jerusalem. Oxford: Clarendon Press, 1984.

William Blake. Oxford: Phaidon Press; New York: E.P.Dutton, 1978.

and Michael Phillips, eds. *William Blake; Essays in Honor of Sir Geoffrey Keynes*. Oxford: Clarendon Press, 1973.

Phillips, Michael, ed. *Interpreting Blake: Essays*. London, New York, Melbourne: Cambridge University Press, 1978.

Punter, David. *Blake, Hegel, and Dialectic*. Amsterdam: Rodopi, 1982.

"Blake: Creative and Uncreative Labor," *Studies in Romanticism* 16 (Fall 1977), 535–561.

"Blake, Marxism, and Dialectic," *Literature and History* 6 (1977).

"Blake, Trauma, and the Female," *New Literary History* 15 (Spring 1984), 475–490.

Rose, Edward J. "Blake and the Double: The Spectre as Doppelganger," *Colby Library Quarterly* 13 no.2 (June 1977), 127–139.

ed. "Perspectives on *Jerusalem*," in *Blake Studies* 7 (No. 1, 1974).

Saurat, Denis. *Blake and Milton*. New York: Russell and Russell, 1965.

Scholz, Joachim J. *Blake and Novalis: A Comparison of Romanticism's High Arguments*. Frankfurt am Main, Berne, Las Vegas: Peter Lang, 1978.

Scrimgeour, J.R. "'The Great Example of Horror & Agony': A Comparison of Søren Kierkegaard's Demonically Despairing Individual with William Blake's Spectre of Urthona," *Scandinavian Studies* 47 (Winter 1975), 36–41.

Shaviro, Steven. "Striving with Systems: Blake and the Politics of Difference," *boundary* 2 10.3 (1982), 229–250.

Simpson, David. "Blake and Derrida – Our Caesars Neither Praised nor Buried," in Hilton and Vogler, pp. 11–25.

Smith, J., ed. *The Literary Freud*. New Haven: Yale University Press, 1980.

Storch, Margaret. "The 'Spectrous Fiend' Cast Out: Blake's Crisis at Felpham," *Modern Language Quarterly* 44 (June 1983), 115–135.

Tannenbaum, Leslie. "Lord Byron in the Wilderness: Biblical Tradition in Byron's *Cain* and Blake's *The Ghost of Abel*," *Modern Philology* 72 (May 1975), 350–364.

"Blake and the Iconography of *Cain*," *Blake in His Time*, ed. Essick and Pearce, pp. 23–34.

Tatham, Frederick. *The Letters of William Blake, Together With a Life*, ed. A.G.B. Russell. New York: Charles Scribner's Sons, 1906.

Trawick, L.M. "William Blake's German Connection," *Colby Library Quarterly* 13, no. 4 (December 1979), 229–245.

Wagenknecht, David. Afterword to *Critical Paths*, ed. Dan Miller et al.

Warner, Janet. "Blake's Figures of Despair: Man in his Spectre's Power," *William Blake: Essays in Honor of Sir Geoffrey Keynes*, ed. Paley and Phillips; pp. 208–224.

Webster, Brenda. *Blake's Prophetic Psychology*. Athens, Georgia: University of Georgia Press, 1983.
Whitehead, Fred. "William Blake and Radical Tradition," *The Weapons of Criticism: Marxism in America and the Literary Tradition*, ed. Norman Rudick. Ramparts Press, 1976, pp. 191–214.
Wilson, Mona. *The Life of William Blake*. London: P. Davies, Ltd., 1932.
Wittreich, J.A. *Angel of Apocalypse: Blake's Idea of Milton*. Madison: University of Wisconsin Press, 1975.

II. KIERKEGAARD

PRIMARY WORKS

Kierkegaard, Søren. *The Concept of Dread*. transl. Walter Lowrie. Princeton: Princeton University Press, 1944.
  The Concept of Irony. transl. Lee M. Capel. Bloomington and London: Indiana University Press, 1965.
  Concluding Unscientific Postscript. transl. David F. Swenson and Walter Lowrie. Princeton: Princeton University Press, 1941.
  Either/Or, vol. I. transl. David F. Swenson and Lillian Swenson. Princeton: Princeton University Press, 1944.
  Either/Or, vol. II. transl. Walter Lowrie. Princeton: Princeton University Press, 1944.
  Fear and Trembling. transl. Walter Lowrie. Princeton: Princeton University Press, 1941.
  Philosophical Fragments. transl. David F. Swenson. Princeton: Princeton University Press, 1936.
  The Point of View for My Work as an Author. transl. Walter Lowrie. New York: Harper & Row, Publishers, Inc., 1962.
  Repetition. transl. Walter Lowrie. Princeton: Princeton University Press, 1941.
  The Sickness Unto Death. transl. Walter Lowrie. Princeton: Princeton University Press, 1941.

SECONDARY WORKS

Agacinski, Sylviane. *Aparté: Conceptions and Deaths of Søren Kierkegaard*, transl. Kevin Newmark. Tallahassee: The Florida State University Press, 1988.

Bigelow, Patrick. "Kierkegaard and the Hermeneutical Circle," *Man and World* 15 (1982), 67–82.
  Kierkegaard and the Problem of Writing. Tallahassee: The Florida State University Press, 1987.

Crites, Stephen. *In the Twilight of Christendom: Hegel Versus Kierkegaard on Faith and History*. AAR Studies in Religion, No. Two, 1972.
"Pseudonymous Authorship as Art and as Act," *Kierkegaard: A Collection of Critical Essays*, ed. Josiah Thompson. Garden City, N.Y.: Anchor Books, 1972, pp. 183–229.

Daise, B. "Kierkegaard and the Absolute Paradox," *Journal of the History of Philosophy* 14 (1976), 63–68.
Dunning, S. N. *Kierkegaard's Dialectic of Inwardness: a Structural Analysis of the Theory of Stages*. Princeton: Princeton University Press, 1985.

Elrod, John W. *Kierkegaard and Christendom*. Princeton: Princeton University Press, 1981.
Evans, C. Stephen. "Is the Concept of an Absolute Duty toward God Morally Unintelligible?", *Kierkegaard's 'Fear and Trembling': Critical Appraisals*, ed. Robert L. Perkins. University, Alabama: University of Alabama Press, 1981, pp. 141–151.
Kierkegaard's 'Fragments' and 'Postscript': the Religious Philosophy of Johannes Climacus. Atlantic Highlands, New Jersey: Humanities Press, 1983.
"Kierkegaard on Subjective Truth: Is God an Ethical Fiction?", *International Journal of Philosophy and Religion* 7 (1976), 288–299.
"Mis-using Religious Language: Something About Kierkegaard and the Myth of God Incarnate," *Religious Studies* 15 (June 1979), 139–157.

Fenger, Henning. *Kierkegaard, the Myths and their Origins: Studies in the Kierkegaard Papers and Letters*. transl. G.C. Schoolfield. New Haven: Yale University Press, 1980.
Friedman, R.Z. "Kierkegaard: First Existentialist or Last Kantian?", *Religious Studies* 18 (June 1982), 159–170.

Jacobs, Louis. "The Problem of the *Akedah* in Jewish Thought," *Kierkegaard's 'Fear and Trembling': Critical Appraisals*, ed. Robert L. Perkins, pp. 1–9.

Kellenberger, J. "Religious Faith and Prometheus," *Philosophy* 55 (October 1980), 497–507.
"Kierkegaard, Indirect Communication, and Religious Truth," *International Journal of Philosophy and Religion* 16 no.2 (1984), 153–160.
Kirmmse, Bruce. *Kierkegaard in Golden Age Denmark*. Bloomington: Indiana University Press, 1990.

Lowith, Karl. *From Hegel to Nietzsche: the Revolution in Nineteenth Century Thought*. transl. David E. Green. Garden City, N.Y.: Doubleday & Co., Inc., 1967.
Lowrie, Walter. *Kierkegaard*. London, New York, and Toronto: Oxford University Press, 1938.

Mackey, Louis. *Kierkegaard: A Kind of Poet*. Philadelphia: University of
    Pennsylvania Press, Inc., 1971.
    Points of View: Readings of Kierkegaard. Tallahassee: Florida State Univer-
    sity Press, 1986.
Malantschuk, Gregor. *The Controversial Kierkegaard*. transl. Howard V.
    Hong and Edna H. Hong. Waterloo, Canada: Wilfred Laurier Uni-
    versity Press, 1980.
    Kierkegaard's Thought. transl. Howard V. Hong and Edna H. Hong.
    Princeton: Princeton University Press, 1971.
Matthis, Michael. "The Social in Kierkegaard's Concept of the Indi-
    vidual," *Philosophy Today* 23 (Spring 1979), 74–83.

Nagley, W.E. "Kierkegaard's Early and Later View of Socratic Irony,"
    Thought 55 (s 1980), 271–282.
Norris, Christopher. "Fictions of Authority: Narrative and Viewpoint in
    Kierkegaard's Writing," in *The Deconstructive Turn: Essays in the Rhe-
    toric of Philosophy*. London and New York: Methuen, 1983, pp. 85–106.

Pailin, David A. "Abraham and Isaac: A Hermeneutical Problem before
    Kierkegaard," *Kierkegaard's 'Fear and Trembling': Critical Appraisals*, ed.
    Robert L. Perkins, pp. 10–42.
Pedersen, B. "Fictionality and Authority: a Point of View for Kierke-
    gaard's Work as an Author," *Modern Language Notes* 89 (December
    1974), 938–956.
Perkins, Robert L. "For Sanity's Sake: Kant, Kierkegaard, and Father
    Abraham," *Kierkegaard's 'Fear and Trembling': Critical Appraisals*, ed.
    Robert L. Perkins, pp. 43–61.
    ed. *Kierkegaard's 'Fear and Trembling': Critical Appraisals*. Alabama: Uni-
    versity of Alabama Press, 1981.
Pletsch, C. "The Self-Sufficient Text in Nietzsche and Kierkegaard," *Yale
    French Studies* no. 66 (1984), 160–188.

Sarf, H. "Reflections on Kierkegaard's Socrates," *Journal for the History of
    Ideas* 44 (April/June 1983), 255–276.
Schleifer, Ronald, and Robert Markley,eds. *Kierkegaard and Literature. Irony,
    Repetition, and Criticism*. Norman: University of Oklahoma Press.
Schufreider, G. "The Logic of the Absurd," *Philosophy and Phenomenological
    Research* 44 (s 1983), 61–84.
Smyth, John Vigneaux. *A Question of Eros: Irony in Sterne, Kierkegaard, and
    Barthes*. Tallahassee: The Florida State University Press, 1987.
Spanos, W.V. "Heidegger, Kierkegaard, and the Hermeneutic Circle:
    Towards a Postmodern Theory of Interpretation as Dis-closure,"
    boundary 2,4 (1976), 455–488.
Stack, George. "The Inward Journey: Kierkegaard's Journals and
    Papers," *Philosophy Today* 23 (Summer 1979), 170–196.

"Repetition in Kierkegaard and Freud," *Personalist* 58 (July 1977), 249–260.

Taylor, Mark C. *Altarity*. Chicago and London: University of Chicago Press, 1987.
Journeys to Selfhood, Hegel and Kierkegaard. Berkeley: University of California Press, 1980.
Kierkegaard's Pseudonymous Authorship: A Study of Time and the Self. Princeton: Princeton University Press, 1975.
Thompson, Josiah. *Kierkegaard: A Biographical Essay*. New York: Alfred A. Knopf, 1973.
ed. *Kierkegaard: A Collection of Critical Essays*. Garden City, N.Y.: Anchor Books, 1972.

III. ROMANTICISM AND THEORY

Adams, Hazard. *Philosophy of the Literary Symbolic*. Tallahassee: University Presses of Florida, 1983.
Abrams, M.H. "Construing and Deconstructing," *Romanticism and Contemporary Criticism*, ed. Morris Eaves and Michael Fischer. Ithaca: Cornell University Press, 1986, pp. 127–182.
ed. *English Romantic Poets. Modern Essays in Criticism*, second edition. London, Oxford, New York: Oxford University Press, 1975.
"English Romanticism: The Spirit of the Age," *Romanticism: Points of View*, second edition, ed. Robert Gleckner and Gerald Enscoe. Detroit: Wayne State University Press, 1979, pp. 314–330.
Natural Supernaturalism. Tradition and Revolution in Romantic Literature. New York: W.W.Norton & Co., Inc, 1971.

Bloom, Harold, et.al., eds. *Deconstruction and Criticism*. New York: The Seabury Press, 1979.
ed. *Romanticism and Consciousness. Essays in Criticism*. New York: W.W. Norton & Co., Inc., 1970.
The Visionary Company. A Reading of English Romantic Poetry. Ithaca and London: Cornell University Press, 1971.
Booth, Wayne C. *A Rhetoric of Irony*. Chicago: University of Chicago Press, 1974.
Bové, Paul A. "Cleanth Brooks and Modern Irony: A Kierkegaardian Critique," in *Destructive Poetics: Heidegger and Modern American Poetry*. New York: Columbia University Press, 1980, pp. 93–130.
Brisman, Leslie. *Milton's Poetry of Choice and Its Romantic Heirs*. New Haven: Yale University Press, 1978.

Cantor, Paul A. *Creature and Creator. Myth-making in English Romanticism*, Cambridge: Cambridge University Press, 1985.

Cooke, Michael. *Acts of Inclusion. Studies Bearing on an Elementary Theory of Romanticism*. New Haven and London: Yale University Press, 1979.
  The Romantic Will. New Haven and London: Yale University Press, 1976.
Cooper, Andrew M. *Doubt and Identity in Romantic Poetry*. New Haven and London: Yale University Press, 1988.

De Man, Paul. *Allegories of Reading. Figural Language in Rousseau, Nietzsche, Rilke, and Proust*. New Haven and London: Yale University Press, 1979.
  The Rhetoric of Romanticism. New York: Columbia University Press, 1984.
  "The Rhetoric of Temporality," *Interpretation: Theory and Practice*, ed. Charles Singleton. Baltimore: The Johns Hopkins University Press, 1969.
Derrida, Jacques. *Of Grammatology*. transl. Gayatri Spivak. Baltimore and London: The Johns Hopkins University Press, 1976.
  "Structure, Sign, and Play," in *The Structuralist Controversy*, ed. Richard Macksey and Eugene Donato. Baltimore: Johns Hopkins University Press, 1972.

Eaves, Morris, and Michael Fischer, eds. *Romanticism and Contemporary Criticism*. Ithaca and London: Cornell University Press, 1986.
Ellis, John M. *Against Deconstruction*. Princeton: Princeton University Press, 1989.

Fischer, Michael. *Does Deconstruction Make Any Difference? Poststructuralism and the Defense of Poetry in Modern Criticism*. Bloomington: Indiana University Press, 1985.
Frye, Northrop. *A Study of English Romanticism*. New York: Random House, 1968.
Furst, Lillian. *Fictions of Romantic Irony*. Cambridge: Harvard University Press, 1984.
  The Contours of European Romanticism. Lincoln: University of Nebraska Press, 1979.

Gleckner, Robert F., and Gerald E. Enscoe, eds. *Romanticism: Points of View*. Detroit: Wayne State University Press, 1975, 1979.
Graff, Gerald. *Literature Against Itself. Literary Ideas in Modern Society*. Chicago and London: University of Chicago Press, 1979.

Handwerk, Gary. *Irony and Ethics in Narrative from Schlegel to Lacan*. New Haven and London: Yale University Press, 1985.
Heller, Peter. *Dialectics and Nihilism. Essays on Lessing, Nietzsche, Mann, and Kafka*. University of Massachusetts Press, 1966.
Hirsch, E.D. *Wordsworth and Schelling. A Typological Study of Romanticism*. New Haven: Yale University Press, 1960.

Validity in Interpretation. New Haven: Yale University Press, 1967.
Hoy, David. "Different Stories." *London Review of Books*, 8 January 1987, 15–17.

Lang, Candace. *Irony/Humor. Critical Paradigms*. Baltimore and London: The Johns Hopkins University Press, 1988.
Lovejoy, A. O. "On the Discrimination of Romanticisms." *Essays in the History of Ideas*. Baltimore: The Johns Hopkins University Press, 1948, pp. 228–253.

McFarland, Thomas. *Romanticism and the Forms of Ruin: Wordsworth, Coleridge, and Modalities of Fragmentation*. Princeton: Princeton University Press, 1981.
McGann, Jerome. *The Romantic Ideology. A Critical Investigation*. Chicago and London: University of Chicago Press, 1983.
Mellor, Anne K. *English Romantic Irony*. Cambridge, Mass., and London: Harvard University Press, 1980.
"On Romantic Irony, Symbolism, and Allegory." *Criticism*, vol. 21, no. 3 (summer 1979), 217–139.
Miller, J. Hillis. *Fiction and Repetition*. Cambridge: Harvard University Press, 1982.
Muecke, D.C. *Irony*. London: Methuen & Co., Ltd., 1970.

Nehamas, Alexander. "The Postulated Author: Critical Monism as a Regulative Ideal." *Critical Inquiry*, vol. 8, no. 1 (Autumn 1981), 133–149.
Nietzsche: Life as Literature. Cambridge and London: Harvard University Press, 1985.
Norris, Christopher. *Deconstruction. Theory and Practice*. London and New York: Methuen & Co., Ltd., 1982.
The Contest of Faculties. Philosophy and Theory After Deconstruction. London and New York: Methuen & Co., Ltd., 1985.
The Deconstructive Turn. Essays in the Rhetoric of Philosophy. London and New York: Methuen, 1983.

Patterson, Lee. *Negotiating the Past. The Historical Understanding of Medieval Literature*. Madison: University of Wisconsin Press, 1987.
Peckham, Morse. "Toward a Theory of Romanticism." *Romanticism: Points of View*, ed. Gleckner and Enscoe, pp. 231–257.
Prickett, Stephen. *Romanticism and Religion: The Tradition of Coleridge and Wordsworth in the Victorian Church*. Cambridge: Cambridge University Press, 1976.

Rajan, Tilottama. "Displacing Post-Structuralism: Romantic Studies After Paul De Man." *Studies in Romanticism*, vol. 24 no.4 (Winter 1985), 451–474.

The Supplement of Reading. Ithaca: Cornell University Press, 1990.

Rorty, Richard. *Contingency, Irony, and Solidarity*. Cambridge: Cambridge University Press, 1989.

Schlegel, F.W. *Dialogue on Poetry and Literary Aphorisms*. transl. Ernst Behler and Roman Stone. University Park: Pennsylvania State University Press, 1968.

"On Incomprehensibility." transl. Peter Firchow. *Friedrich Schlegel's "Lucinde" and the Fragments*. Minneapolis: University of Minnesota Press, 1971, pp. 257–271.

Simpson, David. *Irony and Authority in Romantic Poetry*. Totawa, N.J.: Rowan and Littlefield, 1979.

Thorslev, Peter, Jr. *Romantic Contraries: Freedom versus Destiny*. New Haven and London: Yale University Press, 1984.

Wellek, Rene. "German and English Romanticism: A Confrontation." *Studies in Romanticism* vol. 4 (1964–65), 35–36.

"The Concept of Romanticism in Literary History." *Romanticism: Points of View*, ed. Gleckner and Enscoe, pp. 181–205.

Wessell, Leonard P. *Karl Marx, Romantic Irony, and the Proletariat: the Mythopoetic Origins of Marxism*. Baton Rouge and London: Louisiana State University Press, 1979.

"The Antinomic Structure of Friedrich Schlegel's Romanticism." *Studies in Romanticism* vol. 12, no. 3 (Summer 1973), 648–669.

Woodring, Carl. *Politics in English Romantic Poetry*. Cambridge, Mass.: Harvard University Press, 1970.

Index